Genius on Television

Genius on Television

*Essays on Small Screen
Depictions of Big Minds*

Edited by
ASHLEY LYNN CARLSON

McFarland & Company, Inc., Publishers
Jefferson, North Carolina

LIBRARY OF CONGRESS CATALOGUING-IN-PUBLICATION DATA

    Genius on television : essays on small screen depictions of big minds / edited by Ashley Lynn Carlson.
    p.   cm.
    Includes bibliographical references and index.

    ISBN 978-0-7864-9773-7 (softcover : acid free paper) ∞
    ISBN 978-1-4766-2207-1 (ebook)

    1. Intellect on television.   2. Television series—United States—History and criticism.   I. Carlson, Ashley Lynn, 1981– editor.

PN1992.8.I66G46 2015
791.45'653—dc23
                                          2015023118

BRITISH LIBRARY CATALOGUING DATA ARE AVAILABLE

© 2015 Ashley Lynn Carlson. All rights reserved

No part of this book may be reproduced or transmitted in any form or by any means, electronic or mechanical, including photocopying or recording, or by any information storage and retrieval system, without permission in writing from the publisher.

Front cover images © iStock/Thinkstock

Printed in the United States of America

McFarland & Company, Inc., Publishers
   Box 611, Jefferson, North Carolina 28640
      www.mcfarlandpub.com

Table of Contents

Acknowledgments   viii

Introduction—ASHLEY LYNN CARLSON   1

PART I. GENIUS TYPES: TELEVISION DEFINITIONS OF GENIUS

"Spectacularly ignorant": The Conflicted Representation of Genius—DAVID SIDORE   12

Mediated Genius, Anti-Intellectualism and the Detachment(s) of Everyday Life—JZ LONG   32

The Human Hard Drive: Memory, Intelligence and the Internet Age—ASHLEY LYNN CARLSON   49

Gray Matter: The Malleability of Intelligence in *Fringe* LISA K. PERDIGAO   59

PART II. GENDER AND GENIUS

"Caring is not an advantage": The Triumph of Reason in *Sherlock*—JILLIAN L. CANODE   80

Geeksploitation: Gender and Genius in *The Big Bang Theory* JEFFREY A. SARTAIN   96

The Genius in the Attic: The Female Technologist in *NCIS* and *Criminal Minds*—MARIAN R. HJELMGREN and ASHLEY LYNN CARLSON   113

Gladiators in Dresses: *Scandal*, Femininity and Emotional Genius—JENNIFER KIRBY   124

"I'm not a girl, I'm a genius": The Creative Souls of Brenda Leigh
  Johnson and Cristina Yang—CECILIA J. PANG　　138

PART III. GENIUS, DIFFERENCE AND DEVIANCE

What's the Difference? Pathologizing Genius and Neurodiversity in
  Popular Television Series—CAROL-ANN FARKAS　　156

Temperance Brennan: A Case Study in Genius and Autism
  Spectrum Disorder—KRISTIN LARSON　　175

True Detective or Smooth Criminal? The (Dys)functional
  Genius in Contemporary Detective Shows—LAURA-MARIE
  VON CZARNOWSKY *and* ANNETTE SCHIMMELPFENNIG　　185

"It's the age of the geek, baby": The Intelligent Con Artist,
  Corporate America and the Construction of the Family
  in *Leverage*—HANNAH SWAMIDOSS　　199

About the Contributors　　215
Index　　217

Acknowledgments

I am grateful to many friends and colleagues who have helped me put this project together. Alexandra Bomphray, Bridget Draxler, Zachary Erwin, Kristin Larson, Christine Myers, Jeremy Ricketts, Susie Sanchez, Crystal Walline, Kathryn Will, and David Wright have been instrumental sounding boards as I have sifted through ideas, and I am indebted to each for their encouragement. Marian Hjelmgren has been not only a great collaborator, but also an excellent assistant and extra set of eyes. Finally, thank you to my devoted husband Daniel Chapman, who has been an invaluable support through this and all my various endeavors.

Introduction

ASHLEY LYNN CARLSON

As a culture we are deeply interested in genius, both real and fictional. From Albert Einstein and Stephen Hawking to Gregory House and Sherlock Holmes, highly intelligent individuals and their intellectual feats are a clear source of popular fascination. But what exactly is "genius" and what does it really look like? In the past two decades dozens of television shows have featured highly intelligent main characters, and in the process these shows have constructed many popular beliefs about genius. TV geniuses are capable of amazing mental feats that run the gamut from astounding memory recall (Spencer Reid on *Criminal Minds*, Sherlock Holmes on *Sherlock*, Shawn Spencer on *Psych*) to impressive reasoning and deductive skills (Patrick Jane on *The Mentalist*, Gregory House on *House*, Sherlock Holmes on both *Sherlock* and *Elementary,* Temperance Brennan on *Bones,* Adrian Monk on *Monk*) to remarkable facility with technology (Topher Brink on *Dollhouse*, Leo Fitz on *Marvel Agents of S.H.E.I.L.D.*, Felicity Smoak on *Arrow*, Alec Hardison on *Leverage*). TV geniuses also frequently suffer from mental health issues, such as addiction (Gregory House, Sherlock Holmes, Spencer Reid, Nate Ford on *Leverage*), anxiety disorders (Adrien Monk, Spencer Reid), sociopathy (Sherlock Holmes on *Sherlock*, Dexter Morgan on *Dexter*, Hannibal Lector on *Hannibal*), and a variety of socially awkward behaviors that might also be read as indicative of underlying mental illness (Temperance Brennan, Walter Bishop on *Fringe*, Sheldon Cooper on *The Big Bang Theory*). Contemporary television has provided two overarching narratives of genius, one in which geniuses carry out seemingly superhuman tasks, and one in which geniuses struggle with some of the most basic aspects of everyday human existence. Perhaps unsurprisingly, these two narratives most frequently function in tandem.

This collection had its origins in a conversation with friends about these trends in television, as well as the observation that, while genius has long been of popular interest, it has never been featured so prominently on television as it has been in the past decade. This conversation naturally led to two serious questions, one concerning the realism (or lack thereof) of these portrayals, which signifies a great deal about what it means to be "smart" in today's society, and one concerning the reasons behind the explosive rise of genius characters on TV since the start of the twenty-first century. As a whole, the essays in this collection seek to address these questions.

The essays in the first section interrogate the construction of genius according to television. Therefore, it seems appropriate to first consider what the scientific community has said on the topic. The scientific literature on intelligence is extensive, and to fully examine the topic has been and continues to be the work of many scholars' lives. Still, a brief introduction provides some insight into significant aspects of the narratives about genius that have come from science, and serves as a foundation for considering where the television genius mythos has diverged from scientific understanding.

The definition of "genius" is hardly cut and dried. To some, a genius is a person who has achieved extraordinary things. According to this line of thinking, authors such as Shakespeare and Dickens, scientists such as Einstein and Feynman, and composers such as Mozart and Tchaikovsky are geniuses. Most people would agree that these individuals were geniuses, but does that label come from their recognized contributions to literature, science, or music, or from some innate abilities that their accomplishments only serve to demonstrate? Perhaps more fundamentally, is genius the product of a perfect confluence of ability and circumstance that allows an individual to achieve great things, or is genius an internal potential that exists regardless of actual output?

To phrase this differently, what if Einstein had been born the son of poor farmers during the Dark Ages? In those circumstances, he clearly could not have made the contributions to science that he did in the twentieth century. Does that mean that Einstein, or his Dark Ages double, would not have been a genius? Importantly, Dark Ages Einstein would not have been our Einstein at all, since science has demonstrated time and again that we are products of both our genetics and our environment. Even if we imagine, however, that Dark Ages Einstein somehow developed identically to twentieth-century Einstein, it still isn't clear that he would be a genius. As psychologists Sternberg and Salter point out, "what is intelligent in one culture may be irrelevant in the next."[1] Thus, genius, or maybe even just the potential for genius, may depend more on the culture than the individual.

In contrast with this line of thinking is the concept of innate genius, which suggests that intelligence is rooted within the individual rather than being determined via the individual's social and cultural context. Thus, a four-year-old might be a genius, even if she hasn't done much with her life quite yet, and testing could confirm that Dark Ages Einstein was a genius, even if he was a terribly unsuccessful farmer. This approach to understanding genius has been closely tied to efforts to measure intelligence, and the most famous product of these is the intelligence quotient (IQ). The idea of IQ was invented by a German psychologist named William Stern and was based on Stern's observations of the results of French psychologist Alfred Binet's work in developing tests to measure intelligence in the early twentieth century.[2] Binet's tests were so influential that a revised version, the Stanford-Binet, is still used today. An individual's IQ is determined by one of a number of tests designed to measure intelligence rather than by assessing actual attainments. On IQ tests, 100 is understood to represent average intelligence, the standard deviation is 15. Approximately 95 percent of the population falls within two standard deviations (IQ 70–130).[3] In lay terms, individuals with IQs above 130 are generally considered gifted and those with IQs above 145 are considered geniuses, but the fact is that the scientific community rarely uses the term "genius" at all. Further, measuring IQ has been highly contentious since its very beginning, because scientists have struggled to create tests that truly measure intelligence without cultural bias, because labeling an individual based on a test score (which can be inaccurate) can have disastrous effects, and ultimately because the idea that intelligence can be reduced to a single number ignores the fairly obvious fact that intelligence can be manifest in a variety of ways, not all of which are, or even can be, measured by an IQ test.[4]

IQ is also problematic because measuring intelligence is predicated on the assumption that intelligence has a stable definition that allows it to be quantified. In truth, intelligence is a vague term that is open to multiple interpretations. Psychologist Raymond Cattell first introduced the terms "fluid" and "crystallized" intelligence in the 1960s. Fluid intelligence refers to the capacity to solve problems, whereas crystallized intelligence refers to acquired knowledge. This distinction is important because it recognizes the difference between a type of intelligence (fluid) that is theoretically distinct from the educational and cultural factors that weigh heavily in determining knowledge (crystallized).[5] Around the same time that Cattell introduced fluid and crystallized intelligence, J.P. Guilford presented a model of intelligence that had 120 distinct attributes.[6] Guilford's model was not widely adopted, but it did effectively demonstrate the complexity of human intelligence. In 1983 Howard Gardner published his groundbreaking theory of multiple intelligences. His original model included seven intelligences (music, bodily-kinesthetic, logical-mathematical, linguistic, spatial, interpersonal, intrapersonal), with two more added later (naturalist, existentialist). Gardner's model also included a complex system of determining what constitutes a distinct intelligence.[7] Work such as Guilford's and Gardner's helps explain why attempts to reduce an individual to a numerical IQ has limited usefulness—we are simply too complicated to be assigned a number.

Despite the concerns regarding IQ that have plagued scientists, on television, references to characters' IQs are not uncommon. Characters are frequently assigned extraordinarily high IQs as a marker of their incredible intelligence, but these numbers are almost always provided uncritically. What IQ actually means in the scientific community is only tangentially related to what IQ has come to mean on television. Science recognizes the spectrum and complexity of individual differences, whereas popular culture has tended toward a more simplistic genius-or-not dichotomy. Not surprisingly, therefore, the narratives about genius that have been constructed by contemporary television say a great deal more about popular culture than they do about the limits of human intelligence. That is, television shows about geniuses are rarely, if ever, truly about genius.

The first part of this collection, "Genius Types," includes four essays that consider how geniuses are portrayed on television and what role these portrayals have in the popular imagination. David Sidore begins the section with close readings of *Bones, Sherlock,* and *The Big Bang Theory* that illuminate the ways in which genius has become a spectacle and how this spectacle reinforces negative stereotypes about intellectuals. In the second essay JZ Long discusses the prevalence of anti-intellectual themes in television genius narratives. Next, I examine genius characters whose abilities imitate computer technologies, and demonstrate how television is redefining genius as knowledge-based rather than ability-based. Finally, this part ends with Lisa K. Perdigao's analysis of *Fringe,* in which she engages contemporary debates about intelligence, its measurability, and its potential.

The second part, "Gender and Genius," deals with a more specific, problematic aspect of our culture's construction of genius. For centuries, men have been associated with the head, the logical and rational, while women have been associated with the heart, the emotional. Historically, this perceived dichotomy has meant that genius, understood as the product of rational thinking, has usually been considered the domain of men. With but few exceptions, the classic examples of geniuses are male, and the belief that men are more intellectually capable than women has prevailed. In the nineteenth century, women's minds were considered feeble in comparison to men's, and some health professionals even cautioned that over-educating a woman could pose a serious threat to both her own health and the health of her future children.[8] It was a slow process by which women overcame these strong cultural biases and began to be recognized for their capacity to achieve excellence in their chosen fields of study.

Today, women have made great gains in higher education and the workplace, but significant disparities still exist. Since 2003, women have represented approximately 57 percent of the total number of students enrolled in postsecondary degree-granting institutions.[9] At the same time, women have remained sorely underrepresented in the STEM fields (Science, Technology, Engineering, Mathematics), fields that have been associated with the highest IQs.[10] In 2006, women earned only 29.6 percent of the doctorates in math, 21.3 percent in computer science, 20.2 percent in engineering, and 16.6 percent in physics.[11] Like the usefulness of IQ tests, the paucity of women in STEM fields has been the source of serious contention.

As recently as 2005, Lawrence Summers, the president of Harvard University, argued that biology explains why men outperform women in terms of "overall IQ, mathematical ability, scientific ability."[12] His remarks suggested that when it comes to genius-level researchers, people who are "three and a half, four standard deviations above the mean," small gender differences in intelligence add up and contribute to the lack of women in science and engineering fields. While Summers' statements raised considerable outrage from some corners,[13] they nevertheless laid bare the persistence of the belief that genius is somehow inherently male. In fact, a sizable body of research has demonstrated that cultural biases continue to have a significant impact on women's achievements in the sciences. In a 2010 report addressing the scarcity of women in STEM, the American Association of University Women identified multiple environmental factors that contributed to the gender gap, among them negative stereotypes about women's abilities in math and science and implicit biases against women in STEM subjects.[14] Multiple studies in the past few years have demonstrated the extent to which these biases affect women, by dissuading them from entering certain professions to begin with and by creating disparities in mentoring, hiring, and salaries for those women who do.[15] It is clear that popular beliefs about women's capacity in math and science, which are intrinsically tied to beliefs about women's intelligence in comparison to men's, contribute to gender imbalance in these fields.

Likewise, there is a significant gender imbalance in the number of female geniuses portrayed on television. Moreover, in the existing portrayals of genius women, and particularly women in the sciences, gender disparity abounds. As the essays in the second section demonstrate, television both reflects and perpetuates many of the longstanding stereotypes regarding women and intelligence. Jillian L. Canode's essay on *Sherlock* argues that the show reinforces genius as white and male through the portrayals of Sherlock Holmes and the various women he encounters. Similarly, in his essay on *The Big Bang Theory*, Jeffrey A. Sartain argues that despite the presence of both male and female geniuses, the show ultimately presents repressive and chauvinistic attitudes towards intelligence and gender. Marian R. Hjelmgren and I then discuss the marginalization of female technologists in *NCIS* and *Criminal Minds*. Jennifer Kirby's essay argues for a type of feminine genius as depicted in *Scandal*. Finally, Cecilia J. Pang compares Cristina Yang of *Grey's Anatomy* to Brenda Leigh Johnson of *The Closer* in order to demonstrate how intelligence affects their ability to handle gender-related concerns. All of these essays intersect with questions about women's roles in the workplace and gender imbalances, both perceived and real, that exist in high–IQ occupations.

The last part of the collection delves more deeply into a strain that is introduced in the first section: the portrayal of intelligence as a marker of difference. The essays in this section follow two main lines of discussion: mental illness and crime. The association of mental illness with genius is longstanding; even Aristotle is said to have noted the connection.[16] Cesare Lombroso, the criminologist and "forensic phrenologist" whose theory that physical traits could be used to identify criminals was popular in the late nineteenth century, published *The Man of Genius* in 1889, in which he wrote extensively about connections between genius and insanity. Lombroso cited numerous examples of insane geniuses among artists, writers, and scientists as evidence to support his ideas. He even went so far as to suggest that in the few cases of seemingly sane geniuses the symptoms of insanity had simply been overlooked.[17] Although Lombroso's theories about criminals have long since been debunked, the idea that geniuses are prone to insanity has prevailed. How often, for example, does one hear the story of Van Gogh cutting off his ear or Virginia Woolf drowning herself? Since Lombroso, instances such as these have continued to drive psychologists to study whether a connection exists between intelligence and mental illness, but most recent studies have suggested that mental disorders are more common among those with lower IQs rather than higher IQs.[18] In fact, some evidence suggests that high IQs are associated with a reduced risk of mental illness; intellectually gifted individuals may be less likely than average individuals to develop a mental disorder. There does, however, appear to be one exception: some studies have suggested that highly creative people (as opposed to high IQ people) have a higher incidence of bipolar disorder.[19] Still, a vast number of studies have shown that the idea that highly intelligent people are most often insane is false.

In contrast, the portrayals of geniuses on television very frequently link genius and various types of mental illness. Mental health issues are pervasive among the television geniuses discussed throughout this collection. To open the discussion of this topic in the third section, Carol-Ann Farkas's essay provides a broad analysis of genius as a pathological condition across multiple popular television series, including *The Big Bang Theory*, *Community*, *Homeland*,

Scandal, *House*, *Sherlock*, and *Elementary*. As a follow-up, Kristin Larson's essay focuses specifically on *Bones*, where the main protagonist's behavior is highly suggestive of an autism-spectrum diagnosis, although the show never overtly acknowledges this.

The final two essays look at the intersections between intelligence and criminality, another topic that can be traced back to Lombroso and earlier. In more recent history, the stories of serial killers such as Ted Kazynsky (IQ 155– 165) and Ted Bundy (IQ 136) have contributed to a popular misperception that genius and certain kinds of crime, such as serial murders, are linked.[20] However, research has again suggested that this is untrue. According to the Serial Killer Database created by Radford University and Florida Gulf Coast University, the average serial killer's IQ is actually only 94.1, and the median IQ is even lower, at 86.5.[21] Serial killers tend to be less intelligent that the average population; Bundy and Kazynsky are anomalies. Still, on television, genius murderers are quite popular, from *Hannibal* and *Dexter* to many of the suspects on *Law and Order: Criminal Intent* and "unsubs" on *Criminal Minds*.

In reviewing crimes beyond serial murder, a number of studies have shown that the average IQ among criminal offenders is lower than among the general public.[22] Still, averages don't account for individuals; there is no doubt that some criminals, from serial killers to bank robbers to petty thieves, are in fact geniuses. And, it is hard to deny that these characters make for fascinating stories. Laura-Marie von Czarnowsky and Annette Shimmelpfennig's essay delves into this subject; they discuss the dysfunctional outlaw figure in *Sherlock*, *Hannibal*, *True Detective*, and *Dexter* and illuminate the ways in which these characters are able to cross both social and legal boundaries. Finally, Hannah Swamidoss's essay on *Leverage* connects with both the genius/outlaw dichotomy discussed in the previous essay as well as the genius/nerd stereotypes discussed in several earlier chapters, thus concluding the section with an analysis of how the highly intelligent characters on this show function both within and outside of social, legal, and moral norms.

Intelligence is a complicated and fraught topic in our culture. It stands at the crossroads between our desire to believe that with hard work anything is possible and our knowledge that individual differences are real, and that not everyone has the same capacity for success. Thus, in the popular imagination the genius figure can be either a source of inspiration or an object of envy. As the essays in this book show, whether the genius is a hero or a villain, s/he is always different, strange, or Other. The question, then, is what television's portrayals of the genius ultimately mean for rest of us.

NOTES

1. Robert J. Sternbreg and William Salter, "Conceptions of Intelligence," in *Handbook of Human Intelligence*, ed. Robert J. Sternberg (New York: Cambridge University Press, 1982), 21.

2. John B. Carroll, "The Measurement of Intelligence," in *Handbook of Human Intelligence*, ed. Robert J. Sternberg (New York: Cambridge University Press, 1982), 40.

3. Danuta Bukatko and Marvin W. Daehler, *Child Development: A Thematic Approach*, 6th ed. (Belmont, CA: Wadsworth, 2012), 362–363.

4. David W. Pyle, *Intelligence* (London: Routledge, 1979), 19. In Pyle's words: "Intelligence is not unitary in nature.... However one defines intelligence, it must be seen as multifaceted: many-sided, not one sided" (19).

5. John Duncan, *How Intelligence Happens* (New Haven, Yale, University Press, 2010), 46–47.

6. J.P. Guilford, *The Nature of Human Intelligence* (New York: McGraw Hill, 1967).

7. Howard Gardner, *Multiple Intelligences: New Horizons* (New York: Basic Books, 2006), 8–18.

8. Thomas Addis Emmet, *The Principles and Practice of Gynaecology*, 2nd ed., (Philadelphia, 1880).

9. National Center for Education Statistics, "Table 303.10. Total fall enrollment in degree-granting postsecondary institutions, by attendance status, sex of student, and control of institution: Selected years, 19467–2012, "*Digest of Education Statistics 2012*, retrieved 10 June 2014, http://nces.ed.gov/programs/digest/d13/tables/dt13_303.10.asp.

10. Min-Hsiung Huang studied the relationship between intelligence and various professions, and compiled an list of "high-IQ occupations." Huang found that, in order by rank, mathematical scientists, physicians, lawyers and judges, and architects had the highest average IQs. The average person in each of these professions had an IQ over 120. On Huang's list of high-IQ occupations were many of the usual suspects: chemists (ranked 6th), computer programmers (10th), and engineers (11th). However, his rankings also include a few possible surprises: management analysts (5th), authors (7th), technical writers (8th), and editors and reporters (9th) averaged slightly higher IQs than computer programmers and engineers (Min-Hsuing Huang, "Cognitive Abilities and the Growth of High-IQ Occupations," *Social Science Research* 30 [2001]: 536).

11. Catherine Hill, Christianne Corbett, and Andresse St. Rose, *Why So Few? Women in Science, Technology, Engineering, and Mathematics* (Washington, D.C.: AAUW, 2010), 12.

12. Lawrence Summers, "Remarks at NBER Conference on Diversifying the Science & Engineering Workforce," delivered 14 January 2005, Cambridge, MA, http://www.harvard.edu/president/speeches/summers_2005/nber.php.

13. Scott Jaschik, "What Larry Summers Said," *Inside Higher Ed*, February 18, 2005, http://www.insidehighered.com/news/2005/02/18/summers2_18#sthash.f8V5Ez Lp.dpbs.

14. Hill, Corbett, and St. Rose, *Why So Few?*

15. Ernesto Reuben, Paola Sapienza, and Luigi Zingales, "How stereotypes impair women's careers in science," *PNAS* 111, no. 12 (2014): 4403–4408; Corinne A. Moss-Racusin, John Dovidio, Victoria Brescoll, Mark Graham, and Jo Handelsman, "Science faculty's subtle gender biases favor male students," *PNAS* 109, no. 41 (2012): 16474–16479.

16. Anne Stiles, *Popular Fiction and Brain Science in the Late Nineteenth Century* (New York: Cambridge University Press, 2012), 125.

17. Cesare Lombroso, *The Man of Genius* (New York: Charles Scribner's Sons, 1901), 353.

18. S. Rajput, A. Hassiotis, M. Richards, S.L. Hatch, and R. Steward, "Association between IQ and common mental disorders," *European Psychiatry* 26, no. 6 (2011): 390–5;

Erik Lykke Mortenson, Holger Jelling Sorenson, Hans Henrik Jensen, June Machover Reinisch, and Sarnoff A. Mednick, "IQ and mental disorder in young men," *BJPsych* 187 (2005): 407–415.

19. Tracy C. Misset, "Exploring the Relationship Between Mood Disorders and Gifted Individuals," *Roeper Review* 35 (2013): 47–57.

20. Mike Aamodt, "Serial Killer IQ," Serial Killer Information Center, Radford University. September 16, 2012, http://maamodt.asp.radford.edu/Serial%20; Ben Lawson, Kevin Lillard, and Tim Mayer, "Ted Bundy," Serial Killer Information Center, Radford University, retrieved 14 June 2014, http://maamodt.asp.radford.edu/Psyc%20405/serial%2killers/Bundy,%20Ted%20-%202005.pdf.

21. Mike Aamodt, *Serial Killer Statistics*, October 19, 2013, http://maamodt.asp.radford.edu/serial killer information center/projectdescription.htm.

22. Bruce Bower, "Criminal Intellects: Researchers look at why lawbreakers often brandish low IQs," *Science News* 147, no. 15 (1994): 232–233, 239.

References

Aamodt, Mike G. "Serial Killer IQ." Serial Killer Information Center, Radford University. September 16, 2012. http://maamodt.asp.radford.edu/Serial%20 Killer%20Information%20Center/Serial%20Killer%20IQ.htm.

_____. *Serial Killer Statistics*. October 19, 2013. http://maamodt.asp.radford.edu/serial killer information center/projectdescription.htm.

Bower, Bruce. "Criminal Intellects: Researchers look at why lawbreakers often brandish low IQs." *Science News* 147, no. 15 (1994): 232–233, 239.

Bukatko, Danuta, and Marvin W. Daehler. *Child Development: A Thematic Approach*, 6th ed. Belmont, CA: Wadsworth, 2012.

Carroll, John B. "The Measurement of Intelligence." In *Handbook of Human Intelligence*, edited by Robert J. Sternberg, 29–120. New York: Cambridge University Press, 1982.

Duncan, John. *How Intelligence Happens*. New Haven: Yale University Press, 2010.

Emmet, Thomas Addis. *The Principles and Practice of Gynaecology*, 2nd ed. Philadelphia, 1880.

Gardner, Howard. *Multiple Intelligences: New Horizons*. New York: Basic, 2006.

Guilford, J.P. *The Nature of Human Intelligence*. New York: McGraw Hill, 1967.

Hill, Catherine, Christianne Corbett, and Andresse St. Rose. *Why So Few? Women in Science, Technology, Engineering, and Mathematics*. Washington, D.C.: AAUW, 2010.

Huang, Min-Hsuing. "Cognitive Abilities and the Growth of High-IQ Occupations." *Social Science Research* 30 (2001): 529–551.

Jaschik, Scott. "What Larry Summers Said." *Inside Higher Ed*, February 18, 2005. http://www.insidehighered.com/news/2005/02/18/summers2_18#sthash.f8V5Ez Lp.dpbs.

Lawson, Ben, Kevin Lillard, and Tim Mayer. "Ted Bundy." Serial Killer Information Center, Radford University. Retrieved June 14, 2014. http://maamodt.asp.radford.edu/Psyc.%20405/serial%20killers/Bundy,%20Ted%20-%202005.pdf.

Lombroso, Cesare. *The Man of Genius*. New York: Charles Scribner's Sons, 1901.

Missett, Tracy C. "Exploring the Relationship Between Mood Disorders and Gifted Individuals." *Roeper Review* 35 (2013): 47–57.

Mortenson, Erik Lykke, Holger Jelling Sorenson, Hans Henrik Jensen, June Machover Reinisch, and Sarnoff A. Mednick. "IQ and Mental Disorder in Young Men." *BJPsych* 187 (2005): 407–415.

Moss-Racusin Corinne A., John Dovidio, Victoria Brescoll, Mark Graham, and Jo Handelsman. "Science faculty's subtle gender biases favor male students." *PNAS* 109, no. 41 (2012): 16474–16479.

National Center for Education Statistics. "Table 303.10. Total fall enrollment in degree-granting postsecondary institutions, by attendance status, sex of student, and control of institution: Selected years, 1967–2012." *Digest of Education Statistics 2012.* http://nces.ed.gov/programs/digest/d13/tables/dt13_303.10.asp.

Oleson, J.C., and Rachael Chappell. "Self-Reported Violent Offending Among Subjects with Genius-Level IQ Scores." *Journal of Family Violence* 27 (2012): 715–730.

Pyle, David W. *Intelligence.* London: Routledge, 1979.

Rajput, S., A. Hassiotis, M. Richards, SL Hatch, and R. Steward. "Associations Between IQ and Common Mental Disorders: The 2000 British National Survey of Psychiatric Morbidity." *European Psychiatry* 26, no. 6 (2011): 390–5.

Reuben, Ernesto, Paola Sapienza, and Luigi Zingales. "How stereotypes impair women's careers in science." *PNAS* 111, no. 12 (2014): 4403–4408.

Sternberg, Robert J., and William Salter. "Conceptions of Intelligence." In *Handbook of Human Intelligence*, edited by Robert J. Sternberg, 3–28. New York: Cambridge University Press, 1982.

Stiles, Anne. *Popular Fiction and Brain Science in the Late Nineteenth Century.* New York: Cambridge University Press, 2012.

Summers, Lawrence. "Remarks at NBER Conference on Diversifying the Science & Engineering Workforce." Delivered January 14, 2005, Cambridge, MA. http://www.harvard.edu/president/speeches/summers_2005/nber.php.

Part I
Genius Types: Television Definitions of Genius

"Spectacularly ignorant"

The Conflicted Representation of Genius

David Sidore

> The public is wonderfully tolerant. It forgives everything except genius.—Oscar Wilde[1]

Near the start of the final episode of the first season of BBC's *Sherlock* (2010), Sherlock Holmes takes issue with John Watson's description of him in Watson's blog account of their first case. Although Holmes has no problems with the line "Sherlock sees through everything and everyone in seconds," the subsequent "What's incredible, though, is how spectacularly ignorant he is about some things" strikes a nerve.[2] In the ensuing back and forth about this claim, Watson seems to acknowledge that "who's Prime Minister" and "who's sleeping with who" might be reasonable things not to know, but asserts that "primary school stuff," like the fact that the earth goes around the sun, is not.[3] While I will take up Holmes' justification for this gap in his knowledge below, it is worth noting that this representation of the genius as having dazzling mastery over a vast, but specialized repository of (often scientific and high cultural) knowledge traces back at least as far as Sir Arthur Conan Doyle's original *Study in Scarlet* (1887) on which this scene is based, as does the practice of making a spectacle not only out of acts of "genius," but especially of a genius' blind spots. As Conan Doyle points out in the original version of Watson's line, "His ignorance was as remarkable as his knowledge."[4]

This ignorance is especially worthy of remark because, as both the original stories by Conan Doyle and *Sherlock* make clear (in the same episode), Holmes has a detailed knowledge of astronomy. The spectacle being made of his ignorance, then, serves other purposes. On one level, such slippages address practical, narrative concerns—most notably furthering the plot, delaying the resolution of the enigma at the heart of a story, and keeping the genius from being too godlike in his or her abilities. Yet the primary function of such spectacles lies in the demarcation of difference, marking off the boundary between such exceptional creatures and the norm. The spectacles—and here I include not merely gaps in formal knowledge, but also ignorance of the rules of society and social interactions, both in terms of a genius not understanding those rules and conventions as well as the reasons some geniuses have for ignoring them—serve to identify the genius as an Other, which, as we shall see, reveals a great deal about contemporary perceptions of intelligence, science, and the role of the intellectual in modern society.

Interior Decorating

To pick up where we started, on *Sherlock,* when challenged by Watson about his lack of "common" knowledge, Holmes explains that his brain is his "hard drive" and it can hold only so much information. As such, "it only makes sense to put things in there that are useful ... *really* useful."[5] Unlike most people, Holmes refuses to clutter it up with "all kinds of rubbish" that would make it "hard to get at the stuff that matters!"[6] Viewers can sympathize with the twenty-first century Holmes' selective approach to what he lets onto his "hard drive" in light of the deluge of information characteristic of the contemporary age. As I have already noted, however, this scene and sentiment are actually drawn directly from Conan Doyle's original *Study in Scarlet* (1887). There, when Dr. Watson is similarly surprised by Holmes' ignorance of the solar system, Holmes explains:

> I consider that a man's brain originally is like a little empty attic, and you have to stock it with such furniture as you choose. A fool takes in all the lumber of every sort that he comes across, so that the knowledge which might be useful to him gets crowded out, or at best is jumbled up with a lot of other things, so that he has a difficulty in laying his hands upon it. Now the skillful workman is very careful indeed as to what he takes into his brain-attic. He will have nothing but the tools which may help him in doing his work, but of these he has a large assortment, and all in the most perfect order. It is a mistake to think that this little room has elastic walls and can distend to any extent. Depend upon it there comes a time when for any addition of knowledge, you forget something that you knew before. It is of the highest importance, therefore, not to have useless facts elbowing out the useful ones.[7]

There are practical elements to Conan Doyle's explanation, both in terms of memory and narrative. Holmes studies and generates esoteric forensic knowledge (about ashes, soil, and so on) at a prodigious rate and has a keen eye, often noting that he observes where others merely see. One can easily imagine that maintaining mastery over such a storehouse of knowledge requires careful organization and the frequent and discriminating editing out of "useless" information. This not only makes sense for the character, but also serves Conan Doyle as the storyteller for he knows that if Holmes is too omniscient he becomes narratively boring. Moreover, the gaps in his knowledge can prove useful to the plot.[8]

Contemporary neuroscience suggests that the raw storage capacity of the brain is vast and that humans are highly unlikely to push up against the walls of our "little rooms" even if we live very long, eventful, and "observant" lives. Yet as Maria Konnikova, author of the *New York Times* bestselling book *Mastermind: How to Think Like Sherlock Holmes* (2013), points out, this is not merely a question of raw storage. According to Konnikova, contemporary cognitive science does offer support for the efficacy of Holmes' strategy of organizing one's brain-attic. Cutting down on the clutter and distractions and carefully arranging the information one keeps speaks not only to attending to the content of one's brain, but also to its *structure*:

> The attic's structure is how our mind works: how it takes in information. How it processes that information. How it sorts it and stores it for the future. How it may choose to integrate it or not with contents that are already in the attic space. Unlike a physical attic, the structure of the brain attic isn't altogether fixed. It can expand, albeit not indefinitely, or it can contract, depending on how we use it (in other words, our memory and processing can become more or less effective) ... At the end, it will have to remain within certain confines—each attic, once again, is different and subject to its unique constraints—but within those confines, it can take on any number of configurations, depending on how we learn to approach it.[9]

Although *Sherlock* seems to blur the distinction between them, it would be a mistake to think of that program's "mind palace" as an upgrading of Holmes' brain-attic, for what Conan Doyle is describing is the preparation of a space for thinking and "working" with information rather than merely a mental construct to aid with memorization.[10] While geniuses are often represented as having astonishing or even eidetic memories (something scientists have never confirmed in adults), just being able to recall lots of facts does not make one brilliant. What matters is what one can do with the information.

When we speak of someone having a "big brain," this refers not only to the breadth of one's knowledge, but also to one's "processing power" and ability to hold all of the elements of a complex topic in mind at once, or more precisely, in what is called one's *working memory*.[11] Chess is one of the many markers of intelligence precisely because being good at it requires being able to think several moves ahead, playing the game out in one's mind. The brain-attic is Holmes' mental work space. *Sherlock* offers a representation of this in season three's "The Sign of Three." At nearly an hour into the episode, Holmes enters a council chamber filled with women. He quickly dismisses most of them by pointing and saying, "Not you."[12] He then questions the remaining four (later adding a fifth). When John Watson appears at his side to ask a question it is revealed that Holmes is standing in front of several laptops in the living room at 221B Baker Street. Holmes is using the laptops to chat with the women about a "ghost date." The rest of the scene cuts back and forth between the council chamber and Baker Street, even projecting the information about each woman that Holmes brings up on the laptops onto the faces and bodies of the women in the council chamber, making it clear that this chamber is Holmes' mental workspace, not merely where he goes to retrieve memories. Lest there be any doubt where and what this chamber is, a few minutes later his train of thought leads to Irene Adler (The Woman), who begins to caress his cheek while standing (seemingly naked) in the council chamber. Holmes dismisses her by saying, "Out of my head. I am *busy*."[13]

The television genius, then, is able to recognize what information is relevant, place it into context (often involving identifying unconventional and obscure connections), and see the bigger picture. As "The Sign of Three" plays out, Holmes catches the detail (the middle name "Hamish") and puts together (much of) what is going on as he finishes his toast at Watson's wedding. Such moments of enlightenment offer one of television's favorite spectacles of genius—the epiphany—that moment when the genius stares off into space and the light goes on in his or her eyes, letting the audience know that he or she has connected the dots and can now see the truth. One of the primary functions of the friends and companions of television geniuses is to be in conversation with the genius when this moment strikes, as the character of James Wilson on *House, M.D.* (2008) so ably demonstrates.[14] *Sherlock*'s conceit in "The Sign of Three" is to show us what an epiphany looks like from the inside.

The conception of the genius as one whose brain has been selectively fine-tuned to solve crimes, medical cases, scientific quandaries, or whatever other puzzles or crises come up, also lends itself to one of television's other favorite spectacles of genius: the disjuncture that occurs when the focused mind of a genius encounters the "real world." After all, among the rubbish often discarded to clear the mental space that makes epiphanic moments possible are such mundane topics as politics, current events, popular culture, social conventions, and other basics of "normal" human interaction.

One of the implications of all of this is that the genius processes information about the world differently than the rest of us do, in effect *experiencing* the world differently, leading to the representation of the genius "as otherworldly or in his or her own world, separate from the normal world."[15] While this quote completes my line of reasoning about the representation of genius on television, Anthony Baker wrote it about the depiction of autism in film, where autism "is constructed as ontologically different from the realm of the typical."[16] As we shall see, this linking of genius to mental disorders proves the basis for many of the "spectacles of ignorance" associated with genius.

Remarkable by Implication

The television landscape is full of surprisingly competent and hyperarticulate characters. In order to stand out as truly different, geniuses must be off the scale extraordinary. Giving them (multiple) advanced college degrees (at early ages) and a host of extra skills, expertise, and experiences *tells* us that they are special, but it does not *show* it to us. Too frequent epiphanies undercut their value. How, then, to convey that these characters are off-the-charts brilliant? The answer many programs hit on is by implication. The unconventional set of priorities, intense focus, social awkwardness, and seemingly inappropriate behavior that can signify an "organized" brain dovetail nicely with the public's (mis)perceptions about savantism and the part of the autism spectrum formerly known as Asperger's.

There is nothing, after all, about the organized brain-attic model that requires the selection process be done consciously or precludes it from being the result of biology. Implicit in this connection to autism is the belief that there is a cost for being so mentally different. Stuart Murray identifies *Rain Man* (1988) as "the foundational text for all the various contemporary representations of autism, the breakthrough story that gave the condition a public profile when before it was, to a large degree, confined to medical and educational specialists, and the families of those individuals who had autism."[17] This portrayal has several implications, for the film introduces autism "as being a condition twinned with savantism,"[18] a pairing that reinforces the notion that savantism comes at a price, a fact that informed the name of the condition for many years. As Murray explains, "The degree of awe savant talents produce is matched by the idea that these skills act to compensate for the disability with which they are associated. Hence the common attachment of the word 'idiot' to 'savant,' to designate this double aspect of ability and impairment."[19]

Blurring the line between genius and mental disorders (including not only autism, but schizophrenia and manic-depression) makes whole textbooks of symptoms available to signal atypical cognitive practices. The accumulation of such behaviors functions like negative space. They suggest the extent of a genius' abilities through their perceived role as the paired counterweight or balance. Programs combine socially inappropriate and atypical behavior with the willingness of other characters to tolerate, support, and even enable it to effectively imply just how smart the genius must really be.

The Big Bang Theory (2007) offers an extreme example of using the spectacle of symptoms from various mental disorders to signify great intelligence in this way. The program centers around a quartet of research faculty at Caltech that includes theoretical physicist Dr. Sheldon Cooper, his roommate, experimental physicist Dr. Leonard Hofstadter, mechanical engineer and astronaut Howard Wolowitz, and astrophysicist Dr. Rajesh "Raj" Koothrappali. All are accomplished in their fields and are well versed in science, comic books, video games, science fiction television and films, and the other markers of nerd culture.[20] All display both the vocabulary and various degrees of social dysfunction associated with growing up smart and nerdy.

Sheldon Cooper, however, is not like the others. He is positioned as the primary genius of the show and smarter than all of the rest combined—something he claims often and almost proves when he nearly beats them all in a Physics (Quiz) Bowl singlehandedly (in "The Bat Jar Conjecture").[21] The Physics Bowl performance notwithstanding, because *The Big Bang Theory* is a comedy rather than an investigative procedural, Sheldon has fewer opportunities to impress audiences with acts of extreme intelligence. In order to differentiate Sheldon from his peers, the writers compensate by loading him up with idiosyncratic behaviors typically associated with Asperger's and other mental disorders. Thus, he adheres to a strict and comprehensive routine, scheduling everything from what activities he and his group do on particular nights to the specific times he uses the bathroom every day. Sheldon is very resistant to change, especially to his routine. He also has particular rituals he observes, including sitting in the same spot in the apartment (which predates the couch in his apartment, as the season three episode "The Staircase Implementation"[22] reveals) and an obsessive compulsive door knocking ritual (of three knocks, followed by a name, and done three times) that must be completed even if the door opens before he is done.

A scene from a first season episode, "The Dumpling Paradox," offers a typical example of many of these behaviors when Sheldon finds Penny, his pretty neighbor, asleep on the couch one morning. He is about to sit on her head when Leonard interrupts. Sheldon explains that "every Saturday since we have lived in this apartment, I have awakened at 6:15, poured myself a bowl of cereal, added a quarter cup of 2 percent milk, sat on this end of this couch, turned on BBC America and watched *Doctor Who*."[23] When Leonard counters that Penny's still asleep, Sheldon begins to repeat his explanation, making clear that from his perspective his routine is more important than other niceties, including Penny.

Whereas the other three scientists are socially awkward, especially around women, they are played as merely "geeky." They understand social cues and conventions even if they cannot always conform to them and would be considered largely "neurotypical." Sheldon does not and would not be. He has great difficulty with reading facial expressions and body language as well as perceiving sarcasm and irony. He takes others' comments overly literally and expresses himself in a correspondingly blunt and honest, if pedantic, manner without any sense of how his words affect others, whether boring them or offending them. This proves just as well since he also has a tendency to turn any conversation back to himself and his topics of interest.[24] That he is also uncomfortable with being touched (especially hugged), is mysophobic (more commonly known as germophobic), and has the aforementioned eidetic memory drives home the fact that he is being marked as different even within his specialized and highly intelligent cohort, who regard him as crazy.

One of the effects of this characterization is to infantilize Sheldon. Despite his obvious skills and knowledge, Sheldon often needs to be taken care of (e.g., for rides to work, the dentist, and other errands he wants to run) and comes across as childlike and naïve in social situations, seeking his own goals with directness (and stubbornness) more common to toddlers. As the series progresses, the other characters increasingly treat him like a child, coaxing him to do things with the promise of toys and Disneyland, getting him to go to sleep by counting to three, and so on. Leonard and Penny end up positioned *in loco parentis*.[25] Although this begins more as an association in the third season when a fight between Leonard and Penny reminds Sheldon of similar fights between his parents when he was a child,[26] by the end of the seventh season Leonard tracks Sheldon by his cell phone because, "ever since he wandered off at the swap meet chasing a balloon, I get worried," to which Penny replies, "He can take care of himself. Look, we went over stranger danger and gave him that whistle."[27]

Although television programs like to make use of the symptoms of mental disorders as shorthand to signify intelligence, they rarely actually diagnose the characters and identify them as having specific disorders. Case in point, the writers and producers of *The Big Bang Theory* have denied that Sheldon has Asperger's Syndrome or autism both to interviewers and to Jim Parsons, the actor who plays Sheldon. Many fans of the show, especially those on the autism spectrum, identify with Sheldon and continue to regard him as an "Aspie." Parsons, for his part, maintains that despite the writers' denials "I can say that

[Sheldon] couldn't display more facets of [Asperger's]"[28] and asserts that "the way [Sheldon's] brain works, it's so focused on the intellectual topics at hand that thinking he's autistic is an easy leap for people watching the show to think."[29] Television critic Alan Sepinwall reports that series co-creator Bill Prady told him that the producers of the program did not want to be burdened with accurately portraying a specific condition in a comedy, especially considering the complexity of making comedy out of intellectual disability.[30]

Undiagnosed or not, the linking of genius with mental disorders provides television producers an invaluable method for making something accomplished largely internally (through thought) visible by implication if not presence. The resulting spectacles prove reassuring, suggesting both the balancing of extreme abilities with impairments and that the genius' worldview is merely different, not ultimately better. Making a spectacle of the limitations of genius in this way helps to contain this difference (especially of thought), positioning the genius as a hot house flower, exceptional at what he or she does, perhaps, but not able to survive outside in the "real" world alone.

Squinting at the Screen

Privileging the "real" world and being "human" over the otherness of genius is one of the central themes of another television series, the drama *Bones* (2005). Dr. Temperance Brennan, the title character, is the prototypical television genius. Approaching 30 as the series begins, Brennan is one of the leading authorities in forensic anthropology in the world, is fluent in six languages, and is a bestselling novelist who also happens to be beautiful. Despite all of her achievements, however, Brennan has trouble interacting with "real" people away from a laboratory setting. Her partner, FBI Special Agent Seeley Booth, nicknames her "Bones" and maintains that she is better at "getting information out of a pile of bones" than from live people.[31] Like Sheldon Cooper, she tends to think in terms of logic and reason, to take things literally, and to express herself bluntly without a strong sense of the impact or appropriateness of her comments and actions in any given situation.

Unlike the producers of *The Big Bang Theory*, Hart Hanson, the creator of *Bones*, readily acknowledges that he based Brennan in part on a friend with Asperger's syndrome. He has asserted that he would have "said from the beginning that Brennan has Asperger's" if the show were "on cable" and not constrained by a broadcast network's reluctance to label a central character in any way that might limit that character's appeal to the broadest possible audience.[32] Although he could not come right out and diagnose either Brennan or her primary assistant/protégé Zack Addy as "Aspies," Hanson drops lots of hints in the show, such as having Brennan say the famous line from *Rain Man*, "I'm an excellent driver!" and even having Booth identify it as such (a reference Brennan does not get).[33] Perhaps the closest Hanson comes to a diagnosis occurs in the sixth season episode "The Feet on the Beach" when resident psychologist Dr. Lance Sweets explains that Brennan's "seeming insensitivity and emotional cruelty are merely her way of dealing with an inability to understand or empathize with the feelings of other people."[34]

Since *Bones* is an investigative program (the producers and stars dislike the label "procedural"), Brennan can demonstrate her special talents more clearly than Sheldon can. For example, in the pilot she reads a victim's skeleton:

> I understand Cleo, and her bones are all I've ever seen. When she was seven, she broke her wrist probably falling off a bike and two weeks later, before the cast was even removed, she got right back on that bike and broke it all over again. And when she was being murdered, she fought back hard, even though she was so depressed she could hardly get up in the morning. She didn't welcome death, Cleo wanted to live.[35]

As a result of such scenes, the writers do not have to rely so heavily on psychological "quirks" to imply the breadth of Brennan's intelligence. Eventually the show comes to suggest that Brennan's poor people skills, limited empathy, and logical nature are the result of childhood traumas—notably the loss of her parents and mistreatment in the foster care system—and the cultural isolation of academia and science.

The show's separation of the ivory towers of academia, the hallowed halls of science, and the stuffy world of art and high culture (Brennan and her team work at the Jeffersonian Institute, a museum likened to the Smithsonian) from the "real world" begins in the pilot episode when Booth, our "normal" surrogate on the screen, introduces the term "squints" to refer to Dr. Brennan and her colleagues and to distinguish them from us. To squint is to look closely at something with eyes partially closed in order to block out extraneous stimuli and limit the direction the light can enter in an attempt to see the object of the gaze more clearly. Although applied by the program to all scientists (squinting into their microscopes), the narrowing of focus sounds very akin to the careful organization of worldview and mind detailed in the description of the brain-attic above, although with more negative connotations. The term "squint" strongly implies that scientific work is more akin to putting on blinders than experiencing epiphanic enlightenment. Such tunnel vision produces a useful, but limited understanding of the world. When the scientists argue logic and scientific method in the face of Booth's practical concerns about bringing charges against a U.S. Senator, Booth voices the show's take on science: "This is exactly why squints belong in the lab, you guys don't know anything about the real world."[36]

To reinforce the suggestion that the logical, scientific world Brennan inhabits is what is keeping her out of touch with reality, the program makes a spectacle out of her lack of knowledge about popular culture. An ongoing joke in the series involves her saying, "I don't know what that means," whenever her colleagues make popular culture references (including the *Rain Man* reference above). Such displays suggest the limits of Brennan's knowledge and engagement with the world while at the same time giving the audience (who does get the reference) a sense of being better informed than her on some topics. To make sure we take away the right message from this spectacle, at the end of the pilot Booth tells Brennan, "you need to get out of the lab you know, watch TV, turn on the radio, anything!"[37]

For a program nominally about the use and usefulness of science to solve crimes, *Bones* proves surprisingly anti-intellectual. Booth's directive is not just to get out of the lab and do normal things; he (as the show's mouthpiece) is staking out territory on "what really matters." In another episode, "The Woman in the Garden," Brennan and one of her team, entomologist Jack Hodgins, demonstrate their knowledge of current events and the real world by discussing the ways public policy has produced and perpetuates the poor economic conditions in the barrios of Little Salvador. Booth dismisses their concerns by asking, "What is this, NPR radio? What, are you two running for office?"[38] Despite his advice to "turn on the radio" it cannot be to an "intellectual" or socially conscious channel. The "real world" apparently doesn't think that hard.

The program's disdain for academia comes out often, as when Booth pulls Brennan out of her assistant Zack Addy's dissertation defense saying, "real life murder and mutilation versus academic clap trap? No contest."[39] The show implicitly endorses Booth's interpretation by having Brennan accept this argument and willingly leave with him despite casually commenting in the next scene that Zack has only a "50/50" chance of passing his dissertation defense (presumably less of a chance without her there). That the committee's next question is not about his impressive dissertation work but his appearance— "How do you expect anyone to take you seriously as a working Forensic Anthropologist when you look—the way you do?"—does not inspire much confidence in academia or science as either projects or institutions.[40]

Of course, like Sheldon Cooper, Temperance Brennan is not like the rest of the "squints" on her team. Although scientists, most of them both make and get the cultural references she does not. Despite the broad brush with which the show paints science and academics, only Brennan and Zack truly seem somewhat disconnected from the "normal" world. In the end, the show uses Zack, who also has a very high IQ and is perhaps the only one even more logical, literal, and socially clueless than Brennan, as a cautionary tale about what can happen to one who lives primarily in the sheltered worlds of logic and academia. This "genius" is easily manipulated by the twisted logic of a cannibalistic character that serves as the "big bad" of the show's third season, and thus Zach becomes his apprentice. The message of *Bones* is, as usual, most clearly expressed through Seeley Booth's ongoing quest to bring Brennan as much as he can into the normal world and help her "feel compassion and regret," which he maintains is "what makes us human."[41] The show pursues this goal of grounding her more firmly in the human world through him, eventually having them marry and have a child together.

Living in a World of Goldfish

As we've seen, the spectacles of ignorance serve to delineate the boundary between the world of the genius and the "real" world. Marked by the stigmas associated with mental disorders and the perceived limitations of the out-of-touch academy and the (too?) logical world of science, these displays in *The Big Bang Theory* and *Bones* have highlighted the limitations of their central characters' worldviews. Not every program, however, ultimately privileges conventional thought, behavior, and values over those of the genius. *Sherlock*'s Holmes, for example, has a worldview that *works* and clearly offers him insights not open to ordinary people.

Whereas Sheldon Cooper and Temperance Brennan can be said to have come by their dispassionate insensitivity and social cluelessness "honestly" through Asperger's and personal trauma, the various incarnations of Holmes, including Gregory House and Patrick Jane from *The Mentalist* (2008), are fully aware of how the "real" world works and feel no need to be bound by the normal rules. They know better and choose to encounter the world on their terms. In fact, many of these characters use odd and inappropriate behavior as a means of provoking actions and reactions, often getting others to reveal secrets to their keen observational skills. Dr. Cal Lightmen from *Lie to Me* (2011) and Patrick Jane are walking lie detectors and Holmes demonstrates similar skills on both *Sherlock* and *Elementary* (2012). The spectacles of their social "ignorance" thus serve to display rather than undercut their abilities.

Of course, if the message being conveyed is not that the genius is ultimately limited or "impaired," then the message becomes that *we* are. The producers of *Sherlock* make this clear not just once or twice, but multiple times throughout the opening episode of the series, "A Study in Pink." It begins with our first introduction to Holmes as an intruding, virtual presence at a Scotland Yard press conference. Unable to do more than instruct the assembled reporters to ignore Sherlock's derisive electronic heckling, Detective Sergeant Donovan correctly observes that, "He's making us look like idiots."[42] Nor is Holmes bashful about expressing his condescension in person when others don't see what he regards as "obvious." Standing over the body of the lady in pink he wonders, "Dear God, what is it like in your funny little brains? It must be so boring."[43] Having successfully deduced where the victim's missing pink suitcase must have been and retrieved it, Holmes is even more blunt when Watson rhetorically asks why he himself didn't think of where it must be—"Because you're an idiot," replies Holmes matter-of-factly. Upon seeing Watson's startled and hurt expression, Holmes quickly reassures him, "No, no, no, don't look like that. Practically everyone is." Finally, when he is the only one to realize the significance of the victim's final message, Holmes suggests that we're "not all there" when he says, "You're all so vacant. Is it nice not being me? It must be so relaxing."[44]

Lest we think this derision for the rest of humanity is idiosyncratic of Holmes, the writers of "A Study in Pink" have the other "proper genius" in the episode, Jeff, the serial killing taxi driver, share Holmes' frustration with the rest of the world. As they sit down for their final confrontation, Jeff acknowledges Holmes' website, "The Science of Deduction," as a clear demonstration of *"proper* thinking."[45] Brushing aside Holmes' half-hearted claim that the police and Mrs. Hudson, from whose midst Jeff has just extricated Holmes, are not "*that* stupid," Jeff makes the connection "between you and me sitting 'ere" explicit, asking, "why can't people think?" Echoing Holmes from earlier in the episode, Jeff continues, "Don't it make you mad? Why can't people just *think*?"[46]

Once you start dismissing the vast bulk of humanity as unthinking, it's much easier to start viewing them as less than human. As Sherlock's older and *smarter* brother Mycroft notes in "The Empty Hearse" at the start of season three of *Sherlock*, "If *you* seem slow to me, Sherlock, can you imagine what *real* people are like? I'm living in a world of goldfish."[47] Nor are such characterizations limited to *Sherlock*. When *The Big Bang Theory*'s Sheldon Cooper seeks to convince his friend Howard to show his work to eminent theoretical physicist Stephen Hawking in the fifth season episode "The Hawking Excitation," he uses a very similar analogy: "Try to put yourself in my place. Imagine you're the sole human being living on a planet populated with nothing but dogs. And then it turns out there's another human being."[48] Realizing Howard is getting offended at being likened to a dog, Sheldon quickly tries to substitute in chimps and then dolphins, to no avail. *The Big Bang Theory*'s writers return to this theme the following season, in "The Higgs Boson Observation," when Penny says, "I'm just a blonde monkey to you, aren't I?" to which Sheldon replies, "You said it, not me."[49]

The most extreme rendering of this particular line of thought, however, comes from *House, M.D.* Holmes with a stethoscope, Dr. Gregory House solves mysteries that have diseases as the culprits, but he abuses and manipulates his staff and all those around him with a derisive verve. In the end, however, it is one of his patients, James Sidas, who makes the case for geniuses being a totally different breed.[50] Sidas' backstory is that he was a child prodigy with a promising career as a brilliant physicist, but he gave it all up to be a simple courier married to a simple woman. Over the course of this sixth season episode entitled "Ignorance is Bliss," House and his team come to realize that Sidas has been abusing cough medicine to lower his IQ. When smart, Sidas is lonely and miserable to the point of attempting suicide. When chemically stupefied, he and his wife are happy. As he detoxes and regains his intelligence, his wife becomes less and less attractive to him. As he explains, "Do you know what the difference between her IQ and mine is? 91 points. In relation, she's closer to a gibbon than she is to me. Having sex with her would be an act of bestiality."[51] Lest we mistake who is in the wrong in this situation, Sidas readily concedes that his wife's lack of intelligence is not the problem, he is. When smart, "I'm the one who's a jerk."[52] The episode ends with Sidas choosing his life of cough syrup-induced blissful ignorance, over being a lonely, misanthropic genius.

If such geniuses view most people as less than human, not caring about them is not the price they pay in order to have their profound abilities. Rather, it is a calculated choice. They tend to regard caring about people (and worrying about what others think of them) as low priority distractions. Thus, when Watson reminds Holmes in *Sherlock*'s "The Great Game" that "there are lives at stake, Sherlock—actual human lives" and asks, "just so I know, do you care about that at all?" Holmes is blunt in his reply.[53] Since "caring about them" will not help save them, "I'll continue not to make that mistake."[54] House takes a similar approach to treating patients on *House, M.D.*, which is to say, he avoids them, preferring to deal with them as abstract problems and puzzles to solve, not people. As a result, such geniuses regularly manipulate the other characters, including and perhaps especially their "Dr. Watsons," using them like pieces being moved in a game.[55] That other characters, especially those in law enforcement, go along with and/or put up with such plans (usually without having them fully explained) implies, once again, the full extent of the geniuses' talents and the value of their ability to "close cases" and "save lives" when no one else can.

If these geniuses were altruistic philosopher-kings having us do things for our own good and making the world a better place, that would be one thing. But despite solving crimes and curing patients, most of them are selfish, motivated far more by personal goals and a desire not to be bored than by concern for lesser beings and the common good. When asked by Watson why he puts up with Holmes and his antics, Detective Inspector Lestrade on *Sherlock* observes, "Because I'm desperate ... and because Sherlock Holmes is a great man. And I think one day, if we're very, very *lucky*, he might even be a *good* one."[56] Beyond this hope that Holmes and his ilk can, like Brennan, be made to care about the rest of us, this projection of our hopes and fears about geniuses suggests that underlying our fascination with these exceptional individuals lie serious concerns about letting such logic-minded, emotionally distant, and egomaniacal demi-gods live among us.

Conclusion

Geniuses do amazing things on television. They solve seemingly unfathomable mysteries, perform amazing feats of memory and mathematics, and see things nobody else does. They fascinate, entertain, and (no doubt) get writers out of all sorts of corners into which they've painted themselves. In this chapter, however, I set out to examine what television makes a point of showing us: the things these exceptional people can't do. Not surprisingly, the primary answer to this question turns out to be, *be normal*. Setting aside gaps in the geniuses' knowledge, which are only made into a spectacle if it serves the plot and otherwise merely warrant a little bit of research on the characters' part, what the "spectacles of ignorance" depict is the ignoring of the rules and conventions of the "real" world, which is to say, signs of difference.

Unfortunately, rather than embrace this difference as merely part of human possibility, television programs tend to deploy it as a means of Othering the genius, marking them off as not one of us. As we've seen, this arises in part from the need to differentiate the genius from a television universe that, thanks to scriptwriting and the conventions and economic pressures of television, is already full of amazingly competent, articulate, and insightful characters. As discussed above, aligning genius with mental disorders proves a simple way to signify extreme intelligence while simultaneously limiting and even undercutting its credibility by linking it to the discourses of impairment and the ongoing struggles to remove the stigmas and Othering already associated with mental disability. As a result, most of these spectacles focus on the genius not "properly" engaging with mainstream culture or showing the "appropriate" emotions and empathy that the shows suggest "make us human."

Having decided that geniuses are Others, the programs assume that they, too, would perceive the difference as fundamental and dismiss the rest of us as Other just as we attempt to do to them. While humorous when played for comedy with someone like Sheldon Cooper, this assumption can prove quite disconcerting when projected onto geniuses such as Sherlock Holmes, whose abilities and social skills seem superior to the norm, raising the question of why such amazingly capable creatures should care about and support the simple-minded beasts around them. Maybe we'll make good (or at least amusing) pets.

Perhaps most troubling, however, is the collateral damage that comes with this Othering. The genius is seen as having a unique sense of "what really matters" that grounds his or her insightful perspective on and experience of the world. Marking off the genius as an Other thus involves rejecting what they fundamentally value. Although not quite the "highly evolved creature of pure intellect" Sheldon Cooper aspires to be, genius tends to be associated with reason, logic, science, and intellectual pursuits more broadly. Representing academia, science, and high culture as elitist institutions isolated from the "real" world, and indeed in a show like *Bones* at least partially to blame for Brennan's cultural cluelessness, serves to undermine all of them and reinforce the anti-intellectualism and distrust of science that pervades American culture. Ultimately, then, someone is being "spectacularly ignorant," but it's not the geniuses.

Notes

1. Oscar Wilde, "The Critic as Artist," *The Complete Writings of Oscar Wilde* (New York: Pearson, 1909), 56.
2. Mark Gatiss, "The Great Game," *Sherlock*, season 1, episode 3, directed by Paul McGuigan, aired August 8, 2010, on BBC One.
3. Ibid. Considering the fact that the program makes a point of having Holmes correct grammar and word usage a number of times, most obviously in an interview at the start of this episode, it seems odd that the writers consistently have him say "with who" throughout the series rather than the more proper "with whom."
4. Sir Arthur Conan Doyle, *The Adventures of Sherlock Holmes* (Hertfordshire: Wordsworth Editions Limited, 1995), 15.
5. Gatiss, "The Great Game."
6. Ibid.
7. Conan Doyle, *The Adventures of Sherlock Holmes*, 15.
8. Stephen Thompson, Steven Moffat, and Mark Gatiss, "The Sign of Three," *Sherlock*, season 3, episode 2, directed by Colm McCarthy, aired January 5, 2014, on BBC One. The only time Holmes claims to have actually erased needed information from his brain in *Sherlock* is in "The Sign of Three" episode when Holmes (who made the guest arrangements for the wedding) cannot remember Major Sholto's room number. Holmes' irritated assertion that "I have to delete something!" allows the writers to have Mary Watson provide the room number, which will prove a bit of evidence about her in the next episode. This uncharacteristic gap in Holmes' memory thus appears merely in the service of the series' plot.

9. Maria Konnikova, *Mastermind: How to Think Like Sherlock Holmes* (New York: Penguin, 2013), 26–7.

10. Mind palace and memory palace are contemporary names for the *method of loci*, a memorization technique that dates back to ancient Greece and involves organizing memories by visualizing them in specific locations. After getting shot in "His Last Vow" (the final episode of season three), Sherlock's mental constructs of Molly, Anderson, and Mycroft push him to figure out if he should fall forwards or back before he goes into shock. The construct of Molly slaps him to get his attention and says, "It's all well and clever having a Mind Palace, but you've only three seconds of consciousness left to use it. So, come on—what's going to kill you?" Figuring this out is a matter of thinking, not memory, suggesting some fuzziness on the part of the writer, Steven Moffat, when it comes to just what a mind palace is. The Mycroft construct in Sherlock's mind does appropriately suggest Holmes search his "memory palace" for a calming memory to keep him out of shock a little later, but linking these mental constructs to the notion of the mind palace seems off. Interestingly, the representation of Charles Augustus Magnussen's mind palace in the same episode seems much more in line with the definition of the term.

11. "Working memory" and the related formulation "short term memory" were both developed in the 1960s and, like the hard drive reference in *Sherlock*, are part of the trend to use concepts from computers as analogies for how brains work. In Joanne Ruthsatz and Jourdan B. Urbach's study, "Child prodigy: A novel cognitive profile places elevated general intelligence, exceptional working memory and attention to detail at the root of prodigiousness," *Intelligence* 40, no. 5 (2012): 419–426, the authors found that being a prodigy correlates much more closely with having an exceptional working memory than having a high IQ.

12. Steven Moffat, "His Last Vow," *Sherlock*, season 3, episode 3, directed by Nick Hurran, aired January 12, 2014, on BBC One.

13. Ibid.

14. When someone has just had an epiphany and tells whomever he or she has been talking with "You're a genius!" this harkens back to the origins of the word. From the 14th to mid–17th centuries the term *genius* referred to personal spirits or muses that offered divine insight into the secret workings of the world. By providing the concept or triggering the revelation in some other way, the interlocutor serves as a sort of "tutelary spirit." This seems a kinder reading than the more obvious sense that the person is, in fact, proclaiming his or her own genius.

15. Anthony D. Baker, "Recognizing Jake: Contending with Formulaic and Spectacularized Representations of Autism in Film," in *Autism and Representation*, ed. Mark Osteen (New York: Routledge, 2008), 230.

16. Ibid. As Baker notes, this "otherworldliness is expressed even in titles of films and texts about autism: for example, *Autism is a World*, Gerardine Wurzburg's 2005 award-winning documentary, and *Women from Another Planet*, Jean Kearns Miller's 2003 collection of writings by women with autism. *Time*'s May 6th, 2002, cover story employs the same rhetorical construction: the title 'Inside the World of Autism' is printed in all caps across the torso of a beautiful blond boy with his eyes closed, frozen in the middle of an otherworldly dance" (230).

17. Stuart Murray, *Representing Autism: Culture, Narrative, Fascination* (Liverpool: Liverpool University Press, 2008), 84. There is a certain irony in this being the dominant image of autism since Kim Peek, the man on whom Raymond Babbitt, the central savant and title character of *Rain Man*, is based did not, in fact, have autism. He had a rare genetic condition known as FG syndrome.

18. Ibid.

19. Murray, *Representing Autism*, 66. Intelligence is not, however, a zero-sum game. Only a small percent (typically estimated at between 10 percent and 12 percent) of those with autism are "compensated" for their disabilities with savant-like skills, creating unfair expec-

tations and pressure on those with autism and their families. More troubling still is the fact that, as Baker notes, "autism is a viable plot device—and autistic characters are viable characters—only if a spectacular skill or power is among the character's defining traits. Autistic characters are in the movies only because they have spectacular powers. Remove the savant or supernatural power, the film loses its plot, and the autistic character loses his or her raison d'etre" (see Baker, "Recognizing Jake," 234–5).

20. Henry Jenkins (see Henry Jenkins, *Convergence Culture: Where Old and New Media Collide* [New York: New York University Press, 2006]) and others have noted the ways in which the active and participatory engagement with comic books, video games, (science fiction) television and films characteristic of media fandom have moved from the fringes of society into the mainstream in the past twenty years. As a result, while most of the audience is unlikely to be "superfans" like the characters of *The Big Bang Theory*, it seems likely that what is intended to serve as a stereotypical mark of their difference and alienation as "nerds" is more likely something familiar to audiences in a world where the biggest movies are based on comic books and the annual Comic Con gets covered by the mainstream media as a major entertainment news event.

21. Stephen Engel and Jennifer Glickman, "The Bat Jar Conjecture," *The Big Bang Theory*, season 1, episode 13, directed by Mark Cendrowski, aired April 21, 2008, on CBS.

22. Lee Aronsohn, Steven Molaro, and Steve Holland, "The Staircase Implementation," *The Big Bang Theory*, season 3, episode 22, directed by Mark Cendrowski, aired May 17, 2010, on CBS.

23. Chuck Lorre and Bill Prady, "The Dumpling Paradox," *The Big Bang Theory*, season 1, episode 7, directed by Mark Cendrowski, aired November 5, 2007, on CBS.

24. Shannon Walters makes the very interesting case that despite his atypical approach to social interaction, with surprising regularity "Sheldon is able to communicate with other characters better than any other of the seemingly 'neurotypical' characters" (Shannon Walters, "Cool Aspie Humor: Cognitive Difference and Kenneth Burke's Comic Corrective in *The Big Bang Theory* and *Community*," *Journal of Literary & Cultural Disability Studies* 7.3 [2013], 276). For example, in the pilot Leonard gets tongue-tied trying to invite Penny to lunch and it is only after Sheldon intervenes that the invitation gets conveyed and accepted. Sheldon proves similarly better than the rest at communicating with Raj's date when things go poorly in another episode ("The Grasshopper Experiment").

25. Chuck Lorre, the executive producer of the show, has a tendency to equate sex with adulthood in his sitcoms. As Leonard and Penny's relationship gets more physical and so adult, Sheldon's asexuality results in him being marked as childlike in contrast.

26. Chuck Lorre and Lee Aronsohn, "The Guitarist Amplification," *The Big Bang Theory*, season 3, episode 22, directed by Mark Cendrowski, aired November 9, 2009, on CBS.

27. Eric Kaplan, Jim Reynolds, and Jeremy Howe, "The Status Quo Combustion," *The Big Bang Theory*, season 7, episode 24, directed by Mark Cendrowski, aired May 15, 2014, on CBS.

28. Paul Collins, "Must-Geek TV: Is the world ready for an Asperger's sitcom?" *Slate*, February 6, 2009, http://www.slate.com/articles/arts/television/2009/02/mustgeek_tv.html.

29. Noel Murray, "Interview: Jim Parsons," *A.V Club*, May 1, 2009, http://www.avclub.com/article/jim-parsons-27415.

30. See Walters, "Cool Aspie Humor," for a strong exploration of the complexities of humor when dealing with intellectual disability. She offers a very interesting alternate reading of the motivation behind some of Sheldon's behavior, suggesting that many of his actions could be read in light of a desire to preserve his social group cohesion rather as a sign of autism. The producers of the show, for their part, have tried to vary Sheldon's behavior to make a diagnosis less clear. In the second episode of the eighth season ("The Junior Professor Solution"), for example, Sheldon uncharacteristically changes his knocking ritual, using the speech in between knocks to converse with Human Resources Administrator Janine Davis rather than say her name.

31. Hart Hanson, "Pilot," *Bones*, season 1, episode 1, directed by Greg Yaitanes, aired September 13, 2005, on Fox.
32. Alan Sepinwall, "How TV shows try (or choose not) to depict Asperger's syndrome," *The Star-Ledger* (Newark, N.J.), February 28, 2010.
33. Teresa Lin, "The Woman at the Airport," *Bones*, season 1, episode 10, directed by Greg Yaitanes, aired January 25, 2006, on Fox.
34. Pat Charles, "The Feet on the Beach," *Bones*, season 6, episode 17, directed by Emile Levisetti, aired April 7, 2011, on Fox.
35. Hanson, "Pilot."
36. Ibid.
37. Ibid.
38. Laura Wolner, "The Woman in the Garden," *Bones*, season 1, episode 13, directed by Sanford Bookstaver, aired February 15, 2006, on Fox.
39. Hart Hanson, "Judas on a Pole," *Bones*, season 2, episode 11, directed by David Duchovny, aired December 13, 2006, on Fox.
40. Ibid.
41. Charles, "The Feet on the Beach."
42. Mark Gatiss, "A Study in Pink," *Sherlock*, season 1, episode 1, directed by Paul McGuigan, aired July 25, 2010, on BBC One.
43. Ibid.
44. Ibid. The following season Holmes returns to this formulation, noting near the start of "The Hounds of Baskerville" (Mark Gatiss, *Sherlock*, season 2, episode 2, directed by Paul McGuigan, aired January 8, 2012, on BBC One) that Watson's mind is "so placid, straightforward, barely used. Mine's like an engine, racing out of control; a rocket tearing itself to pieces trapped on the launch pad."
45. Gatiss, "A Study in Pink."
46. Ibid.
47. Mark Gatiss, "The Empty Hearse, " *Sherlock*, season 3, episode 1, directed by Jeremy Lovering, aired January 19, 2014, on BBC One.
48. Bill Prady, Steven Molaro, and Steve Holland, "The Hawking Excitation," *The Big Bang Theory*, season 5, episode 21, directed by Mark Cendrowski, aired April 5, 2012, on CBS.
49. Steven Molaro, Dave Goetsch, and Steve Holland, "The Higgs Boson Observation," *The Big Bang Theory*, season 6, episode 3, directed by Mark Cendrowski, aired October 11, 2012, on CBS.
50. David Hoselton, "Ignorance Is Bliss," *House, M.D.*, season 6, episode 9, directed by Greg Yaitanes, aired November 23, 2009, on Fox.
51. Ibid.
52. Ibid.
53. Gatiss, "The Great Game."
54. Ibid.
55. Even Sheldon from *The Big Bang Theory* gets into the manipulation game. Beyond cajoling others to do his bidding, he also uses operant conditioning to train Penny to give up habits he doesn't like (Lee Aronsohn and Richard Rosenstock, "The Gothowitz Deviation," *The Big Bang Theory*, season 3, episode 3, directed by Mark Cendrowski, aired October 5, 2009, on CBS.)
56. Gatiss, "A Study in Pink."

References

Aronsohn, Lee, and Richard Rosenstock. "The Gothowitz Deviation." *The Big Bang Theory*, season 3, episode 3. Directed by Mark Cendrowski. Aired October 5, 2009, on CBS. *The Big Bang Theory: The Complete Third Season*, DVD. Burbank: Warner Home Video, 2010.

Aronsohn, Lee, Steven Molaro, and Steve Holland. "The Staircase Implementation." *The Big Bang Theory*, season 3, episode 22. Directed by Mark Cendrowski. Aired May 17, 2010, on CBS. *The Big Bang Theory: The Complete Third Season*, DVD. Burbank: Warner Home Video, 2010.

Autism Is a World. Directed by Gerardine Wurzbùrg. DVD. CNN Productions, 2005.

Baker, Anthony D. "Recognizing Jake: Contending with Formulaic and Spectacularized Representations of Autism in Film." In *Autism and Representation*, edited by Mark Osteen, 229–243. New York: Routledge, 2008.

Charles, Pat. "The Feet on the Beach." *Bones*, season 6, episode 17. Directed by Emile Levisetti. Aired April 7, 2011, on Fox. Netflix.com.

Collins, Paul. "Must-Geek TV: Is the world ready for an Asperger's sitcom?" *Slate*, February 6, 2009. http://www.slate.com/articles/arts/television/2009/02/mustgeek_tv.html.

Conan Doyle, Arthur. *The Adventures of Sherlock Holmes*. Hertfordshire: Wordsworth Editions Limited, 1995.

Engel, Stephen, and Jennifer Glickman. "The Bat Jar Conjecture." *The Big Bang Theory*, season 1, episode 13. Directed by Mark Cendrowski. Aired April 21, 2008, on CBS. *The Big Bang Theory: The Complete First Season*, DVD. Burbank: Warner Home Video, 2008.

Gatiss, Mark. "The Empty Hearse." *Sherlock*, season 3, episode 1. Directed by Jeremy Lovering. Aired January 19, 2014, on BBC One. Netflix.com.

———. "The Great Game." *Sherlock*, season 1, episode 3. Directed by Paul McGuigan. Aired August 8, 2010, on BBC One. Netflix.com.

———. "The Hounds of Baskerville." *Sherlock*, season 2, episode 2. Directed by Paul McGuigan. Aired January 8, 2012, on BBC One. Netflix.com.

———. "A Study in Pink." *Sherlock*, season 1, episode 1. Directed by Paul McGuigan. Aired July 25, 2010, on BBC One. Netflix.com.

Goetsch, Dave, and Steven Molaro. "The Grasshopper Experiment." *The Big Bang Theory*, season 1, episode 8. Directed by Ted Wass. Aired November 12, 2007, on CBS. *The Big Bang Theory: The Complete First Season*, DVD. Burbank: Warner Home Video, 2008.

Hanson, Hart. "Judas on a Pole." *Bones*, season 2, episode 11. Directed by David Duchovny. Aired December 13, 2006, on Fox. Netflix.com.

———. "Pilot." *Bones*, season 1, episode 1. Directed by Greg Yaitanes. Aired September 13, 2005, on Fox. Netflix.com.

Hoselton, David. "Ignorance Is Bliss." *House, M.D.*, season 6, episode 9. Directed by Greg Yaitanes. Aired November 23, 2009, on Fox. Netflix.com.

Jenkins, Henry. *Convergence Culture: Where Old and New Media Collide*. New York: New York University Press, 2006.

Kaplan, Eric, Jim Reynolds, and Jeremy Howe. "The Status Quo Combustion." *The Big Bang Theory*, season 7, episode 24. Directed by Mark Cendrowski. Aired May 15, 2014, on CBS. *The Big Bang Theory: The Complete Seventh Season*, DVD. Burbank: Warner Home Video, 2014.

Konnikova, Maria. *Mastermind: How to Think Like Sherlock Holmes* New York: Penguin, 2013.

Lin, Teresa. "The Woman at the Airport." *Bones*, season 1, episode 10. Directed by Greg Yaitanes. Aired January 25, 2006, on Fox. Netflix.com.

Lorre, Chuck, and Bill Prady. "The Dumpling Paradox." *The Big Bang Theory*, season 1, episode 7. Directed by Mark Cendrowski. Aired November 5, 2007, on CBS. *The Big Bang Theory: The Complete First Season*, DVD. Burbank: Warner Home Video, 2008.

Lorre, Chuck, and Lee Aronsohn. "The Guitarist Amplification." *The Big Bang Theory*, season 3, episode 22. Directed by Mark Cendrowski. Aired November 9, 2009, on CBS. *The Big Bang Theory: The Complete Third Season*, DVD. Burbank: Warner Home Video, 2010.

Miller, Jean Kearns. *Women from Another Planet? Our Lives in the Universe of Autism*. Bloomington: 1st Books Library, 2003.

Moffat, Steven. "His Last Vow." *Sherlock*, season 3, episode 3. Directed by Nick Hurran. Aired January 12, 2014, on BBC One. Netflix.com.

Molaro, Steven, Dave Goetsch, and Steve Holland. "The Higgs Boson Observation." *The Big Bang Theory*, season 6, episode 3. Directed by Mark Cendrowski. Aired October 11, 2012, on CBS. *The Big Bang Theory: The Complete Sixth Season*, DVD. Burbank: Warner Home Video, 2013.

Molaro, Steven, Eric Kaplan, and Steve Holland. "The Junior Professor Solution." *The Big Bang Theory*, season 8, episode 2. Directed by Mark Cendrowski. Aired September 22, 2014, on CBS. Amazon Instant Video.

Murray, Noel. "Interview: Jim Parsons." *A.V Club*. 1 May 2009. http://www.avclub.com/article/jim-parsons-27415.

Murray, Stuart. *Representing Autism: Culture, Narrative, Fascination*. Liverpool: Liverpool University Press, 2008.

Nash, J. Madeleine, and Amy Bonesteel. "The Secrets of Autism." *Time*, May 6, 2002, 46.

Prady, Bill, Steven Molaro, and Steve Holland. "The Hawking Excitation." *The Big Bang Theory*, season 5, episode 21. Directed by Mark Cendrowski. *The Big Bang Theory: The Complete Fifth Season*, DVD. Aired April 5, 2012, on CBS. Burbank: Warner Home Video, 2012.

Rain Man. Directed by Barry Levinson. 1988. Netflix.com.

Ruthsatz, Joanne, and Jourdan B. Urbach. "Child prodigy: A novel cognitive profile places elevated general intelligence, exceptional working memory and attention to detail at the root of prodigiousness" *Intelligence* 40, no. 5 (2012): 419–426.

Sepinwall, Alan. "How TV shows try (or choose not) to depict Asperger's syndrome." *The Star-Ledger* (Newark, N.J.), February 28, 2010.

Thompson, Stephen, Steven Moffat, and Mark Gatiss. "The Sign of Three." *Sherlock*, season 3, episode 2. Directed by Colm McCarthy. Aired January 5, 2014, on BBC One. Netflix.com.

Walters, Shannon. "Cool Aspie Humor: Cognitive Difference and Kenneth Burke's Comic Corrective in *The Big Bang Theory* and *Community*." *Journal of Literary & Cultural Disability Studies* 7, no. 3 (2013): 271–288.

Wilde, Oscar. "The Critic as Artist." *The Complete Writings of Oscar Wilde*. New York: Pearson, 1909.

Wolner, Laura. "The Woman in the Garden." *Bones*, season 1, episode 13. Directed by Sanford Bookstaver. Aired February 15, 2006, on Fox. Netflix.com.

Mediated Genius, Anti-Intellectualism and the Detachment(s) of Everyday Life

JZ Long

> Madness and the madman become major figures, in their ambiguity: menace and mockery, the dizzying unreason of the world, and the feeble ridicule of men.—Michel Foucault[1]

> The fundamental cause of the trouble is that in the modern world the stupid are cocksure while the intelligent are full of doubt.
> —Bertrand Russell[2]

The genius is a well-known character in the popular narratives of many cultures, especially on the mass medium of television. As suggested by Robert Sternberg and Stacey Bridges, a genius is "a person [who] produce[s] a product that, in the context of some time and place, is held to be of such extraordinary value that people conclude that the product only could have been produced by someone with absolutely extraordinary talents."[3] The genius is perhaps best represented in popular culture in the form of Sir Arthur Conan Doyle's "master detective" Sherlock Holmes, who has appeared on cinema and television for over a hundred years. Holmes is currently represented in both *Elementary* (2012) and *Sherlock* (2010), two postmodern interpretations which have added a female Watson and a text-savvy Holmes, respectively, to the mix. As the enduring popularity of this character illustrates, it would appear that geniuses remain popular figures in contemporary culture.

In many televisual representations, however, the notion of genius is mediated by a long-running myth of anti-intellectualism which recuperates the characteristics of genius by pathologizing such characters until the already fine line between genius and madness disappears altogether. Thus, while the current resurgence of intellectuals on television can certainly stimulate our own thinking, it also influences our perceptions of genius through repeated portrayals of the genius as tragically flawed. Utilizing established theories and methods from cultural studies, a multiperspectival analysis of these various programs illustrates how the positioning of the genius as tragically flawed allows the viewer to celebrate specific characterizations of intellectuality while maintaining an anti-intellectual stance of detached (anti)-enlightenment.

In unsettled times like these, it is problematic to see how fictionalized representations of genius, rather than improving our intelligence, provide us with both the means and the ends for anti-intellectualizing our own alienation from everyday life. When we come home from the workday, we celebrate as genius after genius solves impossible tasks while distancing ourselves from the various flaws (from addiction and anxiety to disability and depression) which are made to be an integral part of such intelligence. In this way, the combination of these two distinct discourses contributes to the continued growth of anti-intellectualism in today's global cultures. If, as some scholars suggest, the world appears to be getting less intelligent by the day,[4] we could use all the help, including the televisual, that we can get.

Myth-Conceptions

Anti-intellectualism, never far from the surface in American life, is once again on the rise. Etymologically, the term comes from the unique conjunction between the Greek prefix *anti-* ("opposite, against, in exchange, instead, representing, rivalling, simulating") and a new German word, *intellectualismus* ("intellectualism"), and the concept was in wide use by the beginning of the nineteenth century.[5] Intellectualism, according to the *Oxford English Dictionary*, is generally defined in one of two ways: as "the practice of apprehending something only with the intellect; the exercise of the intellect alone (also: devotion to intellectual pursuits)" and, in a more specifically philosophical vein, "the doctrine that knowledge is wholly or mainly derived from the action of the intellect or from pure reason."[6] As both practice and doctrine, then, *anti*-intellectual ideologies are generally opposed not only to an understanding of knowledge as derived from the use of intelligence and reason but also to an understanding of those would use such intelligence and reason to produce knowledge as untrustworthy and suspect.

Though subject to great debates, anti-intellectualism remains a popular theme in contemporary American culture. Recent scholarship, for example, has examined the use of anti-intellectual discourses in such diverse fields as education, law, politics, and science.[7] At present, anti-intellectualism has become part of a wide range of debates playing out in the public sphere over appropriate governmental responses to a number of serious environmental issues,[8] not just in the United States but increasingly in other nations around the world.[9] While anti-intellectualism has once again found a space as a popular trope in our media cultures, it is also, as many intellectuals would certainly call it, a myth.

As a critical concept, myths have long been an integral part of American popular culture. As noted in the *OED*, a myth is most commonly defined as both "a traditional story, typically involving supernatural beings or forces, which embodies and provides an explanation, aetiology, or justification for something such as the early history of a society, a religious belief or ritual, or a natural phenomenon" and "a widespread but untrue or erroneous story or belief; a widely held misconception; a misrepresentation of the truth (also: something existing only in myth; a fictitious or imaginary person or thing)."[10] Myths are both traditional stories and fictitious stories, then, and a lot of other stories in-between. Myth is such versatile concept that it is even versatile grammatically, as it can serve as a noun, an adjective, and verb.

Of the many intellectual analyses of myth, one of the most powerful comes from the work of the late French semiotician Roland Barthes, whose analyses of popular cultural forms introduced semiology and semiotics to whole new audiences. Building on linguist Ferdinand de Saussure's idea of semiology as a new "science that studies the life of signs within a society,"[11] Barthes takes this idea to heart and suggests that one of the key methods for studying contemporary societies is to examine how its popular signs—from logos to ads, from images to texts—both represent and re-present specific ideologies to the public. Examining everything from detergents and toys to chopsticks and stationary, Barthes' semiotic tools have been used to study a wide range of signs and symbols in various popular and media cultures.[12]

At the end of *Mythologies*, a collection of several of his short essays, appears "Myth Today," an extended meditation on the powerful role myths play in structuring culture and society. As Barthes sees it, a myth is a "second-order semiological system [where] ... a sign (namely the associative total of a concept and an image) in the first system, becomes a mere signifier in the second."[13] The problem, for Barthes, is that this second-order system of myths (what Barthes also refers to as metalanguage) increasingly obscures its origins as part of our primary system of signification (signifier + signified = sign; i.e., concept + image = language).

In reconceptualizing myths as a "message," "form," "mode of signification," and "a system of communication,"[14] semiotics can be used as a means of understanding how myths become both embedded in popular cultures and uncritically accepted as a common sense. In lieu of undertaking the hard intellectual work necessary to fix our personal and collective problems, we tend to lapse into the lazy acceptance of "common sense," or popular stories that have been widely disseminated but are not necessarily accurate.[15] Trying to study common sense as ideology is especially difficult, as "we don't often think about ideology, because it has been normalized and naturalized to the point that it's no longer visible to us. It is the air we breathe and the food that we eat. Identifying ideology is the first step in becoming a media-literate society."[16] But when, for example, television, the most popular and ubiquitous mass medium in human history, continues to misrepresent intellectuals as anything but intellectual, that is, as anti-intellectual, then semiologists should take note.

As transmitters of myth, popular cultural forms such as cinema, television, and the internet become important sites for studying and debating how these "materials of mythical speech (the language itself, photography, painting, posters, rituals, objects, etc.), however different at the start, are reduced to a pure signifying function as soon as they are caught by myth."[17] In form and content alike, myths appropriate signs in order to naturalize them as ideologies. For unlike language, the construction of myths is not arbitrary; rather, "it is always in part motivated, and unavoidably contains some analogy."[18] In obfuscating motivation through analogization, Barthes argues that we have now "pass[ed] from semiology to ideology."[19] As a result, the task of the semiologist has significantly increased, for now she must also attempt to discover the ideological content of myths in addition to their linguistic functions, and precisely to illustrate how such popular ideologies become treated as actual facts rather than natural(ized) history.

Our media culture provides us with all manner of mythic symbols, from gods to golems, valkyries to vampires, all represented in myth. In *Popular Culture: An Introductory Text*, Jack Nachbar and Kevin Lause write that there are at least ten popular myths in American culture. These myths are, in alphabetical order, America as a special nation, anti-intellectualism, endless abundance, individual freedom, material success, the nuclear family, romantic love, rural simplicity, technology as protector and savior, and the myth of violence outside the law to achieve justice.[20] In subsequent chapters, analyses of Currier and Ives, Frank Capra, and Joe Cocker deftly illustrate how these myths operate in our cultural unconscious.

Nachbar and Lause's definition of the myth of anti-intellectualism is especially important. According to these scholars, a myth (and its associated heroes, celebrities, stereotypes, and rituals) revolves around the story of "[t]he truly intelligent person [who] translates ideas into practical solutions to real problems, lives 'off' ideas instead of 'for' them, and recognizes that human identity is found essentially in the heart, not the mind."[21] Whether conceptualized "positively" as professionals or "crackerbarrel philosophers" or, more negatively, as "eggheads" and "nerds," Nachbar and Lause suggest that the myth of anti-intellectualism is especially important given that "it is very American and very complex in the manner in which it also embodies other American beliefs and values" as well as other myths and ideologies.[22]

There is no current televisual genre which does not illustrate this anti-intellectual trend. It is evident across such popular television genres as action-adventure (*Breaking Bad, Chuck*), game shows (*Beauty and the Geek, King of the Nerds*), medical comedies (*Childrens Hospital, Doogie Howser, M.D., Scrubs*), news shows (*The Soup, TMZ on TV*); reality television (*Big Brother; Jersey Shore, Keeping Up with the Kardashians, Real Housewives*), science fiction (*Doctor Who, Star Trek: The Next Generation*), talk shows (*The Jerry Springer Show, Maury*), and situation comedies (*The Big Bang Theory, The IT Crowd, Malcolm in the Middle*), especially animated comedies (*Archer, Beavis and Butthead, King of the Hill, The Simpsons*). More than any other contemporary genre, however, the medical drama (*House, Fringe, Mental*) and the police procedural (*Bones, Criminal Minds, Lie to Me, The Mentalist, Numb3rs*) illustrate some peculiar qualities regarding how anti-intellectual ideologies operate across specific texts involving intellectualism.

The use of genre here is especially important. As Jason Mittell has recently suggested, television genres can be interrogated as *cultural categories*, that is, as socially constructed forms. As Mittell describes them,

> Genres work within nearly every facet of television—corporate organizations, policy decisions, critical discourses, audience practices, production techniques, textual aesthetics, and historical trends.... Industries use genres to produce programs, to define brands and identities (channels such as ESPN or Cartoon Network), and to target audiences through scheduling.... Genres help audiences organize fans practices..., guide personal preferences, and frame everyday conversations and viewing practices.[23]

Genre is not simply a narrative style; rather, it is also a critical means of "organizing television practices" themselves. Mittell's conceptualization of television as a "circuit of cultural practice operative in multiple sites, instead of a singular realm of textual criticism or institutional analysis" echoes recent work on the need for a more multiperspectival cultural studies capable of analyzing cultural forms through the multiple (and frequently competing) lenses of political economy, textuality, and audience reception.[24] Triangulation amongst these perspectives contributes to a richer analysis of any media culture, especially once one discovers the similarities and differences unique to each cultural conjunction.

In organizing televisual practices, television genres fulfill a key function of mass media in modern societies: surveillance of the cultural environment. In a classic work in the history of communications theory, American political scientist Harold Lasswell once suggested that

> The communication process in society performs three functions: (a) surveillance of the environment, disclosing threats and opportunities affecting the value position of the community and of the component parts within it; (b) correlation of the components of society in making a response to the environment; (c) transmission of the social inheritance.[25]

But this is, fortunately, far from Lasswell's last word on the subject. In the subsequent paragraph, the final one, Lasswell warns us that

> in society, the communication process reveals special characteristics when the ruling element is afraid of the internal as well as the external environment. In gauging the efficiency of communication in any given context, it is necessary to take into account the values at stake, and the identity of the group whose position is being examined. In democratic societies, rational choices depend on enlightenment, which in turn depends upon communication; and especially upon the equivalence of attention among leaders, experts and rank and file.[26]

As there is a political dimension to ideological obfuscation, it is imperative to critically analyze media cultures in order to identify and deconstruct how specific myths function in specific historical contexts. In the next section, then, multiple television programs will be analyzed for evidence not only of what modes of anti-intellectuality are being represented but also how they are operating in (and on) public consciousness.

Myth-Identifications

The most important example I know of the power of the myth of anti-intellectualism in American televisual culture can be found in Nachbar and Lause's analysis of the short-lived science fiction series *Star Trek* (1966). The core of the series involves the relationships between three main characters: Captain James Tiberius Kirk, First Lieutenant Spock, and Dr. Leonard H. "Bones" McCoy. The dramatic issues involving these characters are excellent examples of how myths like anti-intellectualism come to regulate our common culture. While Spock, a half-human, half-alien being beholden to logical thought, represents an extreme form of intellectualism, Bones' constant emotional outbursts signify the exact opposite. The tension between these two styles of televisual characters, the intellectual and the emotional, drives many of the show's narratives.

This conflict is aptly demonstrated across three Star Trek films—*Star Trek II: The Wrath of Khan* (1982), *Star Trek III: The Search for Spock* (1984), and *Star Trek IV: The Voyage Home* (1986)—which are often thought of, by both fans and critics alike, as an unofficial "trilogy" and the heart of the entire enterprise. Concerned with the death and rebirth of Spock, the three films raise a number of issues about the role of intellectuality in everyday live. In *Star Trek II*, for example, when Spock tells McCoy, "Really, Dr. McCoy. You must learn to govern your passions; they will be your undoing. Logic suggests," McCoy immediately responds with "Logic? My God, the man's talking about logic; we're talking about universal Armageddon! You green-blooded, inhuman..."[27] This triangulation between logic and emotion is further exemplified at the beginning of *Star Trek IV: The Voyage Home*, a film directed by Leonard Nimoy ("Spock") himself. Having been brought back to life, Spock begins the film recovering on his home planet of Vulcan, where he tests his mental prowess by attempting to rapidly answer a series of overlapping questions given to him by a computer: "What is the dilithium crystallization temperature of...? Correct. What is the configuration of a starship in formation...? Correct." All is well until the computer asks Spock, "How do you feel?" His reply? "I do not understand the question."[28] Spock's mother enters the room and informs him that she added the question so that he would learn to utilize his human emotions alongside his Vulcan rationality. Unfazed, Spock leaves the room puzzled by his mother's request. Clearly, this "new" Spock is not yet ready, the viewer is led to believe, to assume command of a starship, let alone his own consciousness.

The primary character, Captain Kirk, is therefore by necessity the captain of the Starship Enterprise. Kirk in is charge of the ship precisely because he embodies both intellectuality and emotionality, utilizing each as needed to make decisions befitting each strange new world, life, and civilization they encounter. This articulation should not be lost on the popular scholar, as it is this ability to balance both sides that makes Kirk so worthy of being captain of the ship. We can only imagine what life aboard a Federation starship would be under the logical command of a Spock or the emotional leadership of a McCoy.

This framework for triangulating between intellectualism and emotionality is also common in other televisual genres. This is especially true in two of the most popular ones: medical dramas and police procedurals. The first two decades of the twenty-first century are producing a number of televisual intellectuals who are easily broken down into a variety of physiological and psychological problems. Whether in medical dramas or police procedurals, geniuses are simultaneously characterized as both mentally gifted and mentally challenged. In constructing the characters in this way, viewers are repeatedly shown representations of genius in such a schizophrenic manner that perceptions of intellectualism and anti-intellectualism become muddled, leading once again to media's target of the lowest common denominator.

One of the most popular recent television shows features the adventures of master surgeon Gregory House. House, the lead diagnostician at a posh New Jersey hospital, is the Sherlock Holmes of the medical ward, deducing diagnoses from the slimmest of symptoms. Featuring an ever-changing team of younger doctors, who themselves exhibit characteristics of both genius and madness, *House, M.D.* (2004) is a key example of how contemporary televisual practices anti-intellectualize genius. As a tagline for the show once put it, "Genius has side effects."

The most obvious evidence of anti-intellectualization occurs in the very conceptualization of the character. Believing that everybody lies, Dr. House does not have time for social interactions. With a bedside manner that offends patients and doctors alike, his character has been referred to as "a world-class jerk and a world-class diagnostician," a "brilliant pill-popping bastard," "maladaptive and destructive," and 'manipulative, sarcastic, and an admitted liar."[29] And these are but a few of the characterizations from just two recent collections of scholarly analyses of the show.[30]

House's character is made even worse insofar as his psychological issues are ascribed to his addiction to Vicodin painkillers as a way to deal with the excruciating pain in his right leg. As House struggles with this pain over the course of the series, he has been fired and arrested multiple times, suffered from hallucinations, been institutionalized in a psychiatric hospital, crashed his car into his ex-girlfriend's living room, and even operated on himself amidst a flow of constant reprimanding and relapsing. Having constantly berated, tricked, and embarrassed almost everyone he ever knew, the series ends with one final lie: after faking his death in a fire à la Sherlock Holmes, House and his cancer-stricken friend Wilson are seen, like Wyatt and Billy in *Easy Rider* (1969), riding off into the distance on their motorcycles. Unlike the tragic conclusion of *Easy Rider*, however, viewers are left to draw their own conclusions about House's fate: while Wilson's cancer is undoubtedly terminal, we can at least believe that, with a clean slate ahead of him, House may yet be redeemed.

Though House is certainly anti-intellectualized, so too, are his rotating team of anti-social doctors. Among the doctors are Dr. Robert Chase, a charismatic doctor who is also an admitted murderer; Dr. Allison Cameron, an empathetic doctor who falls for House before marrying and divorcing Chase; Dr. Remy "Thirteen" Hadley, a bi-sexual with Huntington's disease who killed her own brother; and a variety of short-run characters who are represented in stereotypically anti-social ways, such as poisoning patients (Dr. Travis Brennan), faking credentials (Mr. Henry Dobson), earning multiple academic degrees after graduating from high school at the age of 15 (Ms. Martha Masters), and being represented as a short, bespectacled female Asian doctor who has trouble talking with others (Dr. Chi Park). Working for a psychologically debilitated doctor is bad enough, but all of the show's supporting characters exhibit their own schizophrenic signs of genius and madness. In this way, anti-intellectualism comes to suffuse the entire show; the viewer can enjoy the case-of-the-week resolutions while enjoying the misanthropy of an eccentric team of privileged doctors.

Another excellent example of television's anti-intellectualized intellectual is the brilliant forensic anthropologist Dr. Temperance "Bones" Brennan on *Bones* (2005). Characterized as "hyper-rational," "socially inept and literal to a fault with little popular knowledge," and "aggressive, abrasive, and [with] all the social grace of a snapping turtle,"[31] Dr. Brennan is extremely intelligent in the scientific fields but clueless in many others. Due to her parents' criminal activities, Temperance was raised by foster parents as a teenager, both narratives thus contributing to her already fragile constitution by alienating her from her real parents as well as pre-dispositioning her as of the criminal mind as well. As a result, fans have suggested that, among other things, she "suffers from undiagnosed and untreated PTSD" as a result of her family issues as well as Asperger's due to her "obsession with data and an inability to read other people in social situations."[32]

Bones' other characters do not fare much better. If Brennan is like Spock, then FBI Special Agent Seeley Booth is like McCoy, constantly jumping to conclusions. Other characters who work with Brennan and Booth in the Jeffersonian include Dr. Jack Stanley Hodgins IV, a skilled entomologist who is both secretly wealthy and prone to conspiracy theories, Dr. Lance Sweets, a foster-raised savant with multiple psychology degrees whose young appearance and demeanor often prevent him from being taken seriously, and a revolving cast of interns ("squints," as Booth stereotypically calls them) lacking in a wide variety of social skills, including a young woman who cannot stop talking inappropriately in public and a young man whose 163 IQ is not enough to prevent him from becoming an actual accomplice to a serial killer known as Gorgomon.

Once the show incorporated lead actress Emily Deschanel's real-life pregnancy into the narrative, however, the series shifted into a comfortable procedural where the ebbs and flows of the characters' domestic and professional lives propelled the overall narrative. But Brennan's flaws, especially her emotional detachment and unwillingness to tolerate social niceties, were important to show's development: rather than appealing to audiences with a higher figure like Captain Kirk, *Bones* appealed to a wider audience by following a classic *folie à deux* between Brennan's Spock and Booth's McCoy. What can be seen throughout both of these series, therefore, is intellectuality conceptualized as coextensive with a wide range of maladies and other undesirable traits. While the jury is still out on the precise causes and effects between genius and madness,[33] it is clear that televisual representations of these discourses, in their tendency to conflate the two, contribute to their further correlation.

Myth-Analysis

Whether a House or Brennan, the myth of anti-intellectualism is alive and well in contemporary televisual culture. As the above examples illustrate, one of key ways this anti-intellectualism works to produce surveillance of the environment is by enabling us, on the one hand, to empathize with the shows' characters by desiring the intelligence and reason employed by these intellectuals to solve the problems and paradoxes of their respective fields, while simultaneously disabling us, on the other hand, by representing these intellectuals in such a way as the articulation of psychological deficiencies with intellectual genius allows us to ideologically distance ourselves from these desires (even after discovering the ideological misdirection). That this negation of intelligence and reason appears in two fields, medicine and criminology, that are well understood to require intelligence and reason for their successful operation is especially troubling.

In utilizing subjects from two of the most conservative social institutions, it should not be too surprising to see how their narrative formulas recuperate anti-intellectual ideology time and time again. Medical and criminal discourse themselves surveil both our actual and fictional environments, precisely by intellectually policing the boundaries of what constitutes their respective domains. The work of Michel Foucault proves especially instructive here. In his early essays and books, Foucault outlines a new method of cultural analysis which he has referred to as "archaeology" or "genealogy."[34] Searching the past for exemplary events, Foucault illustrates how social and cultural discourses emerge and coalesce into distinct historical formations or assemblages. In so doing, Foucault's research shows how widely accepted popular discourses like medicine, criminology, and psychiatry were formed through a historical process of articulation and conjunction.

In *Madness and Civilization*, for example, Foucault argues that madness is not inherent in humanity but rather a social construction designed to encircle those individuals who did not conform to the existing structures of society. To further these ends, new discourses on madmen, delirium, and insanity came together to spur the develop of asylums as a legitimate social institution by which, to use Lasswell's terminology, a new group of leaders and experts could emerge to more strictly police the growing rank and file. In *The Birth of the Clinic*, Foucault shows that we become immersed in new disorders, illnesses, and symptoms, which, as a result, lead to the development of the clinic and the hospital as institutional means of regulating not just who is healthy or ill but also who should live and who should die. In *Discipline and Punish*, Foucault famously illustrates how new categorizations, punishments, and panoptical structures emerge as a way for social and cultural elites to better inculcate in their wards the ways and means of policing themselves. And, over three volumes on *The History of Sexuality*, Foucault argues that sexuality is itself nothing but a social construction, an ideological formation that operates by policing the boundaries of what is and is not permissible to say about sex. In each instance, Foucault analyzes how unique social institutions emerge in specific historical times and places in order to make the arduous task of ideological indoctrination proceed largely underneath popular consciousness.[35] What is taken as the natural "order of things" is revealed as its opposite, as the messy, contingent, and complex flows of human life. Given intellectuals' predisposition for questioning the order of anything, it certainly behooves existing elites, including those who control our media, to eliminate the desire for intellectuality as often as possible.

This schizophrenia associated with televisual characterizations of genius, in turn, significantly contributes to intellectualist schizophrenia in the minds of viewers. In "Myth Today," Barthes argues that, in uncritically accepting popular myths, our language itself becomes "depoliticized." As a result, we increasingly inhabit a world "which is trained to *celebrate* things, and no longer to '*act* them.'"[36] Even though television encourages us to celebrate intellectualism, it certainly discourages us from trying, to use Barthes' phrase, to "act them," and it does so by creating a general and pervasive atmosphere of anti-intellectuality. The line between genius and madman is already thin, but the inherent ambiguity in these terms as Foucault sees it is also what allows televisuality to work on those lines, blurring them even further in order to anti-intellectualize its audiences against the growing debates about the conditions of the current structures of our social world. For as Foucault's comment suggests, the madman becomes a popular narrative figure precisely when society needs an ambiguous figure capable of representing "menace and mockery, the dizzying unreason of the world, and the feeble ridicule of men."[37] When coupled with calls, like Russell's, of the general decline of intelligence in the world, the stakes of mediated representations of both genius and madness require close scrutiny. As Steinberg and Bridges suggest, the importance of geniuses and intellectuals is that they "are the people who transform the world so as to make it a very different and better place to live."[38] For when media-controlled images of intellectuality serve to reinforce the "feeble ridicule" of anti-intellectualism, a search for more honest representations is an enlightened place to start.

Notes

1. Michel Foucault, *Madness and Civilization: A History of Insanity in the Age of Reason*, trans. Richard Howard (New York: Vintage, 1988 [1961]), 13.
2. Bertrand Russell, *Mortals and Others* (New York: Routledge, 2009 [1975]), 204.
3. Robert J. Sternberg and Stacey L. Bridges, "Varieties of Genius," in *The Wiley Handbook of Genius*, ed. Dean Keith Simonton (Malden, MA: John Wiley & Sons, 2014), 185.
4. E.g., Isaac Asimov, "A Cult of Ignorance," *Newsweek*, January 21, 1980, 19; Charlotte Thomson Iserbyt, *The Deliberate Dumbing Down of America*, rev. ed. (Ravenna, OH: Conscience Press, 2011); and Charles P. Pierce, *Idiot America: How Stupidity Became a Virtue in the Land of the Free* (New York: Anchor Books, 2010).
5. "anti-, prefix1," *OED Online*, December 2014, Oxford University Press, ttp://www.oed.com/view/Entry/8501?redirectedFrom=anti-intellectual; "intellectualism, n," *OED Online*, December 2014, Oxford University Press, http://www.oed.com/view/Entry/97388?redirectedFrom=intellectualism.
6. "intellectualism, n," *OED Online*.
7. Such fields include education (Rafik Z. Elias, "Anti-Intellectual Attitudes and Academic Self-Efficacy Among Business Students," *Journal of Education for Business* 84, no. 2 [2008]: 110–17; Richard J. Hook, "Students' Anti-Intellectual Attitudes and Adjusting to College," *Psychological Reports* 94, no. 3 [2004]: 909–14), law (Brian J. Foley, "Policing from the Gut: Anti-Intellectualism in American Criminal Procedure," *Maryland Law Review* 69, no. 2 [2009], http://digitalcommons.law.umaryland.edu/mlr/vol69/iss2/4/; Leonard J. Long, "Resisting Anti-Intellectualism and Promoting Legal Literacy," *Southern Illinois University Law Journal* 34, no. 1 [2009]: 1–54), politics (Elvin T. Lim, *The Anti-Intellectual Presidency: The Decline of Presidential Rhetoric from George Washington to George W. Bush* [New York: Oxford University Press, 2008]; Colleen J. Shogan, "Anti-Intellectualism in the Modern Presidency: A Republican Populism," *Perspectives on Politics* 5, no. 2 [2007]: 295–303), and science (Malte C. Ebach and Marcelo R. de Carvalho, "Anti-Intellectualism in the DNA Barcoding Enterprise," *Zoologia* 27, no. 2 [2010]: 165–78; Jonathon Gatehouse, "America Dumbs Down," *Maclean's*, May 15, 2014, http://www.macleans.ca/politics/america-dumbs-down/).
8. See Adam Brophy, "Trusting Science," *Irish Times*, June 14, 2014; John Marcus, "You Can't Tell Me Anything," *Times Higher Education*, October 27, 2011; Shawn Lawrence Otto, "America's Science Problem," *Scientific American* 307, no. 5 (2014): 62–71; Patricia Williams, "Anti-Intellectualism Is Taking Over the U.S.," *The Guardian*, May 18, 2012; and Ray B. Williams, "Anti-Intellectualism and the 'Dumbing Down' of America," *Psychology Today*, July 7, 2014, http://www.psychologytoday.com/blog/wired-success/201407/anti-intellectualism-and-the-dumbing-down-america.
9. Pieter J.D. Drenth, "Growing Anti-Intellectualism in Europe: A Menace to Science,"

Studia Psychologica 45, no. 1 (2003): 5–13; Benjamin J. Glasson, "The Intellectual Outside: Anti-Intellectualism and the Subject of Populist Discourses in Australian Newspapers," *Continuum: Journal of Media and Cultural Studies* 26, no. 1 (2012): 101–14.

10. "myth, n," *OED Online*, December 2014, Oxford University Press, http://www.oed.com/view/Entry/124670?rskey=KjBPEw&result=1&isAdvanced=false.

11. Ferdinand de Saussure, *Course in General Linguistics*, trans. Wade Baskin, ed. Charles Bally and Albert Sechehaye (New York: Philosophical Library, 1959), 16.

12. See, e.g., Roland Barthes, *Mythologies*, trans. Annette Lavers (New York: Hill and Wang, 1972 [1957]); Roland Barthes, *The Eiffel Tower and Other Mythologies*, trans. Richard Howard (New York: Hill and Wang, 1979 [1964]); Roland Barthes, *Critical Essays*, trans. Richard Howard (Evanston, IL: Northwestern University Press, 1972 [1964]); and Roland Barthes, *New Critical Essays*, trans. Richard Howard (New York: Hill and Wang, 1980 [1970]).

13. Barthes, *Mythologies*, 113.

14. Ibid., 107.

15. See Lisa Holderman, ed., *Common Sense: Intelligence as Presented on Popular Television*, (Lanham, MD: Rowman and Littlefield, 2008) and Duncan Watts, *Everything Is Obvious: How Common Sense Fails Us* (New York: Random House, 2011).

16. Leslie A. Grinner, "Bella's Choice: Deconstructing Ideology and Power in *The Twilight Saga*," in *Race/Gender/Class/Media 3.0*, 3d ed. Rebecca Ann Lind (Boston: Pearson, 2012), 203.

17. Barthes, *Mythologies*, 113.

18. Ibid., 124.

19. Ibid., 128.

20. John G. Nachbar and Kevin Lause, *Popular Culture: An Introductory Text* (Bowling Green, OH: Bowling Green State University Popular Press, 1992), 92–98.

21. Ibid., 93.

22. Ibid., 90.

23. Jason Mittell, *Genre and Television: From Cop Shows to Cartoons in American Culture* (New York: Routledge, 2004), xi–xii.

24. Ibid., xii. On "multiperspectival cultural studies," see Douglas Kellner, "Toward a Multiperspectival Cultural Studies," *Centennial Review* 36, no. 1 (1992): 5–42; and Douglas Kellner, "Film, Politics, and Ideology: Toward a Multiperspectival Film Theory," in *Movies and Politics: The Dynamic Relationship*, ed. James E. Combs (New York: Garland Press, 1993), 55–92.

25. Harold Lasswell, "The Structure and Function of Communication in Society," in *The Communication of Ideas: A Series of Addresses*, ed. Lyman Bryson (New York: Cooper Square, 1948), 51. In another classic article in communications theory, "Functional Analysis and Mass Communication," sociologist Charles Wright would later add a fourth characteristic: entertainment. As Wright defines them, "*Surveillance* refers to the collection and distribution of information concerning events in the environment, both outside and within any particular society, thus corresponding approximately to what is popularly conceived as the handling of news. Acts of *correlation*, here, include interpretation of information about the environment and prescriptions for conduct in reaction to these events. In part this activity is popularly identified as editorial or propagandistic. *Transmission of culture* includes activities designed to communicate a group's store of social norms, information, values, and the like, from one generation to another or from members of a group to newcomers. Commonly it is identified as educational activity. Finally, *entertainment* refers to communication primarily intended to amuse people irrespective of any instrumental effects it might have" (emphases added) ("Functional Analysis and Mass Communication," *Public Opinion Quarterly* 24, no. 4 [1960]: 609).

26. Lasswell, 51.

27. *Star Trek II: The Wrath of Khan*, directed by Nicholas Meyer (1982; Los Angeles: Paramount Pictures).

28. *Star Trek IV: The Voyage Home,* directed by Leonard Nimoy (1986; Los Angeles: Paramount Pictures).

29. Respectively, Heather Battaly and Amy Coplan, "Diagnosing Character: A House Divided?" in *House and Philosophy: Everybody Lies,* edited by Henry Jacoby (Hoboken, NJ: John Wiley & Sons, 2009), 235; Henry Jacoby, "Read Less, More TV: A Cranky, Slight Rude, Introduction," in *House and Philosophy: Everybody Lies,* edited by Henry Jacoby (Hoboken, NJ: John Wiley & Sons. 2009), 1; and Brian M. Goldman and Samuel J. Maddox, "Authenticity in the House: Will the Real House Please Stand Up," in *House and Psychology: Humanity Is Overrated,* edited by Ted Cascio and Leonard L. Martin (Hoboken, NJ: John Wiley & Sons, 2011), 36, 21.

30. Ted Cascio and Leonard L. Martin, eds., *House and Psychology: Humanity Is Overrated* (Hoboken, NJ: John Wiley & Sons, 2011); Henry Jacoby, ed., *House and Philosophy: Everybody Lies* (Hoboken, NJ: John Wiley & Sons, 2009).

31. Respectively, "Biography for Dr. Temperance 'Bones' Brennan (Character)," *Internet Movie Database,* last modified 2015, http://www.imdb.com/character/ch0027448/bio; Liz Medendorp, "The Bones in Every Procedural TV Show, Including 'Bones,' are the Characters Themselves," *Pop Matters,* last modified December 12, 2012, http://www.popmatters.com/post/166222-bones-usually-good-but-sometimes-bad/; and "Series: Bones," *TV Tropes,* http://tvtropes.org/pmwiki/pmwiki.php/Series/Bones.

32. Esther Mitchell, "Nature in Conflict: A Character Analysis of Dr. Temperance Brennan," *Decoding BONES: A Fiction Author's Thoughts, Insights and Analysis,* last modified December 3, 2013, https://decodingbones.wordpress.com/2013/12/03/nature-in-conflict-a-character-analysis-of-dr-temperance-brennan/; Melissa Maerz, "'The Bridge Premiere React: Lady Detectives, Asperger's Syndrome, and the Makings of a Compelling New Drama," *Entertainment Weekly,* July 10, 2013, http://popwatch.ew.com/2013/07/10/the-bridge-fx-react-review/, respectively.

33. E.g., Neus Barrantes-Vidal, "Creativity and Madness Revisited from Current Psychological Perspectives," *Journal of Consciousness Studies* 11, no. 3–4 (2004): 58–78; Shelley H. Carson, "Cognitive Disinhibition, Creativity, and Psychopathology," in *The Wiley Handbook of Genius,* ed. Dean Keith Simonton (Malden, MA: John Wiley & Sons, 2014), 198–221; Dean Keith Simonton, "Are Genius and Madness Related? Contemporary Answers to an Ancient Question," *Psychiatric Times* (2005), http://www.psychiatrictimes.com/articles/are-genius-and-madness-related-contemporary-answers-ancientquestion.

34. Michel Foucault, *The Archaeology of Knowledge,* trans. A. M. Sheridan Smith (New York: Routledge Classics, 2002 [1969]); Michel Foucault, "Nietzsche, Genealogy, History," trans. Donald F. Bouchard and Sherry Bouchard, in *Essential Works of Foucault, 1954–1984,* Vol. 2: *Aesthetics, Method, and Epistemology,* ed. James D. Faubion (New York: The New Press, 1998 [1994]), 369–91.

35. Michel Foucault, *Madness and Civilization: A History of Insanity in the Age of Reason,* trans. Richard Howard (New York: Vintage, 1988 [1961]; Michel Foucault, *The Birth of the Clinic: An Archaeology of Medical Perception,* trans. Alan Sheridan (New York: Vintage, 1994 [1963]); Michel Foucault, *Discipline and Punish: The Birth of the Prison,* trans. Alan Sheridan (New York: Vintage, 1995 [1975]); Michel Foucault, *The History of Sexuality,* Vol. 1: *An Introduction,* trans. Robert Hurley (New York: Vintage, 1990 [1976]).

36. Barthes, *Mythologies,* 143.
37. Foucault, *Madness and Civilization,* 13.
38. Steinberg and Bridges, "Varieties of Genius," 197.

References

"anti-, prefix1." *OED Online.* December 2014. Oxford University Press. http://www.oed.com/view/Entry/8501?redirectedFrom=anti-intellectual (accessed February 01, 2015).

Asimov, Isaac. "A Cult of Ignorance." *Newsweek,* January 21, 1980, 19.
Barrantes-Vidal, Neus. "Creativity and Madness Revisited from Current Psychological Perspectives." *Journal of Consciousness Studies* 11, no. 3–4 (2004): 58–78.
Barthes, Roland. *Critical Essays.* Translated by Richard Howard. Evanston, IL: Northwestern University Press, 1972 [1964].
———. *The Eiffel Tower, and Other Mythologies.* Translated by Richard Howard. New York: Hill and Wang, 1979 [1964].
———. *Mythologies.* Translated by Annette Lavers. New York: Hill and Wang, 1972 [1957].
———. *New Critical Essays.* Translated by Richard Howard. New York: Hill and Wang, 1980 [1972].
Battaly, Heather, and Amy Coplan. "Diagnosing Character: A House Divided?" In *House and Philosophy: Everybody Lies,* edited by Henry Jacoby, 222–238. Hoboken, NJ: John Wiley & Sons, 2009.
"Biography for Dr. Temperance 'Bones' Brennan (Character)." *Internet Movie Database.* Last modified 2013. http://www.imdb.com/character/ch0027448/bio.
Bones. Created by Hart Hanson. Produced by Hart Hanson et al. Los Angeles: Josephson Entertainment, Far Field Productions and 20th Century–Fox Television. FOX, 2005–present.
Brophy, Adam. "Trusting Science." *Irish Times,* June 14, 2014: 15.
Carson, Shelley H. "Cognitive Disinhibition, Creativity, and Psychopathology." In *The Wiley Handbook of Genius,* edited by Dean Keith Simonton, 198–221. Malden, MA: John Wiley & Sons, 2014.
Cascio, Ted, and Leonard L. Martin, eds. *House and Psychology: Humanity Is Overrated.* Hoboken, NJ: John Wiley & Sons, 2011.
de Saussure, Ferdinand. *Course in General Linguistics.* Translated by Wade Baskin, edited by Charles Bally and Albert Sechehaye in collaboration with Albert Reidlinger. New York: Philosophical Library, 1959.
Drenth, Pieter J.D. "Growing Anti-Intellectualism in Europe: A Menace to Science." *Studia Psychologica* 45, no. 1 (2003): 5–13.
Ebach, Malte C., and Marcelo R. de Carvalho. "Anti-Intellectualism in the DNA Barcoding Enterprise." *Zoologia* 27, no. 2 (2010): 165–78.
Elias, Rafik Z. "Anti-Intellectual Attitudes and Academic Self-Efficacy Among Business Students." *Journal of Education for Business* 84, no. 2 (2008): 110–17.
Foley, Brian J. "Policing from the Gut: Anti-Intellectualism in American Criminal Procedure." *Maryland Law Review* 69, no. 2 (2009). http://digitalcommons.law.umaryland.edu/mlr/vol69/iss2/4/.
Foucault, Michel. *The Archaeology of Knowledge.* Translated by A. M. Sheridan Smith. New York: Routledge Classics, 2002 [1969].
———. *The Birth of the Clinic: An Archaeology of Medical Perception.* Translated by Alan Sheridan. New York: Vintage, 1994 [1963].
———. *Discipline and Punish: The Birth of the Prison.* Translated by Alan Sheridan. New York: Vintage, 1995 [1975].
———. *The History of Sexuality,* Vol. 1: *An Introduction.* Translated by Robert Hurley. New York: Vintage, 1990 [1976].
———. *Madness and Civilization: A History of Insanity in the Age of Reason.* Translated by Richard Howard. New York: Vintage, 1988 [1961].
———. "Nietzsche, Genealogy, History." Translated by Donald F. Bouchard and Sherry Bouchard. In *Essential Works of Foucault, 1954–1984,* Vol. 2: *Aesthetics, Method, and Epistemology,* Edited by James D. Faubion, 369–91. New York: The New Press, 1998 [1994].
Gatehouse, Jonathon. "America Dumbs Down." *Maclean's,* May 15, 2014. http://www.macleans.ca/politics/america-dumbs-down/.
Glasson, Benjamin J. "The Intellectual Outside: Anti-Intellectualism and the Subject of

Populist Discourses in Australian Newspapers." *Continuum: Journal of Media and Cultural Studies* 26, no. 1 (2012): 101–14.

Goldman, Brian M., and Samuel J. Maddox. "Authenticity in the House: Will the Real House Please Stand Up." In *House and Psychology: Humanity Is Overrated*, edited by Ted Cascio and Leonard L. Martin, 20–36. Hoboken, NJ: John Wiley & Sons, 2011.

Grinner, Leslie A. "Bella's Choice: Deconstructing Ideology and Power in *The Twilight Saga*." In *Race/Gender/Class/Media 3.0*, 3d ed., edited by Rebecca Ann Lind, 198–203. Boston: Pearson, 2012.

Holderman, Lisa, ed. *Common Sense: Intelligence as Presented on Popular Television*. Lanham, MD: Rowman and Littlefield, 2008.

Hook, Richard J. "Students' Anti-Intellectual Attitudes and Adjusting to College." *Psychological Reports* 94, no. 3 (2004): 909–14.

House, M.D. Created by David Shore. Produced by David Shore et al. Los Angeles: Heel and Toe Films et al. and NBC Universal Television Studio et al. FOX, 2004–12.

"intellectualism, n.." *OED Online*. December 2014. Oxford University Press. http://www.oed.com/view/Entry/97388?redirectedFrom=intellectualism (accessed February 1, 2015).

Iserbyt, Charlotte Thomson. *The Deliberate Dumbing Down of America*, Rev. ed. Ravenna, OH: Conscience Press, 2011.

Jacoby, Henry, ed. *House and Philosophy: Everybody Lies*. Hoboken, NJ: John Wiley & Sons, 2009.

Kellner, Douglas. "Film, Politics, and Ideology: Toward a Multiperspectival Film Theory." In *Movies and Politics: The Dynamic Relationship*, edited by James E. Combs, 55–92. New York: Garland Press, 1993.

———. "Toward a Multiperspectival Cultural Studies." *Centennial Review* 36, no. 1 (1992): 5–42.

Lasswell, Harold. "The Structure and Function of Communication in Society." In *The Communication of Ideas: A Series of Addresses*, edited by Lyman Bryson, 37–51. New York: Cooper Square, 1948.

Lim, Elvin T. *The Anti-Intellectual Presidency: The Decline of Presidential Rhetoric from George Washington to George W. Bush*. New York: Oxford University Press, 2008.

Long, Leonard J. "Resisting Anti-Intellectualism and Promoting Legal Literacy." *Southern Illinois University Law Journal* 34, no. 1 (2009): 1–54.

Maerz, Melissa. "'The Bridge' Premiere React: Lady Detectives, Asperger's Syndrome, and the Makings of a Compelling New Drama." *Entertainment Weekly*, July 10, 2013. http://popwatch.ew.com/2013/07/10/the-bridge-fx-react-review/.

Marcus, John. "You Can't Tell Me Anything." *Times Higher Education*, October 27, 2011. http://www.timeshighereducation.co.uk/features/you-cant-tell-me-anything/417881.article.

Medendorp, Liz. "The Bones in Every Procedural TV Show, Including 'Bones,' are the Characters Themselves." *Pop Matters*. Last modified December 12, 2012. http://www.popmatters.com/post/166222-bones-usually-good-but-sometimes-bad/.

Mitchell, Esther. "Nature in Conflict: A Character Analysis of Dr. Temperance Brennan." *Decoding BONES: A Fiction Author's Thoughts, Insights and Analysis*. Last modified December 3, 2013. https://decodingbones.wordpress.com/2013/12/03/nature-in-conflict-a-character-analysis-of-dr-temperance-brennan/.

Mittell, Jason. *Genre and Television: From Cop Shows to Cartoons in American Culture*. New York: Routledge, 2004.

"myth, n." *OED Online*. December 2014. Oxford University Press. http://www.oed.com/view/Entry/124670?rskey=KjBPEw&result=1&isAdvanced=false (accessed February 1, 2015).

Nachbar, John G., and Kevin Lause. *Popular Culture: An Introductory Text*. Bowling Green, OH: Bowling Green State University Popular Press, 1992.

Otto, Shawn Lawrence. "America's Science Problem." *Scientific American* 307, no. 5 (2014): 62–71.

Pierce, Charles P. *Idiot America: How Stupidity Became a Virtue in the Land of the Free*. New York: Anchor Books, 2010.

Russell, Bertrand. *Mortals and Others*. New York: Routledge, 2009.

"Series: Bones." *TV Tropes*. Accessed 2014. http://tvtropes.org/pmwiki/pmwiki.php/Series/Bones

Shogan, Colleen J. "Anti-Intellectualism in the Modern Presidency: A Republican Populism." *Perspectives on Politics* 5, no. 2 (2007): 295–303.

Simonton, Dean Keith. "Are Genius and Madness Related? Contemporary Answers to an Ancient Question." *Psychiatric Times* (2005), http://www.psychiatrictimes.com/articles/are-genius-and-madness-related-contemporary-answers-ancientquestion.

Star Trek. Created and produced by Gene Roddenberry. Los Angeles: Desilu Productions & Paramount Television. NBC, 1966–69.

Star Trek II: The Wrath of Khan. Directed by Nicholas Meyer. 1982. Los Angeles: Paramount Pictures.

Star Trek IV: The Voyage Home. Directed by Leonard Nimoy. 1986. Los Angeles: Paramount Pictures.

Sternberg, Robert J., and Stacey L. Bridges. "Varieties of Genius." In *The Wiley Handbook of Genius*, edited by Dean Keith Simonton, 185–97. Malden, MA: John Wiley & Sons, 2014.

Watts, Duncan. *Everything Is Obvious: How Common Sense Fails Us*. New York: Random House, 2011.

Williams, Ray B. "Anti-Intellectualism and the 'Dumbing Down' of America." *Psychology Today*, July 7, 2014. http://www.psychologytoday.com/blog/wired-success/201407/anti-intellectualism-and-the-dumbing-down-america

Williams, Patricia. "Anti-Intellectualism Is Taking Over the U.S." *The Guardian*, May 18, 2012. http://www.theguardian.com/commentisfree/2012/may/18/anti-intellectualism-us-book-banning.

Wright, Charles. "Functional Analysis and Mass Communication." *Public Opinion Quarterly* 24, no. 4 (1960): 605–20.

The Human Hard Drive

Memory, Intelligence and the Internet Age

Ashley Lynn Carlson

In the episode "The Great Game," from season one of BBC's *Sherlock* (2010), Watson asks Holmes how he can be so ignorant about basic "primary school" knowledge, such as the fact that the earth revolves around the sun. Holmes explains that if he ever knew such information, he "deleted it." He goes on to point at his head and declare "this is my hard drive and it only makes sense to put things in there that are really useful."[1] Sherlock is only one of a breed of new superhumans on television: characters who are not androids, but who function more like computers than humans. These genius characters often have abilities that do not exist in real humans, but that are performed routinely by computers. Specifically, they are able to store large amounts of information with great accuracy, and can recall information with surprising ease. Moreover, like Sherlock, they often demonstrate a diminished capacity for emotional response, making them even more akin to machines. This shift in how genius is understood and represented raises significant questions about our changing values in the internet age.

What Is a "Genius"?

Historically, genius has been used to refer to an individual with superior powers of reasoning or creativity. Cesare Lombroso listed numerous geniuses in his work, *The Man of Genius*, published in 1891, including individuals such as Plato, Aristotle, Mozart, Beethoven, Charles Darwin, George Eliot, and a myriad of other philosophical, political, musical, artistic, scientific, and literary luminaries.[2] Lombroso's geniuses are not only individuals who displayed great intelligence through their life and works, but are also people who made significant contributions to Western culture. Just over 100 years later, Michael J. A. Howe follows Lombroso's example in his examination of genius in *Genius Explained*; he focuses on many of the same people as Lombroso, such as Mozart, Darwin, and Eliot, with the addition of similarly significant twentieth-century figures such as Einstein.[3] From Lombroso to Howe, geniuses are understood to be individuals whose works seem to go beyond the range of human capacity to produce important accomplishments (although Howe's object is to debunk the mythos of genius as mysterious or even magical).

The *Oxford English Dictionary* provides us with numerous definitions of genius, the most apt to the questions raised in this collection being that genius is "innate intellectual or creative power of an exceptional or exalted type, such as is attributed to those people considered greatest in any area of art, science, etc.; instinctive and extraordinary capacity for imaginative creation, original thought, invention, or discovery."[4] The first half of this definition pertains specifically to those geniuses described in *The Man of Genius*, *Genius Explained*, and any number of similar studies from the intervening century: geniuses whose exceptional works have gained public recognition. However, the second half of the definition opens up another side to genius: if genius is demonstrated in extraordinary capacity, rather than production, there may be geniuses among us who are not world-famous scientists, artists, and so on. This definition focuses on the genius' exceptional ability to produce something new: creations, thoughts, inventions, discoveries.

On television, most genius characters have not gained significant renown for their accomplishments within their fictional universes (although some, such as Temperance Brennan on *Bones* (2005), have). More importantly, however, genius on television is usually established through specific cultural markers that are not actually demonstrations of their capacity to produce new inventions or ideas. I do not mean to say that TV geniuses never demonstrate a capacity for imaginative creation or original thought; they often do, and sometimes (although I would argue rarely) their capacities even reach levels that warrant the classification of genius by the traditional terms described above. Instead, my point is that most often we know that characters are geniuses not because of their ability to create, but because they match certain "nerd" stereotypes or, as is more relevant to my project here, because of how much knowledge they have amassed. This is particularly noteworthy given that, until recently, having an extraordinary capacity to remember huge amounts of information has not been considered a feature of genius at all. In fact, in all of the *OED*'s nine definitions of genius, "knowledge" and "information" are never mentioned.

Consider, for example, the opening moments of the pilot episode of *The Big Bang Theory*. We first see Sheldon explaining a physics concept to Leonard, apparently with no point other than that "it's a good idea for a t-shirt."[5] Their clothing establishes them as "nerds," but it is the content of the conversation that tells the viewer that they are smart; the average viewer is unlikely to understand what Sheldon is talking about. In the next moment, they walk into an office where Leonard solves the receptionist's entire crossword puzzle in a few seconds, thus demonstrating that he has broad knowledge. Our suspicion at this point that they are geniuses is reinforced by the realization that they are at a "high IQ sperm bank" where they intend to become donors.[6] Later in the episode we see some evidence of original ideas when they show their formulas to Penny (although Sheldon describes Leonard's work as "derivative") but this is not really how we know they are geniuses. Instead, the audience is made aware of these characters' intelligence specifically through the fact that the characters seem to know so much more than viewer.

On *Criminal Minds* (2005), Spencer Reid's genius is announced directly in the pilot episode when he is introduced to a potential witness. Reid states that he has three Ph.D.s (despite being 23 years old), goes on to say he has "an IQ of 187 and an eidetic memory and can read 20,000 words per minute," and finally declares, "Yes, I'm a genius."[7] Although the show attempts to maintain a level of realism both in terms of the characters and the plausibility of the plots, Reid ascends into the realm of fantasy; the mere suggestion that a person can read 20,000 words (about the length of a novella) with a perfect memory of each page and full comprehension in one minute is perfectly ridiculous.[8] Putting aside Reid's IQ, it is also important to recognize that the other evidence he provides of his genius, his memory and his speed-reading, are both abilities associated with knowledge acquisition rather than original creative or intellectual thought. Further, throughout the pilot Reid's genius in reinforced not by his problem-solving skills or inventiveness, but through his extensive knowledge. For example, he identifies quotes from Beckett and Yoda, and demonstrates expert knowledge of the Chinese board game Go. In short, the foundation for the audience's understanding that Reid is a genius comes from evidence of his vast knowledge, rather than evidence of his ability to create.

Psych (2014), which focuses on the shenanigans of Shawn Spencer, a genius who poses as a psychic detective, also represents the main character's intelligence in a way that emphasizes memorization rather than creation. In the show's opening scene, a young Shawn is shown in a diner with his father. Before his father will let him have a dessert, Shawn must close his eyes and recall details of the room he is in, such as the manager's name (from a nametag he saw on his way in), the number of people wearing hats, and the style of each of the hats.[9] This scene sets up the abilities that the adult Shawn uses throughout the series to help the police solve cases. While Shawn's combination of observational powers and exceptional memory is impressive, these abilities have little to do with the traditional definitions of genius. Instead, the emphasis here again is on Shawn's ability to know more than those around him.

While exceptional memory is used to explain the skills of characters like Spencer Reid or Shawn Spencer, often genius itself is used as an explanation for a character's knowledge. Although Brennan on *Bones* does not have an eidetic memory, on their first case (shown in a flashback during season five) she does inform Booth that she speaks "six languages, two of which you've never heard of."[10] Other TV geniuses, like Gregory House on *House, M.D.* (2004) and Peter Bishop on *Fringe* (2008), also speak multiple languages, and like Brennan, they also demonstrate broad knowledge across multiple fields.

One thing remains clear throughout all of these shows: knowledge has been constructed as a fundamental aspect of genius. While it becomes difficult to assess whether the genius' broad knowledge stems naturally from his or her genius, or whether the accumulation of knowledge is responsible for developing a person into a genius, these portrayals always return to the basic quality of knowing.

"He's more machine now, than man"[11]

The construction of genius as related to knowledge acquisition and retention rather than the production of exceptional, original ideas is striking not only because it represents a break from our historical understanding of genius, but also because it suggests a move towards a definition of genius in which the uniquely human potential for invention is subverted by a computer-like ability for memory storage. The human ideal is thus becoming less human.

Sherlock's assertion that he deletes some information in order to make space for more important information, and that his brain is his "hard drive," is only one way in which his character is associated with technology. Sherlock's first appearance in the first episode, "A Study in Pink," is mediated by technology: before we see his face, he sends text messages to the police and the entire press corps during a press conference.[12] A few scenes later, John Watson, in an effort to learn more about Sherlock, is forced to look him up online after Sherlock proves less than forthcoming with personal details in person. As soon as Sherlock begins investigating the case, typed words appear to represent his thoughts, and later in the episode Sherlock uses a mental map that resembles a GPS system (although it provides even more detail than a standard GPS). Each of these instances and many more throughout the series firmly establish Sherlock as a kind of human computer.

Another obvious feature of Sherlock's behavior that makes him more akin to a computer is his lack of emotion. While this is attributed to the assertion that Sherlock is a sociopath, it nevertheless reduces his human aspect. Watson directly addresses Sherlock's lack of humanity on several occasions, for example when he exclaims, "Why am I the only one ... reacting like a human being!" after Sherlock fails to react with sufficient emotion to the friends' reunification after two years, during which Watson believed Sherlock to be dead.[13] Sherlock also demonstrates an inability to understand other people's emotions, as is clear in numerous instances when he behaves with seemingly callous disregard for people's feelings, and afterwards appears confused by their reactions.

Sherlock is only one of many contemporary television geniuses that lack normal human responses. Temperance Brennan on *Bones*, Gregory House on *House*, and Sheldon Cooper on *The Big Bang Theory*, all demonstrate a limited emotional range and particularly an insensitivity to the feelings of others. As other contributors to this collection note, in each of these cases this abnormal emotional behavior serves to link high intelligence to mental disorders. However, these characters' inability to associate normally with human emotion also specifically dehumanizes them and moves them closer to machines, essentially by removing one of the key features that has always been seen as a fundamental difference between men and machines: the ability to feel.

Additionally, some television geniuses are endowed with specific abilities that humans do not possess, but that computers might. While Spencer Reid on *Criminal Minds* shows an emotional side that many TV geniuses lacks, he demonstrates computer-like capabilities that defy human capacity, such as his aforementioned speed reading ability. While humans are physically incapable of reading at such a speed, a computer can easily scan and store 20,000 words in a minute. Thus, Reid can do what computers can, and humans cannot. Reid is also one of a number of television characters with an "eidetic" memory, which is the scientific term for a photographic memory. However, most of the scientific community agrees that a true photographic memory is a myth. So-called "eidetikers," those who ostensibly possess eidetic memories, sometimes have errors in their recollection of an image and can only describe an image with precision for a few minutes after they have seen it, after which their memory begins to fade.[14] In contrast, Reid is able to recall images long after he has seen them and with literally picture-perfect precision. While humans cannot actually store an image and recall it with perfect detail later, computers most certainly can.

Reid's computational abilities also resemble those of a computer. In the season four episode "The Angel Maker," Reid deciphers a complex binary code by hand. He tells that team that "normally you'd use a computer to run all of these combinations but it was quicker just to do it longhand until I found the right one," thus illustrating that his mind can outperform a computer.[15] In response, his colleague, Emily Prentiss, pokes his cheek and says, "He's so lifelike," thereby insinuating that Reid is some kind of android, rather than a human.[16] Like Sherlock's, Reid's "genius" is tied to his ability to mimic computer technology.

Some shows have even taken this to the next level, by featuring human characters who are directly interfaced with technology and therefore become geniuses. On *Chuck* (2007), the title character accidentally downloads information into his brain. As a result, as CIA agent Sarah Walker explains in the pilot episode, "Chuck *is* the computer."[17] Similarly, the short-lived CBS show *Intelligence* (2014) features a government operative named Gabriel who has a computer chip in his brain. According to the director of his program, the chip gives him "the kind of power that previously had only been found in a machine."[18] Specifically, he is able to access any wireless signal and tap into the global information grid. On the show Gabriel is supposed to be the next evolution in weapons, but for the viewer, Gabriel seems to represent the next evolution in human capacity. His access to vast knowledge via the chip allows him to evolve genius-like capabilities, thereby overtly suggesting that genius is related to knowing more, rather than thinking better.

Although most of the geniuses on popular television shows do not derive their intelligence through a direct interface with technology, it is nevertheless clear that intelligence has been linked to computers through an increased emphasis on information storage and access. Being a genius looks increasingly like being a computer, and on television it seems that the height of human potential is no longer associated with original creative or intellectual achievement, but with knowledge acquisition.

Man Versus Machine

As a facility with memory has become the new standard for "genius" in popular media, its striking difference from earlier definitions of genius forces us to question why our perception of the pinnacle of human existence has shifted away from heightened creativity and towards information and memorization. I posit that two key factors have contributed to this change: first, the accessibility of information via the internet has created anxiety that human memory may become obsolete, and second, the rise of information as a major commodity has created a consumerist model for intellect, in which amassing more information replaces the accumulation of more goods.

In an interview in 2004, Sergey Brin, one of Google's cofounders, commented, "Certainly if you had all the world's information directly attached to your brain, or an artificial brain that was smarter than your brain, you'd be better off."[19] Brin apparently saw his statement as obvious, or "certainly" true, but it struck a number of culture critics as disconcerting. A few years later, Clive Thompson summed up his concerns about relying too heavily on the internet rather than his own memory to store information, saying, "Sure, I'm a veritable genius when I'm on the grid, but am I mentally crippled when I'm not? Does an overreliance on machine memory shut down other important ways of understanding the world?"[20] Similarly, in "Is Google Making us Stupid?" Nicholas Carr notes that his concentration has declined and that he struggles to focus on long texts, changes he attributes to spending too much time online, where Google provides immediate access to an endless supply of information.[21]

Thompson and Carr's concerns that the internet is affecting their intelligence may be legitimate. Patricia Greenfield's review of a number of scientific studies about the effects of visual media on learning led her to conclude that "although the visual capabilities of television, video games, and the internet may develop impressive visual intelligence, the cost seems to be deep processing: mindful knowledge acquisition, inductive analysis, critical thinking, imagination, and reflection."[22] In short, those same features traditionally associated with genius may actually be on the decline as our use of technology increases.

But while scientists and culture critics alike have been worrying about whether the internet is making us stupider, it seems a change has also been underway in what we mean by "smarter." When Carr discussed his anxiety at Brin's worldview, he seemed to recognize this possibility, writing that the idea that we'd be "better off" if the world's information was connected to our brain "suggests a belief that intelligence is the output of a mechanical process, a series of discrete steps that can be isolated, measured, and optimized."[23] Carr fears in part that intelligence is becoming associated with the function of machines rather than minds; looking at the portrayals of genius on television, his concern seems well-founded. The television geniuses do in fact appear more mechanized and optimized, as is particularly noticeable in moments such as when Sherlock uses his mind palace, or Reid chooses to do mental calculations because he is faster than the computer.

Further, Brin's assertion about the benefits of having "all the world's information directly attached to your brain, or an artificial brain that was smarter than your brain"[24] hits precisely at the idea that information is directly equated with smarts. This concept has significant implications across numerous areas. Certainly, we have already seen a shift in world economies, politics, and security as information is regarded as possibly the most important of all assets. Information collected in databases can be worth millions of dollars; information stored on a flash drive can threaten national security; information hidden in our online accounts has become inextricably linked to our identities, which now can be stolen. As the *Sherlock* villain Charles Augustus Magnussen says, "knowing is owning."[25] The implications here for education are also tangible; if 'knowing' is championed as the pinnacle of human achievement, it gives new rise to the banking model of education, and memorization, rather than critical or imaginative thinking becomes the goal. The more knowledge the student can bank, the more they will be considered 'gifted.'

Perhaps most frighteningly, the computer-styled genius has significant implications in how we understand and interpret humanity in today's world. In terms of memory storage, all humans function at a level that is already inferior to the ever-evolving range of technological capacity; without the intervention of technology, we will never be able to perfectly store large amounts of data in our brains. If genius comes to resemble the functional abilities of computers rather people, then truly exceptional human beings cease to appear exceptional. Moreover, those attributes that remain the exclusive realm of mankind, including imagination, empathy, emotions, or morals, are perceived as having diminished importance. We can see this in the way that viewers are expected to forgive characters such as Sherlock, House, or Brennan for their lapses; they are allowed to be rude, insensitive, and sometimes downright amoral because on some level they are better than the rest of us—that is, they have more information than we do. Surely, though, this is not a precedent we should wish to encourage. Will we really be better off if we work to emulate, or even directly plug into, massive data sources? Should we not instead try to foster our potential towards human genius, our innate intellectual, emotional, and creative powers?

Notes

1. Mark Gatiss, "The Great Game," *Sherlock*, season 1, episode 3, directed by Paul McGuigan, aired August 8, 2010, on BBC One.
2. Cesare Lombroso, *The Man of Genius* (London: W. Scott, 1901).
3. Michael J. A. Howe, *Genius Explained* (New York: Cambridge University Press, 1999).
4. "genius, n. and adj," *OED Online* (December 2014, Oxford University Press), http://www.oed.com/view/Entry/77607?redirectedFrom=genius.
5. Chuck Lorre and Bill Prady, "Pilot," *The Big Bang Theory*, season 1, episode 1, directed by James Burrows, aired September 24, 2007, on CBS.

6. Ibid.

7. Jeff Davis, "Extreme Aggressor," *Criminal Minds*, season 1, episode 1, directed by Richard Shepard, aired September 22, 2005, on CBS.

8. To compare, world speed-reading champion Anne Jones reportedly read *Harry Potter and the Deathly Hallows* in only 47 minutes (which comes to around 4200 words per minute). This does not, of course, mean that she achieved Reid's level of perfect recall. Mike Collett-White, "Hurry Potter: Speed-reading Critics Rush Reviews," *Reuters*, July 21, 2007, http://www.reuters.com/article/2007/07/21/us-arts-potter-reviews-idUSL21412654 20070721.

9. Steve Franks, "Pilot," *Psych*, season 1, episode 1, directed by Michael Engler, aired July 7, 2006, on USA.

10. Hart Hanson, "The Parts in the Sum of the Whole," *Bones*, season 5, episode 16, directed by David Boreanaz, aired April 8, 2010, on Fox.

11. As Obi Wan says of Darth Vader in *Star Wars: Return of the Jedi*.

12. Steven Moffat, "A Study in Pink," *Sherlock*, season 1, episode 1, directed by Paul McGuigan, aired July 25, 2010, BBC One.

13. Mark Gatiss, "The Empty Hearse," *Sherlock*, season 3, episode 1, directed by Jeremy Lovering, aired January 1, 2014, on BBC One.

14. William Lee Adams, "The Truth About Photographic Memory," *Psychology Today*, March 1, 2006, https://www.psychologytoday.com/articles/200603/the-truth-about-photographic-memory.

15. Jay Beattie and Dan Dworkin, "The Angel Maker," *Criminal Minds*, season 4, episode 2, directed by Glenn Kershaw, aired October 1, 2008 on CBS.

16. Ibid.

17. Josh Schwartz and Chris Fedak, "Pilot," *Chuck*, season 1, episode 1, directed by McG, aired September 24, 2007 on NBC.

18. Michael Seitzman, "Pilot," *Intelligence*, season 1, episode 1, directed by David Semel, aired January 7, 2014 on CBS.

19. "All Eyes on Google," *Newsweek*, March 28, 2004, http://www.newsweek.com/all-eyes-google-124041.

20. Clive Thompson, "Your Outboard Brain Knows All," *Wired Magazine* 15, no. 10 (September 25, 2007), http://archive.wired.com/techbiz/people/magazine/15-10/st_thompson.

21. Nicholas Carr, "Is Google Making Us Stupid?" *The Atlantic*, July 1, 2008, http://www.theatlantic.com/magazine/archive/2008/07/is-google-making-us-stupid/306868/.

22. Patricia M. Greenfield, "Technology and Informal Education: What Is Taught, What Is Learned," *Science* 323, no. 5910 (January 2, 2009), 71.

23. Carr, "Is Google Making Us Stupid?"

24. "All Eyes on Google."

25. Steven Moffat, "His Last Vow," *Sherlock*, season 3, episode 3, directed by Nick Hurran, aired January 12, 2014, on BBC One.

References

Adams, William Lee. "The Truth About Photographic Memory." *Psychology Today*, March 1, 2006. https://www.psychologytoday.com/articles/200603/the-truth-about-photographic-memory.

"All Eyes on Google." *Newsweek*, March 28, 2004. http://www.newsweek.com/all-eyes-google-124041.

Beattie, Jay, and Dan Dworkin. "The Angel Maker." *Criminal Minds*, season 4, episode 2. Directed by Glenn Kershaw Aired October 1, 2008, on CBS. Netflix.com.

Carr, Nicholas. "Is Google Making Us Stupid?" *The Atlantic*, July 1, 2008. http://www.theatlantic.com/magazine/archive/2008/07/is-google-making-us-stupid/306868/.

Collett-White, Mike. "Hurry Potter: Speed-Reading Critics Rush Reviews." *Reuters*, July 21, 2007. http://www.reuters.com/article/2007/07/21/us-arts-potter-reviews-idUSL2141265420070721.

Davis, Jeff. "Extreme Aggressor." *Criminal Minds*, season 1, episode 1. Directed by Richard Shepard. Aired September 22, 2005, on CBS. Netflix.com.

Franks, Steve. "Pilot." *Psych*, season 1, episode 1. Directed by Michael Engler. Aired July 7, 2006, on USA. Netflix.com.

Gatiss, Mark. "The Great Game." *Sherlock*, season 1, episode 3. Directed by Paul McGuigan. Aired August 8, 2010, on BBC. Netflix.com.

———. "The Empty Hearse." *Sherlock*, season 3, episode 1. Directed by Jeremy Lovering. Aired January 1, 2014, on BBC One. Netflix.com.

"genius, n. and adj." *OED Online*. December 2014. Oxford University Press. http://www.oed.com/view/Entry/77607?redirectedFrom=genius (accessed January 26, 2015).

Greenfield, Patricia M. "Technology and Informal Education: What Is Taught, What Is Learned." *Science* 323, no. 5910 (January 2, 2009): 69–71.

Hanson, Hart. "The Parts in the Sum of the Whole." *Bones*, season 5, episode 16. Directed by David Boreanaz. Aired April 8, 2010, on Fox. Netflix.com.

Howe, Michael J. A. *Genius Explained*. New York: Cambridge University Press, 1999.

Kasdan, Lawrence, and George Lucas. *Star Wars VI: Return of the Jedi*. DVD. Directed by Richard Marquand. Century City, CA: 20th Century–Fox, 2004.

Lombroso, Cesare. *The Man of Genius*. London: W. Scott, 1901.

Lorre, Chuck, and Bill Prady. "Pilot." *The Big Bang Theory*, season 1, episode 1. Directed by James Burrows. Aired September 24, 2007, on CBS. Amazon Prime Video.

Moffat, Steven. "A Study in Pink." *Sherlock*, season 1, episode 1. Directed by Paul McGuigan. Aired July 25, 2010, on BBC One. Netflix.com.

———. "His Last Vow." *Sherlock*, season 3, episode 3. Directed by Nick Hurran. Aired January 12, 2014, on BBC One. Netflix.com.

Schwartz, Josh, and Chris Fedak. "Pilot." *Chuck*, season 1, episode 1. Directed by McG. Aired September 24, 2007, on NBC. Netflix.com.

Seitzman, Michael. "Pilot." *Intelligence*, season 1, episode 1. Directed by David Semel. Aired January 7, 2014 on CBS. Amazon Prime Video.

Thompson, Clive. "Your Outboard Brain Knows All." *Wired Magazine* 15, no. 10 (September 25, 2007), http://archive.wired.com/techbiz/people/magazine/15-10/st_thompson.

Gray Matter

The Malleability of Intelligence in Fringe

Lisa K. Perdigao

The television series *Fringe* (2008) raises questions about the possibilities and limitations of genius. *Fringe* begins as a revision of the Frankensteinian cautionary tale about the dangers of unbridled intellect as Dr. Walter Bishop, a postmodern Victor Frankenstein, has lost everything to science, including control over his own mind. But *Fringe* complicates this narrative by showing what happens after Walter heeds his own warning, altering the course of Mary Shelley's tale. As the series begins, despite his precautionary measures, Walter's plight parallels Victor's: his genius led him to a life of self-isolation. FBI Special Agent Olivia Dunham's discovery of Walter's work and request for his help on a case return him to his lab at Harvard University and reunite him with his son Peter Bishop. Yet Walter remains on the fringe; he is torn between embracing and rejecting the life of the mind. The season two episode "Grey Matters" develops the plot involving the extraction of Walter's brain tissue, a procedure that Walter had requested in an attempt to stop himself from losing his humanity and becoming a "monster." At the series' end, Walter attempts to reconcile his past, present, and future by mending his broken mind, putting the pieces back together so that he can save humanity.

Throughout its five seasons, *Fringe* stages debates about intelligence— natural and artificial, crystallized and fluid. Walter's son, Peter, has an IQ of 190, speaks eight languages, and is able to follow his father's complex research, yet he is a high school dropout. Natural intelligence is again depicted in Olivia, the series' protagonist, who has a photographic (eidetic) memory. However,

Olivia learns that she was part of a series of experiments conducted by Walter when she was a child, and that these changed her: with Cortexiphan in her body, she is able to cross between worlds, transcending her body with her mind. Other participants in the experiments cannot survive the effects; their bodies break down (and even implode) when they try to maximize their minds' potential. Rather than performing a conventional cautionary tale about the unbridled mind, *Fringe* engages contemporary debates about intelligence, the limits and possibilities of measuring intelligence, and increasing potential. As a definitive spectrum of intelligence remains a contested site, *Fringe*'s play in the liminal space, the "gray matter," is reflective of its time. Exploring the fixity and malleability of intelligence in its narratives, *Fringe* expands the boundaries of its own medium.

Shelley's *Frankenstein* is written into *Fringe*'s landscape from the beginning, with an allusive establishing shot in the pilot episode. As a plane travels through a lightning storm, a passenger assures another, "It's just a storm," downplaying its significance.[1] With a nod to the genesis of Shelley's story, recalling the storm that inspired it and the lightning of its film adaptations, *Fringe* sets the stage for its narrative. That connection is reinforced with a title sequence that features a series of words: psychokinesis, teleportation, nanotechnology, artificial intelligence, precognition, dark matter, cybernetics, suspended animation, and transmogrification. Viewers are cast into a strange but not entirely unfamiliar world, much like Olivia and Peter. Olivia discovers Walter's work after searching for information on "tissue hardening" in the attempt to save her partner, John Scott, who has been injured in a chemical explosion. Although Walter appears to be "a gifted scientist accustomed to unlimited exploration and access to the most advanced technology" on paper (or screen), he first appears as a "mad scientist" inside a mental institution.[2] As Sarah Clarke Stuart writes, "Initially, his 'madness' is given greater weight than his scientific ability."[3] To get access to Walter at St. Claire's Hospital, Olivia must first locate his son Peter. Olivia tells Peter that his father's work included "things like mind control, teleportation, astral projection, invisibility, genetic mutation, reanimation, fertility."[4] Introduced to concepts taken from the pages of science fiction, Peter replies, "Excuse me for a sec. Reanimation? Really? So you're telling me what? My father was Dr. Frankenstein?"[5]

The series revivifies the Frankenstein narrative and expands its terms for the twenty-first century. Amy H. Sturgis writes, "It's easy to see parallels between the two characters. Both brilliant scientists mean well: they desire to explore the very nature of reality itself and thus expand the boundaries of human knowledge."[6] *Fringe* follows this course, becoming what Val Nolan refers to as "an experiment, one which tests the social construction of scientists as being 'mad' and 'bad,' and, more specifically, the perceived concurrence of madness with villainy which has been cemented by a century and a half of speculative texts depicting genius scientists as evil madmen."[7] *Fringe*'s depictions of genius most often falls within the "mad scientist" formula, represented by Walter Bishop, William Bell, Massive Dynamic scientists, and "fringe" scientists involved in bioterrorism and genetic manipulation.[8] These examples reflect Darrin M. McMahon's characterization of the "modern genius" who is "believed to possess rare and special powers: the power to create, redeem, and destroy; the power to penetrate the fabric of the universe; the power to see into the future, or to see into our souls."[9] Stuart writes, "In *Fringe* genius is highly prized; the show regularly features brilliant minds exhibiting their power in acts of creation and destruction."[10]

However, *Fringe* is not merely another performance of Shelley's text and reiteration of classical archetypes; instead, its narratives are self-conscious, much like the creature. As a postmodern *Frankenstein* and perhaps post-postmodern Prometheus, *Fringe* takes the theme of "expand[ing] the boundaries of human knowledge" and turns it inward. The pilot episode plays with the reanimation plot: Walter is able to bring John back to life and to Olivia. But the episode goes further than replaying Shelley's story. The key to reanimating John lies in breaking the boundaries of the mind. Where Victor Frankenstein is surprised to learn that his creature possesses a capacity for reason and emotion, Walter's work focuses on the transmission of memories—and consciousness— from an inanimate subject. As Walter creates a state of suspended animation for Olivia to cross over into John's mind, he shows how the minds of his subjects, and not just the imagination of the scientist, are boundless.

Fringe's engagement with and revision of Shelley's text positions it within a larger debate about what constitutes genius, providing contexts in both Romantic and contemporary eras. McMahon identifies the "cultural authority" ascribed to the genius in modern society, writing,

> Enhanced by the pervasive influence of European Romanticism, which further stylized and mystified the genius, this authority was also fortified by an extensive science of genius, which appeared to give sanction—through the measurement of skulls, the analysis of brains, and the identification of pathogens and hereditary traits—to the genius's exceptional nature. The effort to quantify genius that culminated in the elaboration of the intelligence quotient (IQ) at the beginning of the twentieth century seemed to confirm the presence of a power—an exceedingly rare power—that scientists had assumed for over a century.[11]

As *Fringe* studies genius—the cultural authority it assumes (Massive Dynamic's slogan "What do we do? What don't we do?"), its physical manifestations (measurement of skulls, analysis of brains, identification of pathogens and hereditary traits), and the quantification of intelligence (the privileging of IQs)—it presents a case study for how intelligence has been remapped in and for the twenty-first century.[12]

In 1994, the *Wall Street Journal* presented a "unified definition of intelligence" composed by a group of fifty-two experts in "the scientific study of intelligence and allied fields."[13] They concluded that

> intelligence is a very general mental capability that, among other things, involves the ability to reason, plan, solve problems, think abstractly, comprehend complex ideas, learn quickly and learn from experience. It is not merely book learning, a narrow academic skill, or test-taking smarts. Rather, it reflects a broader and deeper capability for comprehending our surroundings—"catching on," "making sense" of things, or "figuring out" what to do.[14]

While the definition may appear "reasonable," as Scott Barry Kaufman acknowledges, "defining a term is one thing, measuring it is another."[15] The appearance of the IQ test in the early twentieth century and subsequent debates about its validity highlight the complexities of identifying what intelligence is and how it performs.[16] McMahon says that the IQ exam "emerged directly out of—and intersected directly with" the "long search for a science of genius that captivated researchers throughout the nineteenth and early twentieth centuries."[17] As N. J. Mackintosh writes, "For the greater part of the twentieth century ... the psychological study of human intelligence attempted to understand how and why people *differ* in intelligence" rather than "study the general nature of human intelligence."[18] McMahon notes that the IQ exam was conceived as a "series of barriers of increasing difficulty that could be used to classify subjects in relation to what was deemed 'normal' for any given stage of development," identifying those "falling below normalcy," but it was soon recognized for its potential: "identifying and ranking individuals whose mental ages were above average."[19] High intelligence and genius emerge as exceptions, even in the test's design.

While seemingly "reasonable," the idea that intelligence is a "very general mental capability" is not without controversy. As Mackintosh notes, responses to Charles Spearman's notion of a generalized intelligence by Louis Thurstone and his followers involved "searching for evidence of the existence of more specialized sites of abilities."[20] They concluded that "intelligence is better conceived as a set of independent faculties or relatively specialized abilities."[21] McMahon distinguishes Thurstone's and Howard Gardner's conceptions of "multiple and varied" intelligences and Spearman's theory of a general intelligence (g), a "single, unitary, measurable 'thing' given at birth, rooted in biological nature, and constant over a lifetime, though protean in its powers."[22]

Fringe focuses on the protean nature of intelligence in its composition of characters. Mackintosh distinguishes two subsets of g present in Raymond Cattell's theory, Gf (fluid ability) and Gc (crystallized ability), writing that Gf was the "biological potential for intelligence, which became manifest in Gc as people acquired knowledge and experience, absorbing the culture in which they lived, and profiting, or not, as the case may be, from the educational system provided by their society."[23] Phillip Ackerman's distinction of "intelligence-as-process," measured by fluid reasoning tests, and "intelligence-as-knowledge," the expertise acquired throughout life, exemplifies the difference between Gf and Gc.[24] *Fringe* highlights the limits and possibilities of knowledge-acquisition, testing the effects of nature and environment on its subjects. Kaufman notes that although the results of studies of Gf and Gc are varied and inconclusive, "they did tell us an important story about the kinds of minds that are attracted to acquiring particular domains of knowledge, and how ability, personality, and interest develop in tandem."[25]

The protean quality of intelligence is reflective of the nature of the debate, particularly in new assessments of the test's—as well as the subjects'—performance. And that performance is itself changing, particularly after a century of circulation. As Kaufman notes, "The twentieth century witnessed a dramatic increase in IQ scores, as much as 3 points per decade."[26] Referencing "The Flynn Effect," Kaufman attributes the perceived rise in fluid reasoning to a changing culture, writing that "today, with more opportunities for educating the scientific mind, more people hold a ticket that gives them the chance to properly develop their abstract reasoning ability."[27] This can be linked to the results in Ackerman's studies where fluid intelligence "was a particularly strong predictor of knowledge in chemistry, physics and biology."[28]

Fringe speculates on the future of human intelligence in relation to developments in artificial intelligence within the twenty-first century. Zak Bronson cites computer scientist and science fiction writer Vernor Vinge's description of "the Singularity," a point where "technology will have developed the ability to reproduce itself so quickly that its intelligence will far surpass that of humans," and locates its possibility—and threat—within *Fringe*.[29] Vinge's approximation of "the Singularity" occurring "within thirty years" parallels the timeline (and multiple timelines) of *Fringe*'s narrative that begins in 2008 and, in the fifth season, moves into the future in 2036.[30] As Bronson notes, *Fringe*'s third season, located in an alternate universe and timeline, begins with alternate opening credits to reflect its position in an Altverse; words emphasized in the sequence include transhumanism, singularity, and transcendence.[31]

Fringe is poised between its visions of the future, offering portraits of worlds with the potential to be improved or destroyed by science and technology. Countering the destructive bent of the Singularity, Ray Kurzweil offers another perspective that the series also takes into account "embrac[ing] the human possibility."[32] According to Kurzweil, the Singularity will "enable humans to transcend beyond the 'limitations of our biological bodies' and 'gain power over our fates.'"[33] However, as Bronson notes, "this transhumanist dream of a transcendent mind abstracted from its body becomes highly problematic as the mind itself is a complex entanglement of mind and matter."[34] The series' interest in the "science of genius" leads the team to "gray matter," through the measurement of skulls, analysis of brains, and identification of pathogens and hereditary traits to locate the exceptional qualities of potential and genius, that singularity.

As the series maps the spectrum of intelligence, it blurs the boundaries between categories, making the study of intelligence appear to be another area of fringe science. The Fringe Team—Olivia, Walter, Peter, and assistant Astrid Farnsworth—is initially defined by natural intelligence. As Olivia travels to Baghdad to retrieve Peter, she outlines his background in a voiceover:

> He's a high school dropout, IQ at 190, which is fifty points north of genius. Misfit, nomad. Hasn't kept a job longer than two months. He's been a wildland fireman, cargo pilot, and briefly a college chemistry professor. He falsified a degree from MIT. He even managed to get a few papers published before he was found out.[35]

Peter is first defined by his IQ and lack of schooling. In "The Arrival," Peter says that Walter kept him up late at night, telling him "how [he'd] squandered [his] above-average intellect and [his] substantial education."[36] As his academic record confirms, Peter is not an ideal student; however, he is able to play the role. Imitating his earlier work at MIT, Peter is recast as scientist, working alongside his father in a Harvard lab. He easily translates his father's complex language and theories to Olivia, Astrid, and the viewers. Here we see a depiction of fluid intelligence—a high capacity for problem-solving independent of education and experience. It is "biological potential." In fact, Walter, explaining his apparent disappointment in Peter's life choices, says, "It has more to do with your potential than anything else. You have no idea what you're capable of, Peter."[37] In "The Same Old Story," Walter tells Peter, "You're a smart boy. But there is much you don't know."[38] Here, the limitations on Peter are imposed by his lack of knowledge, not his ability to understand; after all, he is a "smart boy."

The line between high level intelligence and genius is often blurred in the series. Despite Walter's criticisms, Peter's natural intelligence is foregrounded, and he is repeatedly referred to as a genius. For example, when inquiring about his gambling debt, Olivia says, "I thought you were a genius. You must have had a system," to which Peter replies, "Of course I had a system. The house was cheating."[39] Astrid, a "junior" FBI agent who majored in Linguistics and minored in Computer Science, has an acute ability to recognize and translate foreign languages and complex codes. Astrid is also represented as high functioning in fluid intelligence, but her reasoning is not relegated to the sciences; similar to Peter who is said to be fluent in eight languages, Astrid's skills include deciphering and translating languages. In the season one episode "In Which We Meet Mr. Jones," Astrid is the one to crack the code, a "sequence of three letters that appears on the parasite's DNA."[40] Astrid recognizes that it's "too organized to be accidental" and says that "it's too simple to be plain text" but appears to be "a simple monoalphabetic cipher," likening it to the one purportedly used by Julius Caesar.[41] Olivia notes an acronym she recognizes from John's files, ZFT, thus identifying the terrorist organization behind the recent attacks. Here, Astrid's deciphering skills and Olivia's abilities (information gathered from sharing John's consciousness) combine to interpret the signs.

As the foundation of the Fringe team, Olivia is central to the series' representation of intelligence, particularly in her ability to recognize "The Pattern" of Fringe events that drive the plot. In "The Arrival," Olivia first recognizes a pattern, the appearance of a bald man (who is later identified as an Observer) in a photo of a Brooklyn gas explosion and photos from other cases. She says that she is not good at many things but has always been good at one: "that game, Concentration. Memory. Connecting things. Putting them together."[42] When Olivia introduces the evidence to Agent Phillip Broyles, head of the Fringe Division, he notes that it took his agency a year to spot the man, but it took her only three weeks. The episode "Safe" highlights Olivia's uncanny recall of numbers. When Olivia shows Peter a card trick, he realizes that she can count cards. She admits, "I just have this thing for numbers. I see them once and remember them for the rest of my life. I'm sure if I was a child today I would be diagnosed with something."[43]

Photographic memory is a debated topic and is speculated by many to be a fiction, even a television trope. Real or fictional, it is appealing for serial narratives, particularly forensic series. As an FBI agent with photographic memory, Olivia is part of a field that includes Agent Fox Mulder (*The X-Files*, 1993–2002), Detective Adrian Monk (*Monk*, 2002–2009), Dr. Spencer Reid (*Criminal Minds*, 2005–), Shawn Spencer (*Psych*, 2006–2014), Sherlock Holmes (BBC's *Sherlock*, 2010–), Detective Carrie Wells (*Unforgettable*, 2011–), and Ichabod Crane (*Sleepy Hollow*, 2013–). But Olivia's case is unique. We learn that there is something else at work that is not purely "natural ability"; instead, it involves experiments with adapting the mind and expanding potential, central concepts for the series.

When the pilot episode demonstrates Olivia's ability to cross between worlds, sharing consciousness with John, the experiment's success is initially attributed to Walter's work as a "mad scientist"; however, as the series develops, Olivia's abilities become the focus of the narrative. In the aptly titled season one episode "Ability," Olivia learns that she might have been a subject of Walter's and Bell's experiments in Jacksonville, Florida, when she was only three years old. The plot of "Ability" is driven by Olivia's access to latent powers that ZFT terrorist David Robert Jones says are a result of her exposure to the drug Cortexiphan. Jones' note that accompanies the box he supplies her with reads that although it appears that he has given her a "box of children's games," it's "not a game at all."[44] He identifies it as an "evaluation system. A series of tests designed to cultivate specific innate skills present in particular individuals."[45] Here, Jones' tests, perceived as resembling children's games, can be read as IQ and other intelligence testing measures. And, like those tests, the goal of successfully completing them is maximizing Olivia's potential and displaying her giftedness.

Although Olivia thinks it's all just a "mind game," she begins to question the meaning and larger purpose behind the test—and her results. After she appears to telekinetically turn off lights to stop a bomb from detonating, she follows the Cortexiphan patent to Massive Dynamic and Nina Sharp for answers. Nina says, "Dr. Bell theorized that the human mind at birth is infinitely capable and that every force it encounters—social, physical, intellectual—is the beginning of the process he referred to as 'limitation,' a diminishing of that potential."[46] Nina tells Olivia that Cortexiphan "was meant to limit that limitation, to prevent the natural shrinking of brain power."[47] Nina's statements appear to be consistent with Ackerman's findings that "fluid intelligence tended to *decrease* with age, whereas crystallized intelligence tended to *increase* with age."[48] The trials can be located in the realm of fluid reasoning training, with extraordinary outcomes.

While Olivia's intelligence and photographic memory might be natural, even hereditary, the revelation of the experiments complicates the representation. Stuart writes, "Through scientific ingenuity, Olivia's human limitations have been diminished, which makes her, quite literally, superhuman," or, as Rhonda V. Wilcox puts it, Olivia is "now more able."[49] Telepathic, pyrokinetic, and able to cross between worlds, Olivia emerges as both exceptional and singular test subject. She is contrasted by the trial's other subjects who emerge in Fringe cases. In the season one episode "The Road Not Taken," which features Walter's explanation of a Frostian/Borgesian worldview where all futures are possible and simultaneously exist, twins from two different worlds who had Cortexiphan in their systems are unable to control their pyrokinesis and one self-implodes. In season one's "Bad Dreams," Nick Lane, another test subject, is hyperemotive; unable to control his emotions, he projects them outward. His emotions—and lack of control over them—cause a woman's suicide and, by the episode's end, a mass suicide. Where Walter identifies the potential in Olivia that is a result of the experiments, the other test subjects reveal the dangers of manipulating their minds.

Potential and ability are buzzwords for the series and are part of its mise en scène, invoked in conversations, documents, and advertisements. In the season one episode "Power Hungry," an average man, Joseph Meegar, suffers his mother's reprimands before going to work where an advertisement to "unlock your hidden potential" figures prominently in his locker. The episode's plot reveals how he had volunteered to be part of an experiment to improve his mind, by "realign[ing] the electrical impulses" of his brain.[50] The result is that he becomes, as Peter calls him, "Electroman," unable to control his abilities, transmitting excessive charges that kill those in proximity. This too is a matter of potential, as Walter says, "I say we need to find this person and soon. Before he finds out exactly what he's capable of."[51] Performing "the sort of work [he] was born for," Walter traces Joseph's electromagnetic signature based on the idea that human beings are "highly complex electrical systems."[52] While Walter is always cast as the scientist, he shares the role in this episode. The scientist "improving" Joseph tells him, "You don't realize what you are.... Look what science has made you: special."[53] Joseph plays the roles of both Victor Frankenstein and the creature: he desires to transcend his limitations and becomes a product of science.

The season three episode "The Plateau" shares this theme. It depicts the results of experiments on a mentally challenged individual, Milo Stanfield, who has an IQ of 56 and exhibits "severe cognitive deficiency."[54] To increase his IQ, he is given "smart drugs" that have extraordinary effects on his brain functioning. Milo is an example of *Fringe*'s engagement with transhumanism and reflects Walter's assessment that a "human brain is like a computer. It just needs electricity to function."[55] Using patterns to predict and cause destruction, Milo's transcendence leads him to lose his connection to humanity; at the episode's end, he is rendered as an extension of the machine that "reads" him. Olivia tells his sister, "The drugs have been in his system too long, so the doctors weren't able to reverse the effects. According to the doctors, the patterns that he sees are too complex to put into words. His thoughts now can only be interpreted by a machine."[56] Both "Power Hungry" and "The Plateau" clearly perform as cautionary tales about the dangers of unlocking the mind's potential; however, *Fringe* does not resolve its case. It continually tests and blurs that boundary. Where the episode "Unleashed" features a specific case of a manmade chimera escaping and causing destruction, the idea of "unleashing" potential pervades throughout the series. Even the episode titled "Bound" recalls the series' origin story, with echoes of Prometheus bound and unbound. *Fringe* continually raises the question: although man has the capacity to experiment with and alter the mind, should he?

In contrast to the experiments aimed at improving potential, "The Equation" examines natural giftedness in the form of genius: prodigies are the victims in the case. Finding a pattern in the case of an abducted boy with others involving academics—a "probability theorist" and "structural engineer"—the Fringe team is led back to St. Claire's Hospital and the intersection of genius and madness. Recognizing a detail about red and green flashing lights that induce a hypnotic state for the abducted boy's father, Walter remembers Dashiell Kim, a fellow patient at St. Claire's and former head of Astrophysics at UMASS, and his stories. Although the boy, Ben Stockton, doesn't seem to initially fit the profile of academics, "experts in various fields," his father says that Ben is "kind of an expert himself," a piano prodigy.[57] Even more extraordinary is that Ben never took a lesson and only began to play after waking up from a coma, a result of the car accident that killed his mother. Likening Ben's case to others involving severe brain trauma, the team shifts its focus from his giftedness to the specific details of the piece he obsessively played. When Peter reads Dashiell's equation, he identifies a repeating function and says, "it's a rhythm." Peter asks Walter to convert it to a musical notation, citing that "music is a mathematical language. Chords have numerical values and their notes—one-fourths, one-eighths, one-sixteenths—they're all just fraction variables."[58] After playing the equation, Walter concludes, "Ben's piece is the musical equivalent of Dashiell's mathematical equation."[59]

Identifying a commonality in its representations of discrete types of intelligence (child prodigy and mad genius) with the idea that "curious minds often converge on the same idea," *Fringe* presents a reformulation of contemporary ideas about intelligence, particularly giftedness.[60] Kaufman notes that "multiple studies have also found significant brain plasticity among people engaging in music" and "expert musicians display great gray [matter volume]."[61] Ben's case is particularly revealing of Walter's condition as well. As Walter tries to remember details of a similar story, connecting the case to Dash, he plays Christmas carols in the lab (following the lead of the red and green lights). That mnemonic device leads him to the line "Dashing through the snow..." and the solution. In season three, "The Box" depicts Walter listening to music to "reduce neural activity"; as Walter puts it, listening to harmonic music helps us to "think more clearly when we listen to it."[62] In season five, when Walter is being questioned by the Observer Windmark, Walter tells him that "music helps you shift perspective, to see things differently if you need to."[63]

The episode "The Equation" is a curious meditation on shifting perspectives and seeing intelligence differently. While Ben is reunited with his deceased mother who implores him to complete the rhythm before she decomposes before his eyes, we see the scene from another perspective: Ben is hooked up to wires and a device reminiscent of the ones that Walter uses in his lab. The boy is trapped in a virtual reality. Ben finally completes the sequence and the equation becomes part of the larger Pattern, the intricate web of Fringe events that are under investigation by the Fringe Division; these events signal a breakdown of the boundary between worlds. The formula Ben completes enables members of the bioterrorist group ZFT to pass through solid matter, penetrating bank and prison walls and later the fabric between worlds. Where musical training is aligned in contemporary research with increases in brain plasticity and gray matter, here, Ben's music as mathematical equation enables a dissolution of matter, a transhumanist projection of mind over body, a similar endgame to "The Plateau."

On the other side of the equation, Walter's self-experimentation specifically targets his own mind and the knowledge that he seeks to extract from it. "Grey Matters" reveals the story behind Walter's altered state. Twenty-five years ago, Walter ruptured the fabric between worlds in the attempt to save the "other" Peter; the result of his transgression is the eventual collapse of the boundary separating worlds and, by extension, the very foundations of their world. Walter tries to erase the knowledge of what he can do, in essence, removing the potentiality for destruction. As Claus Penrose, Professor of Endocrinology at Boston College, says, "No one in power should know what he knows."[64] The revelation that others had been implanted with the extracted pieces of his brain introduces new problems (access to those secrets) and possibilities (restoring knowledge) into the narrative, if Walter can put his own mind back together.

It is intriguing that Walter's self-experimentation is directed at what can be interpreted as crystallized intelligence, the culmination of his research and findings. It is knowledge acquired through expertise. In "Grey Matters," in order to decipher The Pattern and his complicity in it, Walter attempts to restore his gray matter. However, he learns that it is an impossible feat. Garth Sundem writes, "Memory is malleable," and this is made explicit as pieces of Walter's brain are extracted, implanted, and destroyed, and, with them, "what memories or knowledge they hold a mystery."[65] As a result, "this broken man is a puzzle to himself, his son, and the viewers."[66] However it is not an entirely bleak picture. Instead, Walter must learn to work with his reconstructed (or rewired) brain and find another course of action. He turns to fluid reasoning, his problem-solving, to connect The Pattern's threads despite missing significant portions of his brain and knowledge. However, Walter's faculties are not entirely impaired. He has a recorded IQ of 196 and retains extensive scientific knowledge that he continually recalls when investigating Fringe cases.[67] Peter complains that Walter recites pi to the 101st digit in order to fall asleep, and, in "Safe," he repeats the Fibonacci sequence in his sleep, providing the clue that links the license plate to the safety deposit box, which turns out to be his own.[68] With each case, he is able to recover and apply knowledge from his former research. He displays fluid reasoning skills like the other members of the Fringe team but most remarkably differs in his vast expertise and knowledge base, which, as Heather M. Porter concludes, are central to his decision and the series' plot.[69] His wisdom is what initially led him to alter his brain.

Yet, in the worlds of *Fringe*, "There's More Than One of Everything," including (and perhaps especially) causes and effects. In the series' alternate course, following a season three reboot that saves their world from imminent destruction, Walter is able to regenerate his brain with a serum. Restoring his knowledge, crystallized intelligence, is part of the solution to the Observers' threat in season five. The other facet, though, is Olivia's extraordinary ability to cross between worlds and regenerate herself after being shot by Walter in the season four finale "Brave New World, Part 2." From the pilot episode onward, Olivia's work is facilitated by Walter's knowledge and resources. The two characters and methodologies exist in tandem, operating on the fringe. Throughout its five seasons, *Fringe* is continually poised between models of intelligence, and the series is sustained by play in the liminal space between absolutes.

While the definition of intelligence and the measures to quantify it have been contested for centuries, as Kaufman notes, there are recurring themes, one being "adaptation to the environment."[70] *Fringe*'s interest in adaptation is expansive, including its use of source material, "monster of the week" transformations, and larger narrative arc that depicts characters navigating a world that is fundamentally changed by science, technology, and their knowledge. By the series' end, the characters must adapt to survive in a world overrun by intelligent design. The risk that the Observers present is evolving too far, becoming wholly intellect, unemotional.[71] Where the risks of utilizing "potential" are destruction and self-implosion for Joseph Meegar ("Power Hungry"), twins Susan Pratt and Nancy Lewis ("The Road Not Taken"), and Olivia, Milo Stanfield's case ("The Plateau") most clearly parallels the evolution evidenced by the Observers. And, like Milo, Peter also almost entirely adapts into a machine, in an imitation of the Observers. In season five, Peter, distraught over his daughter's murder and seeking vengeance, finally utilizes his potential, though not in the way that Walter intended. Peter seizes an Observer's technology and implants it into his own body. Capable of telepathy and teleportation, Peter is "more able" to kill Observers; however, the risk is that he will lose his humanity.

Here, *Fringe*'s representation of the transhumanist future is glimpsed in Peter's transformation, and it emphasizes both the possibility (transcending the body and its limitations) and dangers (removing gray matter from the equation). Bronson writes, "much of transhumanist research sees the mind as easily transferred into other forms—into computers, machines, new version 2.0 bodies—an image that is a frequent occurrence in *Fringe*."[72] Like Milo, Peter becomes a computer, a predictor of what will happen, in essence, suggesting not only the results of increasing intelligence but also the mechanics of the test itself, even—or particularly—its limitations. Kaufman writes that "statistical predictions only tell us what a person is *likely* to achieve in the future, not whether they are *capable* of achieving the outcome."[73] As Kaufman notes, potential is a "constantly moving target," and "The more we engage in something, the more potential grows."[74] He says that "The latest research on the dynamic, nonlinear, and probabilistic nature of human development suggests that it's best to conceptualize potential as *readiness for engagement*."[75] This very logic is what led Walter and Bell to attempt to weaponize children in the Cortexiphan trials in the first place—creating an army of super-soldiers to fight in and for a future world irreparably changed by technology. As Porter notes, the characters in *Fringe* "possess an immeasurable amount of intelligence and potential, but what matters within the parameters of the series is how they use this vast ability."[76]

Fringe ultimately turns its experiments to the viewers, asking that they, too, make sense of The Pattern. Memory is again the key to solving the cases. In season one, Olivia realizes that she must revisit her old cases to figure out who is responsible for Fringe events; everything is connected. In season five, the Fringe team returns to its former cases from earlier seasons, employing that evidence—and technology—in its fight against the Observers. Written into *Fringe*'s mise en scène is its self-reflexivity, its awareness of its source material that begins with Shelley and includes its own narratives. *Fringe* performs as a version of Olivia's favorite game, "Concentration," which depends upon memory and focuses on "Connecting things. Putting them together."[77]

This is part of the series' play from the beginning, evidenced in its opening credits. Glyphs of a butterfly, sea horse, frog, flower, and hand with six fingers appear in the title sequence.[78] These glyphs also introduce the commercial breaks (or momentary fades on DVD and Blu-Ray), with some additions: twin embryos, an apple, and a leaf.[79] As Victor Hernández-Santaolalla and Javier Lozano Delmar state, "The very action of decoding messages is obvious in the final moment of the title sequence when the letters are recomposed in an organic way to present the title of the series to the spectator," a template for viewers to follow when the glyphs reappear in the episodes' structured breaks, an "invitation to reveal hidden content" as "every glyph contains within it another reference or hidden image that alludes ... to the narrative universe of the series."[80] Stuart notes co-producer Jeff Pinker's statement at the 2009 New York Comic-Con that "they were indeed implementing a code that would be difficult to decipher"; however, fans cracked it by the end of season one, "revealing the solution to be a simple substitution process" that generated words foreshadowing the next episode.[81] These images also are embedded in the series' mise en scène; for example, in "6955 kHz," a sea horse is on a book and a leaf appears on a lamp in "The Plateau."[82] Another "Easter egg" in the series is the appearance of one or more Observers in every episode, oftentimes in a crowd scene; fans have dubbed the search "Where's Baldo?," another return to a simple yet complex game for children.[83]

In her analysis of the series' relationship with its fans, Stuart refers to an idea circulating in the fan community that "the Observers represent the show's viewers," granting the viewers omniscience, a kind of omnipotence, and perfect memory "even when the main characters may have forgotten."[84] Julie L. Hawk traces the Observers' evolution in the narrative to that of the viewers, writing, "The movement of the Observers from the fringes of the show to the center of the narrative suggests a stronger, more empowered role for the observers at home, the viewers"; they are "participant observers."[85] This is a convincing argument in an age when viewers "have an opportunity to interpret, reframe, and even reimagine the television narrative," but perhaps Walter again offers a more compelling theory.[86] At the end of season five, Walter is presented with a unique opportunity to rewrite his past by accompanying the boy Observer Michael, a mistake in genetic engineering that allowed both intellect and emotion (IQ and EQ?) to coexist, into the future. The result of this act is a reboot of time, a return to a past before the Observers' invasion. Before they leave, Michael touches Walter, giving him access to his lost memories, including those of his son that were erased when Peter sacrificed himself to save the world at the end of season three.

At the series' end, Walter is a "complete man, as he has back all the pieces of his brain."[87] He is able to reclaim his lost knowledge, in essence, replaying *Fringe*'s complete narrative. The viewers are afforded this position, Walter's position, of revisiting the narrative, working at the nexus of fluid and crystallized knowledge. As Michael offers the possibility of a better future by bridging the divide between the Observers and humanity, the series privileges different ways of knowing. The viewers' work is quite similar to that of the Fringe team, tasked with trying to remember their world and put it back together. Intelligent television has that potential.

Notes

1. J.J. Abrams, Alex Kurtzman, and Robert Orci, "Pilot," *Fringe*, season 1, episode 1, directed by Alex Graves, aired September 9, 2008, on Fox.
2. Sarah Clarke Stuart, *Into the Looking Glass: Exploring the Worlds of* Fringe (Toronto: ECW Press, 2011), 15. Heather M. Porter defines the "mad scientist" archetype as "usually a genius, with a questionable ethics and a lack of moral standards, on a search for answers to particular questions (e.g., how to cure Alzheimer's disease), for knowledge (Is there life "out there"?), for justice, or just for a way to rule the world" but notes that Walter Bishop "provides a different take on the mad scientist paradigm" with his introduction as a broken man. "'You're a Smart Boy. But There Is Much You Don't Know': A Quantitative Examination of Intelligence, Wisdom and Family Relationships," *The Multiple Worlds of* Fringe: *Essays on the J. J. Abrams Science Fiction Series*, ed. Tanya R. Cochran et al. (Jefferson, NC: McFarland, 2014), 94.
3. Stuart, *Into the Looking Glass*, 15. Stuart writes, "Presumably he was more than just an absent-minded professor. His was the profile of a megalomaniacal genius—a danger to himself and the rest of the world." Ibid., 15.
4. Abrams, Kurtzman, and Orci, "Pilot."
5. Ibid.
6. Amy H. Sturgis, "In Search of Fringe's Literary Ancestors," *Fringe Science: Parallel Universes, White Tulips, and Mad Scientists*, ed. Kevin R. Grazier (Dallas: BenBella, 2011), 19.
7. Val Nolan, "'The Whole World Is Their Lab': The Scientist as Villain, the Scientist as Hero," in Cochran et al., *The Multiple Worlds of* Fringe, 14.
8. Stuart notes, "Walter is certainly not the only 'Frankenstein' in *Fringe*," as "many of the Massive Dynamic scientists and the followers of ZFT are modeled on this archetype." Stuart, *Into the Looking Glass*, 18.
9. Darrin M. McMahon, *Divine Fury: A History of Genius* (New York: Basic Books, 2013), 21. Nook file.
10. Stuart, *Into the Looking Glass*, 91.
11. McMahon, *Divine Fury*, 21.
12. N. J. Mackintosh writes, "No one has supposed that genius is simply a matter of having an unusually high IQ score, but many writers have thought it probably important (surprisingly enough, even Gardner, 1997, accepts this), and some, such as Eysenck (1995) and Simonton (2003), have argued that a high IQ is a necessary precondition of genius." *IQ and Human Intelligence*, 2d ed. (Oxford: Oxford University Press, 2011), 207.
13. Scott Barry Kaufman, *Ungifted: Intelligence Redefined* (New York: Basic Books, 2013), 291.
14. Ibid.
15. Ibid.
16. Mackintosh writes, "Ever since IQ tests were first developed, a common argument has been that they measure only a narrow aspect of (largely academic) intelligence." Mackintosh, *IQ and Human Intelligence*, 222.
17. McMahon, *Divine Fury*, 235.
18. Mackintosh, *IQ and Human Intelligence*, 1.
19. McMahon, *Divine Fury*, 236. Binet and Henri's 1895 test aimed to measure "ten separate abilities: memory, imagery, imagination, attention, comprehension, suggestibility, aesthetic sentiment, moral sentiment, muscular strength/willpower, and motor ability/hand-eye coordination." Kaufman, *Ungifted*, 23.
20. Mackintosh, *IQ and Human Intelligence*, 42.
21. Ibid., 42–43.

22. McMahon, *Divine Fury*, 241. Gardner's *Frames of Mind: The Theory of Multiple Intelligences* (1983) identifies "seven independent intelligences: logical-mathematical, linguistic, spatial, bodily-kinesthetic, musical, interpersonal, and intrapersonal," and, most recently, "naturalistic intelligence." Kaufman, *Ungifted*, 77.

23. Mackintosh, *IQ and Human Intelligence*, 76–77.

24. Kaufman, *Ungifted*, 177.

25. Ibid., 178.

26. Ibid., 210.

27. Ibid. Kaufman identifies other "social multipliers" cited in Dickens and Flynn's work, including "increased nutrition, increased literacy, increased test familiarity, video games, complexity of TV shows and movie plotlines, modernization, decreased prevalence of infectious diseases and parasites." Ibid., 213.

28. Ibid., 177.

29. Zak Bronson, "'We Were Trying to Make You More Than You Were': The Singularity, Transhumanism and Shapeshifting," Cochran et al., *The Multiple Worlds of* Fringe, 60.

30. Ibid.

31. Ibid., 61.

32. Ibid.

33. Ibid.

34. Ibid., 66.

35. Abrams, Kurtzman, and Orci, "Pilot."

36. J. J. Abrams and Jeff Pinker, "The Arrival," *Fringe*, season 1, episode 4, Paul Edwards, aired September 30, 2008, on Fox.

37. David H. Goodman and Jason Cahill, "Safe," *Fringe*, season 1, episode 10, directed by Michael Zinberg, aired December 2, 2008, on Fox.

38. Jeff Pinker, J. J. Abrams, Alex Kurtzman, and Roberto Orci, "The Same Old Story," *Fringe*, season 1, episode 2, directed by Paul Edwards, aired September 16, 2008, on Fox.

39. Goodman and Cahill, "Safe."

40. J. J. Abrams and Jeff Pinker, "In Which We Meet Mr. Jones," *Fringe*, season 1, episode 7, directed by Brad Anderson, aired November 11, 2008, on Fox.

41. Ibid.

42. Abrams and Pinker, "The Arrival."

43. Goodman and Cahill, "Safe."

44. David H. Goodman, Glen Whitman, and Robert Chiappetta, "Ability," *Fringe*, season 1, episode 14, directed by Norberto Barba, aired February 10, 2009, on Fox. *Fringe: The Complete First Season* (Burbank: Warner Home Video 2010), Blu-ray.

45. Ibid.

46. Ibid.

47. Ibid.

48. Kaufman, *Ungifted*, 177.

49. Stuart, *Into the Looking Glass*, 5, Rhonda V. Wilcox, "Women with the Agency: Dana Scully, Temperance Brennan, and Olivia Dunham," Cochran et al., *The Multiple Worlds of* Fringe, 52.

50. Jason Cahill and Julia Cho, "Power Hungry," *Fringe*, season 1, episode 5, directed by Christopher Misiano, aired October 14, 2008, on Fox.

51. Ibid.

52. Ibid.

53. Ibid.

54. Alison Schapker and Monica Owusu-Breen, "The Plateau," *Fringe*, season 3, episode 3, directed by Brad Anderson, aired October 7, 2010, on Fox.

55. Abrams and Pinker, "In Which We Meet Mr. Jones."

56. Schapker and Owusu-Breen, "The Plateau."

57. J. R. Orci and David H. Goodman, "The Equation," *Fringe*, season 1, episode 8, directed by Gwyneth Horder-Payton, aired November 18, 2008, on Fox.
58. Ibid.
59. Ibid.
60. Ibid.
61. Kaufman, *Ungifted*, 205.
62. Josh Singer and Graham Roland, "The Box," *Fringe*, season 3, episode 2, directed by Jeffrey Hunt, aired September 30, 2010, on Fox.
63. J. H. Wyman, "Transilience Thought Unifier Model-11," *Fringe*, season 5, episode 1, directed by Miguel Sapochnik and Jeannot Szwarc, aired September 28, 2012 on Fox.
64. Abrams, Kurtzman, Orci, "The Same Old Story."
65. Garth Sundem, "The Malleability of Memory," *Fringe Science*, 99, Porter, "You're a Smart Boy," 95.
66. Porter, "You're a Smart Boy," 95.
67. J. R. Orci and Zack Whedon, "The Transformation," *Fringe*, season 1, episode 13, directed by Brad Anderson, aired February 2, 2009, on Fox.
68. Milo's "unnatural" intelligence—or genius—is a contrast; Milo is able to recite pi to the 1000th place after being part of the drug trial. Schapker and Owusu-Breen, "The Plateau."
69. Porter writes that "intelligence is only part of the equation. How that intelligence is used is another. The study of intelligence use in the form of wisdom has become the forefront of intelligence research recently, and like intelligence, wisdom is not easily defined." After summarizing the results of her quantitative study, Porter concludes that Walter's final choice is "made with wisdom." "You're a Smart Boy," 98, 105.
70. Kaufman, *Ungifted*, 294. According to Kaufman, from Alfred Binet and David Wechsler to Robert Sternberg, adaptation has been central to the study of intelligence. Ibid., 295.
71. Bronson writes that the Observers "literalize the transhumanist dream of a human identity located purely in the mind, but in so doing, they ultimately sacrifice their material connections—to themselves, others, place, or their environment." "More Than You Were," 72.
72. Ibid., 65–66.
73. Kaufman, *Ungifted*, 305.
74. Ibid.
75. Ibid.
76. Porter, "You're a Smart Boy," 95. Here, Porter specifically refers to Walter and Peter, but her terms are indicative of the principles at the foundation of *Fringe*'s world(s) and its narratives.
77. Goodman and Cahill, "Safe."
78. Víctor Hernández-Santaolalla and Javier Lozano Delmar, "Teasing the Audience: Construction of Meaning Through the Opening Title Sequence," Cochran et al., *The Multiple Worlds of* Fringe, 215.
79. Ibid.
80. Ibid., 215–216.
81. Stuart, *Into the Looking Glass*, 165–166.
82. Ibid., 167.
83. Stuart refers to "Where's Baldo?" as a "good, old-fashioned seek-and-find challenge." Ibid., 162. She also makes note of ways that the series has been extended for fans with transmedia storytelling, with examples being a real-life scavenger hunt at Comic-Con, Imagine the Impossibilities, the SearchForThePattern, and Complete the Pattern websites. Ibid., 159–160.
84. Ibid., 171.
85. Julie L. Hawk, "Observation on the Fringe: September's Observation and Narrative

Participation as a Template for Viewer Agency," Cochran et al., *The Multiple Worlds of* Fringe, 201, 204.
  86. Stuart, *Into the Looking Glass*, 173.
  87. Porter, "You're a Smart Boy," 97.

References

Abrams, J. J., and Jeff Pinker. "The Arrival." *Fringe,* season 1, episode 4. Directed by Paul Edwards. Aired September 23, 2008, on Fox. *Fringe, The Complete First Season*, Blu-ray. Burbank: Warner Home Video, 2009.
_____. "In Which We Meet Mr. Jones." *Fringe,* season 1, episode 7. Directed by Brad Anderson. Aired November 11, 2008, on Fox. *Fringe, The Complete First Season*, Blu-ray. Burbank: Warner Home Video, 2009.
Abrams, J. J., Jeff Pinker, Alex Kurtzman, and Roberto Orci. "The Same Old Story." *Fringe,* season 1, episode 2. Directed by Paul Edwards. Aired September 16, 2008, on Fox. *Fringe, The Complete First Season*, Blu-ray. Burbank: Warner Home Video, 2009.
Abrams, J. J., Alex Kurtzman, and Robert Orci. "Pilot." *Fringe,* season 1, episode 1. Directed by Alex Graves. Aired September 9, 2008, on Fox. *Fringe, The Complete First Season*, Blu-ray. Burbank: Warner Home Video, 2009.
Bronson, Zak. "'We Were Trying to Make You More Than You Were': The Singularity, Transhumanism and Shapeshifting." In *The Multiple Worlds of* Fringe: *Essays on the J. J. Abrams Science Fiction Series*, edited by Tanya R. Cochran, Sherry Gin, and Paul Zinder, 60–76. Jefferson, NC: McFarland, 2014.
Cahill, Jason, and Julia Cho. "Power Hungry." *Fringe*, season 1, episode 5. Directed by Christopher Misiano. Aired October 14, 2008, on Fox. *Fringe, The Complete First Season*, Blu-ray. Burbank: Warner Home Video, 2009.
Goodman, David H., and Jason Cahill. "Safe." *Fringe,* season 1, episode 10. Directed by Michael Zinberg. Aired December 2, 2008, on Fox. *Fringe, The Complete First Season*, Blu-ray. Burbank: Warner Home Video, 2009.
Goodman, David H., and J. R. Orci. "The Equation." *Fringe,* season 1, episode 8. Directed by Gwyneth Horder-Payton. Aired November 18, 2008, on Fox. *Fringe, The Complete First Season*, Blu-ray. Burbank: Warner Home Video, 2009.
Goodman, David H., Glen Whitman, and Robert Chiappetta."Ability." *Fringe,* season 1, episode 14. Directed by Norberto Barba. Aired February 10, 2009, on Fox. *Fringe, The Complete First Season*, Blu-ray. Burbank: Warner Home Video, 2009.
Hawk, Julie L. "Observation on the Fringe: September's Observation and Narrative Participation as a Template for Viewer Agency." In *The Multiple Worlds of* Fringe: *Essays on the J. J. Abrams Science Fiction Series*, edited by Tanya R. Cochran, Sherry Gin, and Paul Zinder, 201–208. Jefferson, NC: McFarland, 2014.
Hernández-Santaolalla, Víctor, and Javier Lozano Delmar. "Teasing the Audience: Construction of Meaning Through the Opening Title Sequence." In *The Multiple Worlds of* Fringe: *Essays on the J. J. Abrams Science Fiction Series*, edited by Tanya R. Cochran, Sherry Gin, and Paul Zinder, 209–224. Jefferson, NC: McFarland, 2014.
Kaufman, Scott Barry. *Ungifted: Intelligence Redefined*. New York: Basic Books, 2013.
Mackintosh, N.J. *IQ and Human Intelligence*, 2 ed. Oxford: Oxford University Press, 2011.
McMahon, Darrin M. *Divine Fury: A History of Genius*. New York: Basic Books, 2013. Nook file.
Miller, Ashley, and Zack Stentz. "Grey Matters." *Fringe,* season 2, episode 10. Directed by Jeannot Szwarc. Aired December 10, 2009, on Fox. *Fringe, The Complete Secone Season*, Blu-ray. Burbank: Warner Home Video, 2010.
Nolan, Val. "'The Whole World Is Their Lab': The Scientist as Villain, the Scientist as Hero."

In *The Multiple Worlds of* Fringe*: Essays on the J. J. Abrams Science Fiction Series*, edited by Tanya R. Cochran, Sherry Gin, and Paul Zinder, 13–30. Jefferson, NC: McFarland, 2014.

Orci, J. R., and Zack Whedon. "The Transformation." *Fringe*, season 1, episode 13. Directed by Brad Anderson. Aired February 3, 2009, on Fox. *Fringe, The Complete First Season*, Blu-ray. Burbank: Warner Home Video, 2009.

Porter, Heather M. "'You're a Smart Boy. But There Is Much You Don't Know': A Quantitative Examination of Intelligence, Wisdom and Family Relationships." In *The Multiple Worlds of* Fringe*: Essays on the J. J. Abrams Science Fiction Series*, edited by Tanya R. Cochran, Sherry Gin, and Paul Zinder, 93–107. Jefferson, NC: McFarland, 2014.

Schapker, Alison, and Monica Owusu-Breen. "The Plateau." *Fringe*, season 3, episode 3. Directed by Brad Anderson. Aired October 7, 2010, on Fox. *Fringe, The Complete Third Season*, DVD. Burbank: Warner Home Video, 2011.

Singer, Josh, and Graham Roland. "The Box." *Fringe*, season 3, episode 2. Directed by Jeffrey Hunt. Aired September 30, 2010, on Fox. *Fringe, The Complete Third Season*, DVD. Burbank: Warner Home Video, 2011.

Stuart, Sarah Clarke. *Into the Looking Glass: Exploring the Worlds of* Fringe. Toronto: ECW Press, 2011.

Sturgis, Amy H. "In Search of Fringe's Literary Ancestors." In *Fringe Science: Parallel Universes, White Tulips, and Mad Scientists*, edited by Kevin R. Grazier, 17–36. Dallas: BenBella, 2011.

Sundem, Garth. "The Malleability of Memory." In *Fringe Science: Parallel Universes, White Tulips, and Mad Scientists*, edited by Kevin R. Grazier, 97–112. Dallas: BenBella, 2011.

Wilcox, Rhonda V. "Women with the Agency: Dana Scully, Temperance Brennan and Olivia Dunham." In *The Multiple Worlds of* Fringe*: Essays on the J. J. Abrams Science Fiction Series*, edited by Tanya R. Cochran, Sherry Gin, and Paul Zinder 43–59. Jefferson, NC: McFarland, 2014.

Wyman, J. H. "Transilience Thought Unifier Model–11." *Fringe*, season 5, episode 1. Directed by Miguel Sapochnik and Jeannot Szwarc. Aired September 28, 2012, on Fox. *Fringe, The Complete Fifth and Final Season*, Blu-ray. Burbank: Warner Home Video, 2013.

PART II
GENDER AND GENIUS

"Caring is not an advantage"

The Triumph of Reason in Sherlock

JILLIAN L. CANODE

Over the last decade, television has portrayed genius in a variety of ways. Shows ranging in genre from comedy to drama depict their geniuses differently, but they share the common underlying belief that geniuses are those who cherish reason above all else. TV geniuses, lately, are most commonly portrayed as detectives, where their uncanny, almost superhuman abilities lend themselves to benefitting the greater good by solving crimes. One of the more recent and most successful incarnations of the genius on television is a revival of Sir Arthur Conan Doyle's "Consulting Detective"[1] Sherlock Holmes on the BBC's *Sherlock*. His ability to solve crimes using deductive reasoning is unparalleled, and those who rely on his skills do so sometimes begrudgingly. Sherlock is frequently downright cruel in his emotional insensitivity to others, but because he is so effective with his methods, many are willing to overlook his emotional ignorance in favor of solving crimes. Indeed, they forgive his social ineptitude not only because he is often the only one capable of catching the criminals, but also because his abilities are marvelous.

Steven Moffat and Mark Gatiss' *Sherlock* takes Holmes to levels of inhumanity Conan Doyle did not elaborate upon in his stories. To be sure, Sherlock Holmes always had a kind of preternatural gift for seeing details others missed and using logic to solve crimes, but *Sherlock* takes viewers deeper into the psyche of the detective, where we learn more about why he is so good at his job. Sherlock has the ability to separate himself from his emotions, to quash the effects his body might have on his mind, and to avoid, as much as possible, caring about anything other than solving cases. We are drawn to Sherlock because he is a crime-solving machine, for better or worse.

This Sherlock Holmes, this most unkind and least gentle version of the detective who is brought to life by Benedict Cumberbatch, is enormously popular, not only because the show's stories and cast of characters are entertaining and the acting is excellent, but also because Sherlock represents for us, on a more subconscious level, the triumph of mind over body something we in the West have been obsessed with since the ancient Greeks. We love geniuses like Sherlock so much because they remind us of what we could be capable if we stopped emotion from getting in our way. This essay will argue that our cultural love affair with reason—expressed in its highest human form as the genius—endures, as evidenced by the immense popularity of Cumberbatch's portrayal of the sleuth. Furthermore, I will demonstrate not only that we still value reason at the expense of emotion, but, given that the majority of geniuses portrayed on television over the last decade have been men, and that the women on *Sherlock* are portrayed as shrews, airheads, or temptresses, we also hold fast to the idea that the dichotomy between reason and emotion aligns with the dichotomy between men and women.

In a time when we need to see more representative characters on our televisions, *Sherlock,* though rightfully beloved for a number of reasons, serves as a reminder that our culture continues to celebrate those who fit the description of genius as it was defined centuries ago, when reason, whiteness,[2] and maleness were valued above all else.

Why Genius?

Thousands of years have passed since the Ancient Greek philosophers asked questions about human nature, knowledge, truth, justice, beauty, love, and reason, but those questions linger, especially among modern day philosophers. Philosophers are not the only ones concerned with sussing out the answers to these major questions, though they are stereotypically portrayed as the ones who sit and ponder them for pay. We find those wondering about the answers to these great questions in any number of places, but artifacts of popular culture pose queries for us to contemplate in ways proven to be more accessible than the ivory tower provides. We have had a very long love affair with figuring ourselves out. In certain realms of popular culture, such as television, part of how we figure ourselves out is through examining the characters we love to see on the small screen. To which characters we are attracted and to whom we find ourselves returning again and again can tell us any number of things about what we value and the kind of people we wish to be. If we look to the productions of Western popular culture, especially those of television over the last decade, we cannot help but see the massive popularity of the genius on the small screen.

Why the genius, though? As I mentioned earlier, the genius is often portrayed as someone so smart they can't really function very well in the world (they are sometimes considered disordered in some way), or, at least, they do not function in the "normal" way we expect them to. It is as if their brains are so full of knowledge they do not have room for all the messy stuff we cram into our heads day-in and day-out. Sherlock Holmes, in Moffat and Gatiss' adaptation of Conan Doyle, is a man who is well aware of his own mental capacity, careful to store only the most pertinent information in his "hard drive."[3] That Sherlock has no idea that the Earth revolves around the Sun is a point of particular disbelief for John. "It's primary school stuff, Sherlock,"[4] John remarks with an incredulous look on his face, throwing Sherlock into a rant about useless and useful knowledge.

Sherlock is massively popular for numerous reasons, and the fascination with the Sherlock Holmes character is far from new. But I think part of the popularity of Moffat and Gatiss' incarnation of Sherlock is that he is so brilliant, he's practically inhuman. We are drawn to Sherlock's inhumanity for two main reasons: first, we want to be him; second, we thank our lucky stars that we are not him, and therefore we take comfort in the fact that we can hold a sort of moral high ground because we are able to care, though we wish we didn't have to. It seems strange that we could entertain these reasons for attraction simultaneously, but that we do demonstrates that we are still ruled by reason. Sure, we know that Sherlock needs John to balance him out, to be his moral and emotional compass at times, but it is Sherlock who is the star because it is Sherlock who gets the job done. The genius does the work, and we sit in awe of him, just like John does. We, the spectators, are in many ways represented by John. He is the human being, Sherlock is the machine.

Our Love Affair with Reason and the Genius

We know emotions are necessary. But that doesn't mean we have to like them. And the history of Western thought has borne out for us both the fact that we dislike emotions and why, in fact, we are right to dislike emotions. To understand why we love this acerbic, high-functioning sociopath[5] so much, we have to trace a line through the history of the productions of culture in the West. As we know, what we value today is an amalgamation of religious, cultural, political, and economic influences. At the center of all of these aspects of our lives lies reason, and Enlightenment thinkers helped ensure reason's primacy. Logic is of course a powerful tool; to be able to construct arguments in order to persuade others of the rightness of one point or another is an acquired skill. But, we use reason to convince others of the rightness of our beliefs. Well-reasoned arguments receive far more accolades than arguments based on intuition, even if intuition often helps to inform some of our reasoning. Still, our long-held belief that through excellent use of reason we can acquire the answers to life's most burning questions has turned us against anything that may threaten our ability develop our faculties of reason.

From where does this obsession with reason come? As I mentioned earlier, in philosophy at least, the quest to attain knowledge and truth is thousands of years long and will continue, I hope, for thousands more. Philosophers have argued that part of the ability to attain knowledge comes through divorcing oneself from the body; it is only through use of the intellect and through clean, careful reasoning that we can acquire useful knowledge. Descartes most famously severed any connection between mind and body, thereby positioning the body as something that really only gets in the way and messes stuff up for us. Even the empiricists like Locke and Hume granted that while we need the body to be able to function in the world, we should never let the body be our sole guide; reason should always take the lead.

In part, the question of the legitimacy of the rule of reason has come from feminist philosophers who were and continue to be concerned with how the body has been relegated to an undesirable status in theory. Although these ideas about reason and the body took root hundreds of years ago, their influence is still palpable, especially for those who are more immediately affected by them. The stakes of this forced division of reason and emotion are high, though, and we should not ignore them. Epistemologist Lorraine Code explains the implications of the divide beautifully:

> Reason is not an independent item one simply comes across in the world. It is symbolically, metaphorically constituted all the way down: its constitution in association with ideal masculinity stakes out a rational domain that is inaccessible, or accessible only uneasily and with difficulty, to people whose traits and attributes do not coincide with those by which ideal white masculinity has defined itself. The conceptual-symbolic dichotomies that such alignments generate—of which reason/emotion, mind/body, abstract/concrete, objective/subjective are typical samples—align also with a male/female dichotomy, both descriptively and evaluatively. And those dichotomies work to establish the features of ideal, universally valid knowledge as a product of rational endeavor, and to separate it from opin-

ion, hearsay, particularity which come to be associated with (stereotypical) femininity.[6]

Code makes it easy to see why the genius has, for ages, been portrayed as a man. These divides, which have dominated the history of Western thought and culture for centuries, indicate that men are capable of complex, detached, scientific thought, and women are better suited for more practical tasks that do not require higher order thought. Our insistence on maintaining the stereotypes these divisions have produced has had lasting, damaging effects on both men and women. To see how these dichotomies still adversely affect women, one need only look at the speculation in *The Washington Post* over how a potential run for office will affect Hillary Clinton's family,[7] or witness *Today* anchor Matt Lauer's concern about whether a female CEO can be an executive and good mother.[8] These are issues men simply do not have to face because it is still assumed that they naturally are able to handle business and politics in isolation from other personal concerns.

Times have been slow to change, and Moffat and Gatiss' Sherlock conforms to the ideal genius perfectly. To be fair, Arthur Conan Doyle's Sherlock Holmes was a white male, so we may expect the twenty-first century Sherlock to be as well. But *Sherlock* is an adaptation; Moffat and Gatiss already take a number of liberties with the original stories. The show is set in present-day London, after all. So, we should wonder why, if they can transport Sherlock to the current century, give him all kinds of technology and equipment heretofore unavailable to the Holmes of the nineteenth century, he is still an upper-class, white male. It would seem the imagination can only accommodate so much.[9] Whatever the reason Sherlock Holmes remains unchanged biologically, and there are a number of reasonable excuses as to why people maintain him in at least part of his original incarnation, the lack of women geniuses on television is telling, and the way women are written on *Sherlock* is even more revealing. I will come to this last point a bit later on.

Consulting Genius

People want to say the primacy of reason is dead, and that we're all much more touchy-feely than we used to be, and that we realized, long ago, that even scientists cannot be completely objective and divorce themselves from emotion. Still, there is overwhelming evidence to suggest that we still would much rather have intelligence than be in touch with our feelings. The proliferation of genius-centered television shows in the last decade suggests that we remain fascinated with the genius because he[10] is who we wish we could be, who we believe we should be, who we know we cannot be, and who we are relieved not to be. We don't want to eschew the body wholesale. After all, we need to be able to take a break from all that thinking now and then.

We love Sherlock because he's so good at what he does; he can separate himself from his emotions, employ reason to take down criminals and solve mysteries no one else can crack. Curiously, there is a running commentary throughout the series on Sherlock's sexuality (or lack thereof). Sherlock is not interested in sex; he is not unaware of people making sexual advances toward him, nor is he unaware when people find him attractive. Indeed, he uses his body and its apparent desirability to Molly and Janine to his advantage. But Sherlock's apparent disinterest in sex frustrates and confuses others. Moriarty refers to Sherlock as "The Virgin,"[11] and Mycroft jabs at Sherlock for his presumed ignorance when it comes to sex.[12] Even Janine, who Sherlock pretended to love, is disappointed in their complete lack of sexual intimacy.[13] These characters' reactions to Sherlock's ability to transcend sex are indicative of the disdain we often feel for people who are able to get beyond the trappings of the body. It's a kind of jealous reaction because Sherlock can do what we cannot. Our sexual desire reminds us that the body will pull us from pure rationality time and again.

I will not spend a long time dwelling on whether Sherlock is in fact asexual, though there are many who contend he is.[14] Legions of fans of the show wish dearly that Sherlock and Molly would have paired off, or that Sherlock and Janine would have been a real, lasting couple, or, of course and very popularly, that Sherlock would have married John instead of John marrying Mary. But such pairings would never work. Sherlock sometimes doesn't want to eat because food will slow down his rational processing; why on earth would he be interested in sex? In the "Unaired Pilot," John and Sherlock's conversation in the restaurant goes a bit differently than it did in the first aired episode of the series, "A Study in Pink." When John asks Sherlock if he's going to eat, Sherlock asks John what day it is.[15] This, of course, indicates not only that Sherlock does not eat every day, but also that his obsessive personality interferes with his diet; his very thin frame supports this. When John insists that Sherlock needs to eat, our favorite detective quickly retorts: "No, *you* need to eat. I need to think. The brain's what counts. Everything else is transport."[16]

Sherlock's ability to divorce himself from sex, to compartmentalize and delete information that doesn't help solve cases, and to abstain from food shows his difference from the rest of us. He is very nearly a being of total reflection and thought, the mind in its highest and best form. This Sherlock has even beaten a drug habit (though his stint as an undercover heroin addict in the third season makes us doubtful of his rehabilitation), and, despite the occasional nicotine rage when he isn't distracted by work,[17] Sherlock very nearly achieves enlightened status of the kind where the ties of the human body no longer bind. He is the type of genius that Marjorie Garber calls "the post–Enlightenment equivalent of sainthood."[18] He is a saint not only because he seemingly works miracles in his cases, but also because he has transcended the trappings of the body.

In That Moment, We Were All John Watson

Moffat and Gatiss' Sherlock still embodies much of the original Holmes character with many of the elements of the traditional genius, and we find comfort in the familiarity of such a character. Garber puts the lure of the genius succinctly, saying, "The genius was, and to some extent continues to be, the Romantic hero, the loner, the eccentric, the apotheosis of the individual. The further our society gets from individual agency ... the more we idealize the genius, who is by this definition the opposite of the committee or collaborative enterprise."[19] In the West, we are highly individualistic and meritocratic; we love to get by on our own steam. As Garber points out, the smaller the world gets, the less able we are to remain the lone wolf. Sherlock is so appealing to us because even though he'd "be lost without his blogger"[20] and can't seem to operate without an assistant, he still does all the real work—the brainwork—himself.

Sherlock insists, and the show bears this out, that he is the only person capable of doing what he does, hence his status as loner. He is the intellectual superhero, and his superpower is his ability to use reason and deduction. Just like when the police in Gotham City use the bat signal to call for Batman's help, "when the police are out of their element, which is always,"[21] they call Sherlock Holmes. Though he is the least gracious hero people have ever encountered, John serves to humanize him a bit, especially as the show progresses and his fame grows. Part of the superhero attraction, and subsequently, part of Sherlock's attraction as a genius, is that even though we can rely on him to figure out the whole mystery, now and then he needs inspiration; he needs John Watson. We are attracted to the idea that we could be that source of inspiration. We want Sherlock's backhanded compliment to John—"Some people who aren't geniuses have the amazing ability to stimulate it in others"[22]—leveled at us.

John serves as an apt reflection of the feelings we experience in relation to the genius we find in Sherlock. His awed expressions and unintentional outbursts of praise for Sherlock's deductive powers delight us, for we feel the same way. John reacts to Sherlock's speed-talking his way through a particularly complex deduction as a child would to a magic trick. Like a spider with a fly, Sherlock lures John into his little crime-solving web when they first meet in "A Study in Pink" and Sherlock asks, "Afghanistan or Iraq?" From that moment, John is hooked, and so are we. Sherlock continues to impress John when they are in the taxi en route to a crime scene in Brixton where Sherlock explains how he figured out that John was a soldier and has a sibling who drinks too much. After Sherlock unfurls the immensely complex train of thought that got him to the question of location he posed, John is so amazed he's almost angry about it. When he tells Sherlock his deduction is amazing and gets a "Really?" in reply, John says, "Of course it was. It was extraordinary. It was quite extraordinary."[23] The juxtaposition in the demeanors of John and Sherlock in scenes such as this, where Sherlock deduces and John is left awestruck, is indicative of the overall positioning of the common person in relation to the genius. We are merely children, our brains incapable of understanding how the genius works.

Betrayed by the Body, Saved by the Mind

Sherlock never misses an opportunity to remind people how inadequate their minds are compared to his. Like some other fictionalized geniuses,[24] Sherlock enjoys pointing out how intelligent he is. On more than one occasion, he marvels at how it's possible for average people to function properly without a brain like his.[25] Sherlock wields his intellect like a weapon; it is both his source of power and his defense mechanism. We all seek power in some form; power not only goes hand-in-hand with the individualism Western culture celebrates, but it is also protective. The genius exerts his intellectual power over others because that is the only power he has. The thing about the kind of power the genius has, and a major reason why we are so attracted to that power, is that while physical power, monetary power, social power, and military power can always be challenged, intellectual power is less vulnerable to attack. A self-proclaimed show-off,[26] Sherlock bullies via brainpower, often targeting those who have targeted him. Sherlock's exceptionally mean-spirited moments of snark are some of the more celebrated scenes in the series, inspiring viewers to wish they had an Anderson they could tell to shut up because he "lowers the IQ of the whole street"[27] when he speaks aloud.

We love Sherlock because he doesn't care. He doesn't have to care. Mycroft says that "caring is not an advantage,"[28] and Sherlock reminds John why caring makes no difference: caring does not solve crimes faster, caring does not keep people from dying, and caring is, in fact, a hindrance.[29] While Sherlock shuns emotion, he cannot deny the role the body must play in his work. For Sherlock, the body is a useful tool: he relies heavily on his senses to aid his deductive process, but the body, we must remember, is merely transport. The real work happens after the senses have had their moment to shine. In "The Hounds of Baskerville," we see what happens when Sherlock allows emotion to cloud his judgment. As he and John sit by the fire after their encounter with the hound, Sherlock drinks alcohol and speaks to John with hands shaking: "Look at me. I'm afraid, John. Afraid." He continues, saying angrily, "Always been able to keep myself distant, divorce myself from feelings. You see? Body's betraying me. Interesting, yes? Emotions. The grit on the lens. The fly in the ointment."[30] If there is anything Sherlock likes the least, it's being a person with emotional weaknesses. We sympathize with Sherlock in his moment of anger and disappointment, even though, ironically, he's having a temper tantrum. We love Sherlock for his ability to be an uncaring, calculating, crime-solving machine, and we can't help but care when emotion gets in the way of that. We care because we understand the disappointment he feels. We care. Sherlock doesn't. This, he would tell us, is our primary error.

Though we identify with the disappointment Sherlock experiences when his body betrays him, we are disappointed in Sherlock as well. We are let down because despite our ability to sympathize with his frustration, we expect him to be above emotion. When he fails, we are devastated; we believe he is above error. As the intellectual superhero and genius saint, when he falls from grace, it is painful for the mere mortals who witness it. His fall is a literal one in "The Reichenbach Fall,"[31] and the scene just before Sherlock steps off the roof of St. Bart's hospital is especially heartbreaking. After Sherlock is dead, and John is standing at his grave, mourning the loss of his best friend and begging him for a resurrection miracle, we beg with him. We share in John's refusal to believe that Sherlock is a fraud or that he really is dead; no one that smart could die so simply. Of course, we learn Sherlock survived the fall. Genius allows Sherlock a kind of immortality, as he was able to devise a plan to sacrifice himself very publicly in order to spare those he put in danger by making the mistake of caring for them.

Through his knowledge and his sacrifice, Sherlock becomes a kind of messiah. Perhaps this is the true reason we love the genius Sherlock Holmes so much: he can save us when no one else can, and there is something intoxicating about being able to depend on someone in that way. Garber explains the draw of the genius-as-savior, saying, "Deep within us lies a certain strain of longing for genius, a genius worship, that might be described as messianic: the hope that a genius will come along to save us from our technological, philosophical, spiritual, or aesthetic impasse."[32] We know we are flawed and tragic and broken and messy, so when the genius comes along, he makes everything seem like it will be all right. He assures us that it will be, for he is full of swagger, confidence, and answers. He is not like us; he is not a complicated tangle of emotion and reason. And though he may be "the most unpleasant, rude, ignorant, and all-around obnoxious asshole that anyone could possibly have the misfortune to meet,"[33] we forgive him these faults because we recognize that he is superior to us.

We strive to be better than we are, and we love Sherlock because somewhere deep down we think it may be possible that if we practice our deductive powers, we could be like him. We think perhaps that we, too, could be geniuses and saviors. Sherlock seems to think it is possible for other people to become geniuses, though it is highly unlikely. He laments people's inability to think properly,[34] though he does encourage John to try his hand at deduction now and then.[35] Usually his encouragements end in a scathing comment, so people will not often try to reach his level of detection. Part of the draw of the series itself is that we can play detective too. We have access to the same clues and information Sherlock does—though we can't see the world the same way—and we are shielded from the verbal blows he lobs at lesser minds. The more observant viewers may be able to follow Sherlock's trail for a while, but it is impossible to keep track of him the entire time; after all, he is a genius and we are not. We thrill at the idea of getting close to solving a case, much like John does when he believes a cat scratch caused a tetanus death,[36] but we are put in our place just as John is when Sherlock swoops in and in less than a minute shatters any illusion that we are even close to his level of brainpower.

Gifts like Sherlock's are rare, innate and, in his case, genetic.[37] Still, we persist in our paradoxical belief that while we know it's impossible to be a genius like Sherlock, we think perhaps we could be with enough practice. We may love the genius detective because he is fiercely independent and solves crimes through his own labor, but we still wish such a level of intelligence would come through cultivation. Of course it never will, so we return to Sherlock and marvel because while "ordinary mortals can achieve many things by dint of hard work ... the natural and effortless gifts of a true genius ... will forever elude the diligent overachiever ... genius, and geniuses, cannot be made, only born."[38] If Garber is correct in her assertion about how geniuses the likes of Sherlock come to be, television's depictions of geniuses take her sentiment a step further: if the shows on television featuring geniuses provide any evidence, then the genius is not merely born, but born white and male as well.

Women and Sherlock

Our longing to be the genius is grounded by our contempt for emotion, and, subsequently, the body. We have been taught to value rationality and devalue emotion. As I pointed out earlier, the body has been aligned, traditionally, with the feminine, and the feminine, of course, with women. For those who choose to believe this dichotomy no longer exists, *Sherlock* serves as a harsh reminder that reason and maleness are still privileged over emotion and femaleness. Despite the fact that we know that not all men are rational and not all women emotional, we still maintain that suppressing emotion in favor of reason is paramount to success. To see just how valued men and reason are in the world of Sherlock, we need only look at how this celebrated character treats the women in his life. As I discussed earlier, each of the women with whom Sherlock interacts is portrayed as a mere extension of a body; even the "smart" ones are relegated to the status of nothing more than their sex, and they each embody various female stereotypes, all tied to emotion and the body in some way. Sally Donovan is vindictive and cruel, Molly is awkward, submissive, and lovesick, Mrs. Hudson is a former exotic dancer, who is now an airheaded nag, Irene Adler uses her body as a weapon, Janine is gullible because she dares to love, and Mary is a psychopath in a wedding dress. Sherlock easily undermines any power these women may gain throughout the series, proving again and again that the mind will always be superior to the body.

The most telling and most obvious indicator of how reason triumphs in *Sherlock* comes in the form of Irene Adler. In the original Conan Doyle story, "A Scandal in Bohemia," she is merely an intelligent woman who manages to outwit Sherlock Holmes, thereby earning her respected status as "the woman."[39] In Moffat and Gatiss' *Sherlock*, however, Ms. Adler is inexplicably turned into a dominatrix. One could argue, perhaps, that making her a dominatrix is way of allowing her some kind of autonomy through sexual freedom, ownership of her own sexuality, and love of her body, but we cannot take such a theory seriously for long. Sherlock reminds both her and the viewers that while she may be intelligent, she isn't a match for his genius because he can ignore the body. Sherlock uses his intellect as a weapon and for self-defense; Adler uses her body in the same way, but Sherlock shames her for it when she can't follow his logic in solving the case of the dead hiker. When Adler expresses her confusion and inability to follow Sherlock's line of thought, he berates her, sniping viciously, "you cater to the whims of the pathetic and take your clothes off to make an impression. Stop boring me and think. It's the new sexy."[40]

Despite Sherlock's apparent distaste with Adler's chosen profession, he is intrigued by her, and he enjoys showing off in front of her just like he enjoys showing off for John. Nearing the end of "A Scandal in Belgravia," Sherlock appears to have been beaten by Adler, and Mycroft has upbraided him for his slip in letting his emotions get the best of him. In the usual way television and films like to give the audience a bit of exposition, Adler explains how she went about defeating Sherlock. The next moments of the episode are telling, as the audience is made privy to the fact that Irene Adler was not the mastermind behind bringing the British government to heel; that honor belonged to the evil genius, James Moriarty. Through Adler's own words we see that she is incapable of coming up with a sufficient plan of attack; she is the body, and Moriarty is the brains.

However, when Sherlock realizes Adler has not, in fact, beaten him, he does so because he understands that her weakness is emotion, and emotion proves to be her undoing. Some of the series' best comments revealing the creators' ideas about the body and emotion feature in this episode, as it is in this episode that we see Sherlock show some sign of emotional weakness for the first time. Adler is intelligent, and her intellect intrigues Sherlock, but she concentrates her efforts on seduction, and this proves to be her undoing. Sherlock revels in his impending victory, chastising Adler for falling victim to emotion. And as he explains to her and Mycroft how he figured out how to unlock her secrets and, incidentally, her phone, he shames her much like he did when they first met. Had she not fallen in love, had she not let her heart rule her head, she would have stood a better chance of winning. Instead, she was a woman who fell victim to her inability to control herself. Adler's downfall serves as the proof that "sentiment is a chemical defect found in the losing side."[41] Sherlock reminds her that as long as one is enslaved to the body and doesn't see the cultivation of reason as paramount, one will always fall prey to the "dangerous disadvantage"[42] of loving.

The frivolity of the female characters in *Sherlock* acts as a constant reminder to the detective of how one ought not to be. They are emotional foils to his ideal, intellectual hero. Though Irene Adler is the most intense female presence in the series, Mrs. Hudson, with her motherly comportment, and Molly, with her permanent schoolgirl-like crush on Sherlock, play integral roles in Sherlock's world. These women are repeatedly ridiculed and humiliated in the service of demonstrating Sherlock's superiority. And though he also insults the men in his life in equal measure, when he attacks women, he levels his attacks at their bodies and how their bodies make them lesser than he. Even Sherlock's mother, a genius mathematician who we meet in the third season, is not granted the dignity of being an intelligent person whose worth lies in her intellect. Instead, it is not only implied that she's a bit insane, but we learn she gave up her career for motherhood—apparently the writers do not think a woman can be an academic and a mother—and she brushes off her intelligence as if it were merely a fluke.[43]

We see the contempt Sherlock harbors for everyone come through most brazenly in the nasty way he treats the women he encounters. Because women are still connected so intimately to the body in the collective cultural psyche, Sherlock—a fictional character obsessed with reason, whose lines are written by real human beings with deep-seated opinions about men and women—punishes women the most. He uses the follies of the women to demonstrate the superiority of the mind over all things physical. Sherlock's astonishing intellect and powers of deduction baffle and amaze us; we submit willingly to his authority. However, the constant and various ways his authority is used to devalue emotional affect and praise reason are indicative of the general disdain we harbor for the body in the West.

Vulnerability and Representation

The Sherlock Holmes of Moffat and Gatiss is not completely incapable of emotional experience. He is, however, always on alert, fending off any attacks from gathering sentiment. He is not always successful in remaining unattached, and he grows quite fond of John Watson. The moments in which we see Sherlock caring for and about John are immensely rewarding to us, but in the third episode of the third season, "His Last Vow," we see the fallout of allowing emotion to have too strong of a foothold within us. Sherlock, in his attempt to protect John and Mary, falls victim to a trick, and Augustus Magnussen gains the upper hand. Sherlock believes his only option to keep John and Mary safe is to shoot Magnussen in the head, though his explanation for why he will pull the trigger is that he's a sociopath. However, we know Sherlock is vulnerable to emotion from time to time, and because he lets emotion get the best of him, he commits murder and is sent away to work on a case that will most certainly ensure his death.[44]

Even when Sherlock looks like he may fail, ultimately, he triumphs. His genius, expertise, and ability to outthink everyone else set him apart. His uniqueness as the genius is what draws people to him; it is certainly what draws us as viewers and keeps us on edge during the nearly two-year gap between seasons of the show. I am definitely one of the people who bemoan the wait. The popularity of the series, though, is in large part due to the fact that Sherlock assures us and reminds us that the picture we have in our minds of the genius is correct, and we are comforted by that. We have come to expect geniuses to look a certain way because the television shows (and stories on which those shows may be based) and movies that feature geniuses only depict them as looking a certain way: white and male.

The shift in the types of people we see on the small and large screens is encouraging. We are pushing for more representative figures in our entertainment; we demand that the worlds we allow our imaginations to inhabit resemble our own. However, the old ideas about the type of person that we are willing to believe can successfully fill a certain role still hold enormous sway. The predominance of the genius on television in the last ten years reflects our cultural obsession with rationality; we long to be the one with cool self-control, super intelligence, and superior problem-solving skills. However, it also reflects our cultural belief that, with very few exceptions, the genius is a man. We still cling, perhaps even accidentally, to the idea that a person who achieves pure rationality—the kind of unfettered, emotion-free reason men have striven to achieve for centuries—has reached the ideal state of being, and our love of the genius in popular culture confirms this. Future television and film geniuses may begin to represent accurately the wonderful variety of people there are in the world. And while the external profiles of the genius may change, it seems unlikely that we will ever call anyone a genius who does not fit a certain internal profile. Pure, detached, abstract reason rules, and if our love for the genius on television is anything to go by, the reign of reason will endure.

Notes

1. Steven Moffat, "A Study in Pink," *Sherlock*, season 1, episode 1, directed by Paul McGuigan, aired October 24, 2010, on BBC One.
2. As my focus lies mainly on gender and reason in *Sherlock*, I will not elaborate on the issue of race and representations of race on television beyond pointing out how very white TV geniuses are and how problematic underrepresentation is.
3. Mark Gatiss, "The Great Game," *Sherlock*, season 1, episode 3, directed by Paul McGuigan, aired November 7, 2012, on BBC One.
4. Ibid.
5. Moffat, "A Study in Pink."
6. Lorraine Code, "Epistemology," *A Companion to Feminist Philosophy*, ed. Alison M. Jaggar and Iris Marion Young (Malden, MA: Blackwell, 2000), 174–175.
7. Chris Cillizza, "Why Hillary Clinton Shouldn't Run for President in 2016," *Washington Post*, May 27, 2014, http://www.washingtonpost.com/blogs/the-fix/wp/2014/05/27/why-hillary-clinton-shouldnt-run-for-president-in-2016/.
8. "Mary Barra: Gender Played No Role in Me Becoming a CEO" (interview by Matt Lauer), *Today*, aired June 26, 2014, on NBC.
9. CBS' *Elementary* managed to change John Watson to Joan Watson, and the world did not end, so there is hope for other shows.
10. I'm using the masculine pronoun to emphasize the predominance of the TV genius as male.
11. Steven Moffat, "A Scandal in Belgravia," *Sherlock*, season 2, episode 1, directed by Paul McGuigan, aired May 6, 2012, on BBC One.
12. Ibid.
13. Steven Moffat, "His Last Vow," *Sherlock*, season 3, episode 3, directed by Nick Hurran, aired February 2, 2014, on BBC One.
14. One need only read the extensive works of fan fiction written about the show to see these theories in very loving detail.

15. Steven Moffat, "Unaired Pilot," *Sherlock*, season 1, episode 0, directed by Coky Giedroyc, n.d.
16. Ibid.
17. Mark Gatiss, "The Hounds of Baskerville," *Sherlock*, season 2, episode 2, directed by Paul McGuigan, aired May 13, 2012, on BBC One.
18. Marjorie Garber, "Our Genius Problem," *The Atlantic*, December 1, 2002, http://www.theatlantic.com/magazine/archive/2002/12/our-genius-problem/376720/?single_page=true.
19. Garber, "Our Genius Problem."
20. Gatiss, "The Great Game."
21. Moffat, "A Study in Pink."
22. Gatiss, "The Hounds of Baskerville."
23. Moffat, "A Study in Pink."
24. I'm thinking specifically of Sheldon Cooper from *The Big Bang Theory*.
25. Moffat, "A Study in Pink."
26. Gatiss, "The Hounds of Baskerville."
27. Moffat, "A Study in Pink."
28. Moffat, "A Scandal in Belgravia."
29. Gatiss and Moffat, "The Great Game" and "His Last Vow."
30. Gatiss, "The Hounds of Baskerville."
31. Steve Thompson, "The Reichenbach Fall," *Sherlock*, season 2, episode 3, directed by Toby Haynes, aired May 20, 2012, on BBC One.
32. Garber, "Our Genius Problem."
33. Steve Thompson, Steven Moffat, and Mark Gatiss, "The Sign of Three," *Sherlock*, season 3, episode 2, directed by Colm McCarthy, aired January 26, 2014, on BBC One.
34. Moffat, "A Study in Pink."
35. Gatiss, "The Great Game."
36. Ibid.
37. Mycroft Holmes has moments in the series where his deductive powers outshine Sherlock's.
38. Garber, "Our Genius Problem."
39. Arthur Conan Doyle, "A Scandal in Bohemia," in *The Complete Sherlock Holmes: All 4 Novels and 56 Short Stories* (New York: Doubleday, 1986), 161.
40. Moffat, "A Scandal in Belgravia."
41. Ibid.
42. Ibid.
43. Moffat, "His Last Vow."
44. Moffat, "His Last Vow."

References

Cillizza, Chris. "Why Hillary Clinton Shouldn't Run for President in 2016." *Washington Post*, May 27, 2014. http://www.washingtonpost.com/blogs/the-fix/wp/2014/05/27/why-hillary-clinton-shouldnt-run-for-president-in-2016/.

Code, Lorraine. "Epistemology." In *A Companion to Feminist Philosophy*, ed. Alison M. Jaggar and Iris Marion Young, 173–184. Malden, MA: Blackwell, 2000.

Conan Doyle, Arthur. "A Scandal in Bohemia." In *The Complete Sherlock Holmes: All 4 Novels and 56 Short Stories*, 161–175. New York: Doubleday, 1986.

Garber, Marjorie. "Our Genius Problem." *The Atlantic*, December 1, 2002. http://www.theatlantic.com/magazine/archive/2002/12/our-genius-problem/376720/?single_page=true.

Gardener, Judith Kegan. "Men, Masculinities, and Feminist Theory." In *Handbook of Studies on Men and Masculinities*, ed. Michael S. Kimmel, Jeff Hearn, and R. W. Connell. PDF e-book. Thousand Oaks: Sage, 2012.

Gatiss, Mark. "The Great Game." *Sherlock*, season 1, episode 1. Directed by Paul McGuigan. Aired November 7, 2012. *Sherlock Season One*, DVD. Upper Boat, Wales: BBC Home Entertainment, 2010.

———. "The Hounds of Baskerville." *Sherlock*, season 2, episode 2. Directed by Paul McGuigan. Aired May 13, 2012. *Sherlock Season Two*, DVD. Upper Boat, Wales: BBC Home Entertainment, 2012.

Held, Virginia. "Care and Justice in the Global Context." *Ratio Juris*, no. 17–2 (2004): 141–155.

"Mary Barra: Gender Played No Role in Me Becoming a CEO" (interview by Matt Lauer). *Today*, aired June 26, 2014, on NBC. http://www.today.com/video/today/55512578#55512578.

Moffat, Steven. "His Last Vow." *Sherlock*, season 3, episode 3. Directed by Nick Hurran. Aired Febrary 2, 2014. *Sherlock Season Three*, DVD. Upper Boat, Wales: BBC Home Entertainment, 2014.

———. "A Scandal in Belgravia." *Sherlock*, season 2, episode 1. Directed by Paul McGuigan. Aired May 6, 2012. *Sherlock Season Two*, DVD. Upper Boat, Wales: BBC Home Entertainment, 2012.

———. "A Study in Pink." *Sherlock*, season 1, episode 1. Directed by Paul McGuigan. Aired October 24, 2010. *Sherlock Season One*, DVD. Upper Boat, Wales: BBC Home Entertainment, 2010.

———. "Unaired Pilot." *Sherlock*, season 1, episode 0. Directed by Coky Giedrovc. *Sherlock Season One*, DVD. Upper Boat, Wales: BBC Home Entertainment, 2010.

Percy, Walker. "The Loss of the Creature." In *The Message in the Bottle: How Queer Man Is, How Queer Language Is, and What One Has to Do with the Other*. Kindle edition. Open Road Media, 2001.

Szalavitz, Maia. "What Genius and Autism Have in Common." *Time*, July 10, 2012. http://healthland.time.com/2012/07/10/what-child-prodigies-and-autistic-people-have-in-common/.

Thompson, Steve. "The Reichenbach Fall." *Sherlock*, season 2, episode 3. Directed by Toby Haynes. Aired May 20, 2012. *Sherlock Season Two*, DVD. Upper Boat, Wales: BBC Home Entertainment, 2012.

Thompson, Steve, Steven Moffat, and Mark Gatiss. "The Sign of Three." *Sherlock*, season 3, episode 2. Directed by Colm McCarthy. Aired January 26, 2014. *Sherlock Season Three*, DVD. Upper Boat, Wales: BBC Home Entertainment, 2014.

Geeksploitation

Gender and Genius in The Big Bang Theory

Jeffrey A. Sartain

Since its debut in 2007, *The Big Bang Theory* has become one of the most popular television shows in the country. Created by Chuck Lorre and Bill Prady, *The Big Bang Theory* focuses on a group of friends who are scientists and engineers in the San Francisco Bay area. An episodic sitcom, the show has been a top primetime earner for CBS, scoring high ratings consistently and earning numerous awards throughout its run. Many critics have praised the show for its portrayal of intelligent characters, which ostensibly brings positive attention to intelligence, intellectualism, and scientific pursuits in the mainstream media. In "The Quantum Mechanics of The Big Bang Theory: Inside Geek Chic," series creator Chuck Lorre says, "To my knowledge, I'm not sure there's been a comedy about this level of brilliance, genius really. This is a level of intelligence that's never been looked at before and these are characters that actually change the world."[1] While Lorre may be correct about the lack of intelligent characters on television, the show's potentially positive portrayals of intellectualism and intelligence are complicated because *The Big Bang Theory* explicitly ties intelligence to the stereotype of the geek, "previously a liminal masculine identity" that "gets rehabilitated and partially incorporated into hegemonic masculinity during the period from the early 1980s through the present."[2] Specifically, the various male and female characters identified as geeks reify dualistic and misogynistic constructions of gender and intelligence, tying pursuits of the mind to the false ideal of masculinized abstraction, which affirms existing structures of inequity and repression around women in scientific pursuits.

Instead of delving deeply into the intricacies of the scientific disciplines or the geek subcultures represented in the show, *The Big Bang Theory* only engages with inaccurate, stereotypic, surface-level representations of both. The surface level understanding of geek culture on display in *The Big Bang Theory* further reinforces existing anti-intellectual and potentially damaging stereotypes about gender and intelligence. A writer for the UCSD *Guardian*, Melissa Martinyak, critiques *The Big Bang Theory* for the show's bastardization of geek culture, which turns the vast variety of intellectual interests and hobbies characterized as geek chic into a flattened monoculture:

> The main issue with the show is that in terms of geek culture, the show overextends itself. Go to any Con and look around—the anime fans are not in any way like the Browncoats, the Trekkies are doing their own thing. I've been to Comic-Con twice, and I can tell you that I have still never read manga (pronounced with a long "a"). Take Sheldon and Leonard's apartment as an example. What the set designers think the room screams (look at these huge nerds!), screams a Think Geek.com advertisement to everybody else. "Hmm," you can practically hear them thinking. "What do nerds like?" Clearly, the consensus was molecular structures, Green Lantern memorabilia and Rubik's Cubes. "Ha ha," laughs Middle America. "I have seen these items before and identify with how they frame nerd culture."[3]

What Martinyak is noting is the often strictly enforced subcultural divide between geek chic, an exploitative mainstream appropriation, and actual geek culture. The humor in *The Big Bang Theory* is voyeuristic, where the show's main characters' eccentricities are pure spectacle, an exaggerated parody of geek culture so extreme that it explicitly reinforces normative stereotypes about gender and intelligence.

The Big Bang Theory's humor, predicated as it is on a voyeuristic perspective on geek culture, lends itself to a mere surface understanding of geeks and the intelligence that they represent. While popular attention towards intelligence and intellectualism is generally a welcome reprieve from the overwhelming amount of anti-intellectualism on television, *The Big Bang Theory* refuses to portray the characters as anything other than the thinnest of punchlines for jokes about intelligence and geek culture. By refusing complexity and depth in favor of cheap laughs predicated on stereotypes, *The Big Bang Theory* participates in an emerging subgenre of film and television, geeksploitation, that utilizes the stereotyped and spectacularized image of the geek for exploitative purposes, furthering a misogynist hegemony that views intelligence and the life of the mind as male pursuits.

The stereotypical image of the geek must be analyzed because, as Judith Butler writes, "any uncritical reproduction of the mind/body distinction ought to be rethought for the implicit gender hierarchy that the distinction has conventionally produced, maintained, and rationalized."[4] Rather than approach geeks with a nuanced understanding of gender, *The Big Bang Theory* reiterates gendered stereotypes, recreating and reinforcing misogynist ideology in every episode's performance of gender. The show represents its intellectual characters with all the trappings of the cultural stereotype of the geek in both its male and female forms, based on the misogynist implications of repressive Cartesian thinking. By explicitly linking intelligence to geeks, *The Big Bang Theory* implicitly argues that intellectualism must be tied to the kinds of socially repressive attitudes and representations embodied in the cultural stereotype of the geek.

Cartesian Dualism and the Geek Stereotype

The Big Bang Theory's portrayal of gender is a remarkably simplistic binary predicated on the terms of Cartesian dualism, the tenets of which it reifies with every episode. As Butler observes, cultural texts like *The Big Bang Theory* are deeply implicated in structures of inequity because "terms of gender designation are thus never settled once and for all but are constantly in the process of being remade," and cultural productions are a vital source of the remaking.[5] *The Big Bang Theory* is but one text within the entirety of popular culture, but the popularity of its stereotypic portrayals of geeks suggests, as Susan Bordo asserts, "that even in this era of postmodern pastiche racial clichés and gender taboos persist."[6] Such gender taboos around intelligence are endemic to the cultural myths about science and technology. Claudia Henrion, in *Women in Mathematics*, names the stereotype of the individualist masculine intellectual "The Mathematical Marlboro Man," who is "a tough, independent hero taming uncharted terrain" using the abstract, disembodied powers of "imagination and reason."[7] These are the classical delineations of Cartesian dualism, which "succeeded in linking the mind/body opposition to the foundations of knowledge itself, a link which places the mind in a position of hierarchical superiority over and above nature, including the nature of the body."[8] Following the logic of these classically sexist constructions of gender, the world of abstraction is reserved as an Edenic paradise for men; an unsullied, unconquered intellectual terrain awaiting conquest.

For women laboring under the assumptions of Cartesian dualism, access to the abstract is always contingent on an individual's ability to circumvent or transcend their own embodiment. This results in the two versions of the female geek stereotype, both equally repressive and misogynistic. Most commonly, female geeks are portrayed as intelligent but frumpy, asexual individuals who are divorced from their own embodiments. On the rise, though, is the image of the female geek who is fully embodied and empowered by her own sexuality, but her beauty and sexuality are always contained within the male gaze as an object of sexual desire. The female geek, then, suffers the classic double bind that Naomi Wolf describes in *The Beauty Myth*, where women can never really achieve mastery over their own image and are therefore subjected to constant demands to be more beautiful, regardless of their accomplishments in other spheres of life.[9]

Lori Kendall asserts that the masculinized stereotype of the geek and the current emphasis on geek chic is a result of the success of the computer industry and the alignment of geeks and intelligence with the computer.[10] Feminine identification with the term geek is much more problematic, as the stereotype is one that has found particular currency with the terms of masculinity set forth by American westward expansionism. The alignment of the geek with terms of individualism, mastery, (virtual) mobility, and abstract order have made the geek a suitable heir to these terms of nineteenth-century American masculinity, which found expression in the image of the cowboy, the explorer, and the frontiersman. The geek's genius and reliance on intellect has allowed the classic masculine traits of ruggedness and athletic prowess to be supplanted by intellectual certainty and technological dexterity, both abstract notions that can be safely disembodied from the messiness of the material—a key feature of the geek's masculine position in Cartesian epistemologies.

For example, Dr. Sheldon Cooper (Jim Parsons) is the show's most idealized example of the male geek stereotype. He is brilliant, but as predicted by the geek stereotype, his brilliance comes at a price—he is socially awkward, obsessive, juvenile, and asexual. Indeed, in many ways he is the ultimate expression of the geek stereotype, which at its most fundamental level divorces intellect from embodiment, reinforcing ideological constructions of gender that dictate the mutual exclusivity of the pursuits of mind and body. Sheldon best articulates the gendering of mind and body in season six's episode, "The Egg Salad Equivalency," where he disciplines his female research assistant, Alex, for being romantically interested in his roommate, Dr. Leonard Hofstadter (Johnny Galecki). Sheldon misogynistically compares women to "an egg salad sandwich on a warm Texas day" stating that they are "full of eggs and only appealing for a short time."[11] He then adds the following rationale to his earlier articulations of misogyny: "Now, please understand, I don't hold you responsible for your behavior because, see, from an evolutionary standpoint you're a slave to your desire to reproduce."[12] This episode is the most pointed encapsulation of the sexist rhetoric that surrounds intelligent women in Cartesian epistemologies. As Grosz articulates in *Volatile Bodies*:

> Relying on essentialism, naturalism, and biologism, misogynist thought confines women to the biological requirements of reproduction on the assumption that

because of particular biological, physiological, and endocrinological transformations, women are somehow *more* biological, *more* corporeal, and *more* natural than men. The coding of femininity with corporeality in effect leaves men free to inhabit what they (falsely) believe is a purely conceptual order while at the same time enabling them to satisfy their (sometimes disavowed) need for corporeal contact through their access to women's bodies and services.[13]

So, as the apotheosis of geek stereotypes, Sheldon demonstrates an idealized version of masculinity tied to abstract intelligence. Even in his disembodied abstraction, though, Sheldon frequently places the women of the show in maternal roles, demanding that they care for him when he is sick and comfort him when he is sad.

The show's other male main characters, Dr. Leonard Hofstadter, Howard Wolowitz (Simon Helberg), and Dr. Rajesh Koothrappali (Kunal Nayyar) demonstrate varying degrees of the same Cartesian thinking that informs the Sheldon character. All three are awkward around women and lack the physical mastery that marks stereotypic men from earlier centuries' versions of masculinity. Like Sheldon, all three supplant the physical mastery of masculinity with intellectual mastery, demonstrating how the stereotypes deployed in service of misogynistic ideals are revised and updated through cultural texts. Tellingly, all four male principal characters are frequently emasculated by the women in their lives, prefiguring women as threats to their masculine identities. For Sheldon, Leonard, and Howard, the castrating image of woman takes the form of their mothers, each a hovering and controlling presence in their lives. For Rajesh, though, the emasculation is extended to all women, as the show demonstrates with his pathological inability to talk to women while sober. In each case, the male geeks of the show seek romantic relationships with women who will cater to their needs and provide a form of maternal nurturing in their lives that was not provided by their mothers, frequently placing the burden of care on the woman across the hall, Penny (Kaley Cuoco-Sweeting).

Within the show's deployments of misogynist stereotypes, Penny is the female side of the Cartesian gender binary that Sheldon epitomizes. She is beautiful, embodied, sexual, and unintelligent. Frequently, Penny's lack of intelligence is the subject of the show's running jokes, including an entire subplot where she goes back to community college to finish her degree and hides the fact from her boyfriend, Leonard. She is always portrayed as the object of sexual desire for Leonard, perfectly demonstrating Suzanne Franks's assertion: "When nerds are only men, then women can only be Whores.... In this theorem, sexual attractiveness in women negates their competence and proves that they are, in reality, dumb."[14] Even when the show's chauvinist ideology seems to relent in moments where Penny solves a problem with common sense, the viewer gets the feeling that the commonality of Penny's sense is precisely the point. She does not think on the levels of abstraction that the show's main characters do, and therefore her intelligence must be grounded in the material world of the everyday, the common. She is uneducated and driven by the material demands of embodiment, demonstrated in her predilections towards alcohol and casual sex. And finally, her common sense wisdom is located in the maternal care that she displays most frequently towards Sheldon and Leonard, but which is present in all of her relationships with the show's geeks. In this case, Penny's common sense serves to reify the insistence of the material and the embodied that is an essentialized part of her femininity according the show's fundamentally dualistic understanding of gender and intelligence.

The show's chauvinistic ideology even appears in the naming conventions about Penny. Every other character's name, qualifications, and background are detailed exactingly, but the show's lead female character is left with but a single signifier. The singularity of the name itself suggests a kind of universalization and objectification of the character. In the vagueness of her name, Penny is an Everywoman in *The Big Bang Theory*, a universal signifier for the feminine qualities valued within the show's chauvinist ideology. And if Penny is prefigured as the universal ideal of woman, it is a decidedly retrograde and repressive portrayal that values women as mere material objects of sexual desire and comfort for men.

The binary between the abstract and the material is not restricted to just Penny, but permeates the performance of gender indicated in all the show's female characters. Such dualistic constructions of gender are the source of many damaging and repressive attitudes about women and intelligence. Dr. Amy Farrah Fowler (Mayim Bialik) and Dr. Bernadette Rostenkowski-Wolowitz (Melissa Rauch) are subject to the demands of the Cartesian stereotype even though, on the surface, these intelligent female characters seem like a nod towards more progressive ideals regarding women in science. Upon closer examination, though, even these characters reinforce Cartesian assumptions about intelligence. For example, while Amy is a scientist and an accomplished intellectual, she is constantly denigrated by Sheldon for what he views as the substandard scientific merit of her field, neurobiology, wrapped up as it is with the messiness of embodiment. She is often represented as more sexually active and experimental than Sheldon, but again, his attitudes reify geek stereotypes as he frequently chides her for being beholden to the biological imperatives of the body. In all cases, it is Amy's status as a woman that inevitably grounds her intellectualism in the body and makes it less worthy than the supposedly pure abstractions of intellect offered by Sheldon's field of theoretical physics.

Additionally, as one of the accomplished, intelligent woman on the show,

Amy bears the burden of representation for modern women. However, her character falls directly into line with the schematic binaries predicted by Cartesian logic. She is intelligent and accomplished, therefore abstracted and distanced from her embodiment, but not entirely distant, and therefore caught in a problematic double bind. For example, Amy is critiqued for her social awkwardness and abstraction where Sheldon is admired. Amy cannot live up to the double standard for women set up by Cartesian logic, which dictates that brains and beauty are mutually exclusive. So even when she begins to master her own embodiment and express her sexual needs, she is portrayed as a threatening sexual aggressor towards Sheldon, a kind of predator to Sheldon's meek, asexual abstraction. Amy's efforts at reclaiming her repressed sexuality are always immediately disciplined and re-contained within by Sheldon's expression of the show's Cartesian logic.

The gender binary appears to have been at least partially deconstructed in the case of Bernadette. She is both intelligent and beautiful, but she is simultaneously constructed as the most amoral, competitive, and unethical of all the characters, which makes her a significant threat to the masculinity of the men around her. The writing infers that her aggressively individualistic approach to work and competition results from her upbringing with five siblings and a very masculine father, an ex-cop named Mike (Casey Sander). He is the most visible symbol of traditional masculinity in the series, drinking beer, watching football, and generally harboring a distaste for the intellectual pursuits of his son-in-law (although he does begrudgingly acknowledge the masculinized bravery it takes for Howard to go to the International Space Station). Mike's traditional hypermasculinity, though, seems to have been passed down to Bernadette, who actively embodies many of the worst traits associated with masculine stereotypes while simultaneously appropriating the role of emasculating matriarch in her relationship with Howard. Thusly, Bernadette's supposed liberation from the strict gender roles of the geek stereotype is negated as these gender roles are reasserted with more vehemence than ever because she is an attractive female geek with mastery in both the embodied and abstract spheres, but the positivity of her mastery is undercut by her domineering, threatening, and emasculating characteristics. Additionally, Bernadette continually questions her mastery of the material sphere of beauty and sexuality by comparing herself to Penny, whom she views as more attractive and more sexual in a damaging instance of the female competition described in Wolf's articulation of the beauty myth.[15]

In *The Big Bang Theory*, the geek in both its male and female forms is mere stereotype, pure geeksploitation unconnected with reality, a malicious parody of geek culture that is designed for cheap laughs and profit generating capabilities. A veritable industry of *The Big Bang Theory* related products has sprung up, ranging from the commonplace to the ridiculous. For some, the kinds of geeksploitation represented here are untroublesome because they are expected from the Hollywood sausage machine that churns out situation comedies for primetime on one of America's big three networks. The popularity of the show is especially concerning, though, because of the way it valorizes overtly repressive stereotypes about women and intelligence. In an era when the image of the female geek that predominates the media is one of an asexual and frumpy or objectified and beautiful woman, there seems to be little room left for characters with depth, complexity, and writing that does not fall directly into the worst repressive stereotypes about women and intelligence. In actuality, there are such representations in literature, film, and television (the works of Richard Powers come to mind); however, their voices are drowned out by the overwhelming exploitation and repression in television like *The Big Bang Theory,* which draws more than 20 million viewers a week at its peak. And while Amy and Bernadette may be, in some people's views, a step in the right direction, I propose that this is a one-step-forward, two-steps-back dilemma, easily demonstrated through close readings of some of *The Big Bang Theory*'s most indicative moments.

To see the show's attitudes towards intelligence and gender, it is useful to closely examine a selection of exemplary episodes. Beginning with the first scene of the first episode, the show establishes gender, embodiment, and intelligence as some of its most important concerns. As the show opens, we see Leonard and Sheldon approaching a receptionist in a doctor's office. "Is this the high IQ sperm bank?" Leonard asks shyly, to which the receptionist responds, "If you have to ask, maybe you shouldn't be here."[16] After receiving their forms, Leonard objects to the donation of sperm because it is potentially "genetic fraud."[17] The argument that follows reveals that they were there to proffer their sperm for the funds to increase the bandwidth of their internet connection at the apartment. This scene, as noted by numerous viewers and fan websites, is not usually shown in syndication, although it does appear on the various video releases. The reasons for editing episodes in syndication are generally material in nature, as contemporary television episodes tend to lose a few seconds of show time every year to make more time for commercials, so the fact of the scene being trimmed is not necessarily surprising in and of itself. The effect of this deleted scene on the meaning of the text, though, is much larger than the length of the scene would suggest.

For instance, the scene quoted above is the cold open for the "Pilot" episode of *The Big Bang Theory.* As the first encounter viewers ever have with these characters, it sets up important character information and tone for the audience. In this case, it sets up both Leonard and Sheldon as more sexual and comfortable in their embodiment than later seasons and syndicated reruns imply. The significant shift this scene lends to the Sheldon character demands analysis. Rather than the completely asexual geek that Sheldon is written to become in later seasons, the first episode establishes him as much more comfortable with his embodiment and sexuality than he is later, especially in his relationship with Amy Farrah-Fowler. The conclusion that one can draw when watching the existing seasons of *The Big Bang Theory* in order is that Sheldon's character has been consistently written to be *more* geeky, *more* uncomfortable with his embodiment, and *more* phobic about human connection as the series continues. The amplification of these attributes in Sheldon follows the characteristics of the male geek stereotype, and it certainly appears that the show's writers are amplifying these dimensions of the character as they continue to script Sheldon as the archetypal geek.

Many of the issues of gender, intelligence, and power that are at the heart of the geek stereotype are also clearly articulated in the season one episode, "The Jerusalem Duality," where the characters' university is interviewing an adolescent prodigy named Dennis Kim (Austin Lee). Threatened by Kim's abilities, confidence, and swagger, Sheldon, Howard, Raj, and Leonard conspire to derail his research and hiring prospects by getting age appropriate girls interested in Kim. Once he is distracted by the sexual pursuit of women, the characters are sure that they can accomplish more and continue in their pursuits unthreatened by this younger, more masculine counterpart. Sheldon, at the end of one of the episode's last scenes, demonstrates the show's ideological valuation of abstract intelligence. When Kim does, indeed, get distracted by a teenage girl, Sheldon assures the audience of university personnel at the mixer, "While Mr. Kim, by virtue of his youth and naivety, has fallen prey to the inexplicable need for human contact, let me step in and assure you that my research will go on uninterrupted, and that social relationships will continue to baffle and repulse me."[18] As the show's hierarchy demonstrates, the top intellectual in this circle is Sheldon because he appears to have transcended his own embodiment and need for human contact. Next is the youthful genius, Dennis Kim, who has not transcended his embodiment, but can at least negotiate relationships with women on his own. Finally, in liminalized and subordinate positions are Leonard, Howard, and Raj. As early as this episode is in the show's run, there are no prominent representations of female geeks, and that omission alone demonstrates one aspect of the gendered understanding of intelligence that comes with the show's Cartesian dualism.

As misogynistic as these moments from the "Pilot" and "The Jerusalem Duality" episodes are, they are relatively early in the series and the female geek characters had not yet been introduced. Later in the series, there is a single episode that captures the repressive attitudes about gender and the vicious double bind suffered by female geeks in one magnum opus of stereotypes and repressions writ large. In season six's "The Contractual Obligation Implementation," Leonard enlists Howard and Sheldon in an effort to fulfill their university's service requirements. They decide to focus their efforts on the underrepresentation of women in scientific fields, and the plan they decide on attempts to make science cool for a classroom of middle school girls. In one of the episode's subplots, Amy, Bernadette, and Penny have all called in sick from work to spend a girls' day at Disneyland receiving Princess Makeovers. In the episode's main plot, Sheldon, Leonard, and Howard fail to convince the young women that science is cool in ways that demonstrate exactly how incompetent they are at dealing with women. They turn to Bernadette and Amy to rescue their failed presentation, using a smartphone to allow the women to speak to the roomful of students. In what could be the show's most progressive moment, Amy tells the students, "The world of science needs more women, but from a young age we girls are encouraged to care more about the way we look than the power of our minds."[19] Bernadette follows up with the affirmation, 'Every one of you has the capacity to be anything you want to be."[20] This potentially progressive moment is immediately contained, undercut, and collapsed, though, when the editing shows audiences the context in which Amy and Bernadette are talking. They are wearing full Princess Makeover costumes, with each of them dressed like one of Disney's famous damsels in distress. Further, their costumes are used for pure sexual objectification, as each of the women demonstrates in the closing sequence. All three women do their best to seduce their respective partners while in costume, with only Amy failing as Sheldon stereotypically responds with an abstracted and annoyed dismissal of Amy's desires. In this episode, the female geeks own their own sexuality and embodiment in a way that their male counterparts never do when they dress up in idealized male costumes. Unfortunately, though, Sheldon's reception to Amy's sexual advances in this episode is indicative of the double bind containment strategies of misogyny—the sexually empowered and intelligent woman must be marginalized because of the totalizing mastery she represents. In this case, Amy's sexuality is dismissed again by Sheldon, with his lack of response putting the ultimate reinforcement on the Cartesian stereotypes, literally giving the last word of the episode to repression and misogyny.

While *The Big Bang Theory*'s popularity and praise signal a popular acceptance of the show's portrayal of intelligence, it is the participation in this show of actual scientists and technologists that demonstrates the show's real commitment to misogynist constructions of gender and intelligence. Throughout the show's run, it has included prominent guest stars from the fields of science and technology who appear in the show playing themselves, including astrophysicist Stephen Hawking, physicist Brian Greene, astronaut Buzz Aldrin, astrophysicist George Smoot, children's television science host Bill Nye, children's radio science host Ira Flatow, astronaut Mike Massimino, astrophysicist Neil de Grasse Tyson, and Apple Computer co-founder Steve Wozniak. The appearances by these luminaries lend legitimacy to the show's representations of intelligence, gender, and science. The representations, though, are clearly hyperbolized and unrealistic, geared for maximum objectification and exploitation of the show's male and female geek characters. In each appearance of a real life individual, there is a moment where the real world scientist asserts his dominance and masculinity over the show's geeks, either in a friendly competition or a scholarly dismissal of their research, thereby reinforcing (with the added legitimacy of real life scientists) the show's gendered portrayal of intelligence. Once again, potentially progressive moments in the show are undercut because they are already contextualized within the misogynist ideology of *The Big Bang Theory*, making it an almost passé observation that every single luminary from science and technology featured on the show has been male. Indeed, the only women allowed to play themselves have been three prominent science fiction actors whose fame is inextricably linked with their characters' sexual embodiment in their respective series: Carrie Fisher of *Star Wars* fame, Katie Sackhoff from *Battlestar Galactica* reboot, and Summer Glau from *Firefly*.

Geek Culture and Gender Today

Noting specific valances and repressions of the geek stereotype in cultural productions such as *The Big Bang Theory* is vital to understanding the nature of the geek stereotype and how gender repressions continue to seize cultural forms as a part of the ongoing backlash against progressive gender politics. Recently controversies in the last quarter of 2014 around gender in science and technology, including the gamergate, shirtstorm, and Ubergate scandals, as well as the "Male Allies" panel at the 2014 Grace Hopper Celebration of Women in Technology have highlighted the persistent and overt oppression women have faced when taking on traditionally masculine roles in areas of abstract intelligence, such as programming, engineering, or theoretical science.

The gamergate controversy erupted in August of 2014 after game developer Zoe Quinn was accused of having an inappropriate relationship with gaming journalist, Nathan Grayson, to promote her latest game, *Depression Quest*. Quinn then became the target of malicious cyberattacks that released her personal information to the world, as well as misogynistic personal attacks that threatened her with everything from slander to physical violence.[21] The controversy around Quinn's game quickly grew into a much larger discussion about the role of women in gaming and the ethics of gaming journalism. The rhetoric of the gamergate debate quickly polarized, and misogynistic rhetoric and personal threats to feminist game commentators and critics amplified. One of the most visible instances of misogyny surrounding gamergate occurred in October 2014. Anita Sarkeesian, a game industry and popular culture critic, cancelled a scheduled talk at Utah State University after receiving death threats that promised a "Montreal Massacre style of attack," referring to the 1989 shooting of 28 people in Canada.[22] After receiving the threat, Sarkeesian requested that metal detectors and pat down searches be implemented for her talk at the University, but police and University official refused, citing Utah's open carry firearm laws. At the time of this writing, the gamergate controversy still rages, but the number of issues being discussed under the gamergate rubric do not truly coalesce into a distinct movement, as several different camps have emerged with vastly different agendas, all sporting the gamergate tag on their rhetoric.

November 2014 saw the controversy dubbed "shirtstorm" erupt when lead scientist Matt Taylor of the European Space Agency wore a bowling shirt featuring pinup images of women during interviews around the Rosetta space probe landing.[23] As the first space probe to ever land on a comet, Rosetta was covered by every major news agency in the world and Taylor's image was broadcast globally. Feminists chided Taylor and the European Space Agency for the casual sexism the shirt represented, which resulted in "a frothing torrent of backlash misogyny [that] swept over social media" where anti-feminists reacted in Taylor's defense.[24] Taylor has since apologized for his choice of attire, but the entire incident highlights the sexism endemic to science and technology fields. The shirtstorm incident, in many ways, is like the appearance of the real world scientists on *The Big Bang Theory*, showing the chauvinism and repression that is commonplace and assumed in science and technology fields. Indeed, the *Harvard Business Review*'s Center for Work-Life Policy recently published the study *The Athena Factor: Reversing the Brain Drain in Science, Engineering, and Technology*. Among this study's numerous findings regarding women in SET (Science, Engineering, and Technology) fields, the authors identified "Hostile macho cultures" as one of the top antigens to women entering and persisting in SET fields.[25] The study is of vast economic and social importance because it seeks to reveal the reasons that out of the 41% of women on the lower rungs of private sector SET firms, "over time, fully 52% of highly qualified females working for SET companies quit their jobs, driven out by hostile work environments and extreme job pressures."[26] As *The Athena Factor* and the shirtstorm incident make clear, the culture of sexism is a clear and present force in science and technology.

Most recently, journalist Sarah Lacy published articles that highlighted the culture of sexism in the administration of the tech company, Uber, which provides taxi services based on a mobile phone application. Lacy, a senior editor of the *PandoDaily* tech site, wrote several articles in 2014 that were critical of Uber's sexist business practices. In response to Lacy's critiques, Uber's Senior Vice President of Business, Emil Michael, suggested that the company launch a million dollar investigation into tech journalists' personal lives. The threat of a major company (valued at $17 billion in June 2014) launching a smear campaign against journalists sparked immediate and vocal backlash from the journalistic community, quickly dubbed "Ubergate," and Uber has been fighting a major public relations battle since Michael's comments. While the Uber controversy is more directly about journalism and business ethics than it is about gender, the instigating spark is, yet again, a backlash against perceived feminist criticisms of the tech industry.

Perhaps 2014's most disappointing moment in the discussion of women in science and technology occurred at the Anita Borg Institute's Grace Hopper Celebration of Women in Computing. On October 8, 2014, the Grace Hopper Celebration hosted the "Male Allies" panel for prominent tech figures to weigh in on the role of women in technological fields. The panel included Facebook's CTO, Mike Schroepfer, Google's Senior VP of Search, Alan Eustace, GoDaddy's CEO, Blake Irving, and Intuit's CTO, Tayloe Stansbury. Penny Herscher, president and CEO of FirstRain moderated the panel. Feminist tech commentators from the groups Geek Feminism, the Ada Initiative, and Model View Culture had such low hopes for the discourse of this panel that they printed "Ally Bingo" cards that were handed out to the audience.[27] The bingo cards included numerous phrases that are standard sexist rhetoric in the tech industry, including such tired rhetorical moves as "My mother taught me to respect women," and "[The speaker] quotes woman he has power over in the workplace."[28] As commentator Selena Larson notes, "In essence, [the panelists'] advice to women was: Work harder, build great things, speak up for yourself, *lean in*."[29] In Larson's coverage, she quotes several of the lowlights of the panel, including Eustace offering this worn out chestnut of advice to women: "The best thing you can do is excel, and push through whatever boundaries you see in front of you. Just continue to push and be great."[30] Irving is quoted as stating, "The only thing I would add is speak up.... Speak up and be confident," following with, "When a guy has an idea, he gets really pumped up about it, really vocal about it. Back to that notion of speaking up, if you have an idea ... tell people your story and then execute it."[31] This particular panel was the only one at the conference that did not feature a Q&A session after the presentation, further highlighting the ways that issues around women in technology are discursively silenced. Additionally, while the panel was live streamed online, the video has since been removed from the Grace Hopper Celebration's website and can no longer be found. While feminist tech commentators did not predict particularly progressive rhetoric from this panel, the sexist missives and stereotypes on display during the panel were a distinct marker of how far the tech industry still must go to redress the culture of misogyny.

As all of these very recent controversies reveal that stakes for issues of gender in technology and science are very real, and the predominating epistemology in all of these cases tends towards a dualistic understanding of gender and intelligence. Representatively, these sexist attitudes are encapsulated in *The Big Bang Theory*, the most popular show on television, boasting a peak of 23.4 million viewers and already appearing multiple times a day in syndication.[32] The show's influence has been extended, too, with the negotiations in place to continue the show through the 10th season. At the 2013 Paley Center for Media celebration, PALEYFEST Jim Parsons voiced that he thinks the show will go through ten seasons as well, and his seems to be the most important voice that decides the future of the show because his character is the center of the action in recent seasons.[33]

When the most watched comedy on television is predicated on the flimsy portrayal of scientists, geeks, and intellectuals that actually reifies existing misogynistic discourse and ideology, it can only be an exploitative effort worthy of the term geeksploitation, where the geekery is merely window dressing for exhausted sexist tropes. Cultural productions such as *The Big Bang Theory* demonstrate that in popular culture, images of intelligence cannot yet be extracted from longstanding cultural suppositions about gender, abstraction, and embodiment. *The Big Bang Theory* is lauded by some critics for its portrayal of intelligence and scientific pursuits by male and female characters, and on the surface, the show occasionally seems to be a progressive appraisal of genius and gender. Upon closer reading of how the show's geeksploitation functions, though, one can see that the ideology represented in *The Big Bang Theory* is an explicit reification of an outmoded misogynist ideology in science and technology fields that specifically codes intelligence and abstraction as masculine pursuits.

Notes

1. "The Quantum Mechanics of The Big Bang Theory: Inside Geek Chic," DVD extra feature, *The Big Bang Theory. The Complete First Season* (Burbank: Warner Home Video, 2008), DVD.
2. Lori Kendall, "Nerd Nation: Images of Nerds in U.S. Popular Culture," *International Journal of Cultural Studies* 2, no. 2 (1999): 261.

3. Melissa Martinyak, "For Nerd Culture, It's Just a Big Bang Bust," *UCSD Guardian*, November 8, 2012, http://ucsdguardian.org/2012/11/08/for-nerd-culture-it%E2%80%99s-just-a-big-bang-bust/.

4. Judith Butler, *Gender Trouble: Feminism and the Subversion of Identity* (New York: Routledge, 1990), 12.

5. Judith Butler, *Undoing Gender* (New York: Routldege, 2004), 10.

6. Susan Bordo, *The Male Body: A New Look at Men in Public and Private* (New York: Farrar, Straus and Giroux, 1999), 193.

7. Claudia Henrion, *Women in Mathematics: The Addition of Difference* (Bloomington: Indiana University Press, 1997), 4.

8. Elizabeth Grosz, *Volatile Bodies: Toward a Corporeal Feminism* (Bloomington: Indiana University Press, 1994), 6.

9. Naomi Wolf, *The Beauty Myth: How Images of Beauty Are Used Against Women* (New York: Wm. Morrow, 1991), 27–29.

10. Kendall, "Nerd Nation," 262–63.

11. Steven Molaro, Eric Kaplan, and Maria Ferrari, "The Egg Salad Equivalency," *The Big Bang Theory*, season 6, episode 12, directed by Mark Cendrowski, aired on January 3, 2013, on CBS.

12. Ibid.

13. Grosz, *Volatile Bodies*, 14 (original italics).

14. Suzanne E. Franks, "Suzy the Computer versus Dr. Sexy," in *She's Such a Geek: Women Write About Science, Technology, and Other Nerdy Stuff*, ed. Annalee Newitz and Charlie Anders (Emeryville, CA: Seal, 2006), 92.

15. Wolf, *The Beauty Myth*, 27–29.

16. Chuck Lorre and Bill Prady, "Pilot," *The Big Bang Theory*, season 1, episode 1, directed by James Burrows, aired on September 24, 2007, on CBS.

17. Ibid.

18. Steven Molaro and David Goetsch, "The Jerusalem Duality," *The Big Bang Theory*, season 1, episode 12, directed by Mark Cendrowski, aired on April 14, 2008, on CBS.

19. Steven Molaro, Jim Reynolds, and Maria Ferrari, "The Contractual Obligation Implementation," *The Big Bang Theory*, season 6, episode 18, directed by Mark Cendrowski, aired on March 7, 2013, on CBS.

20. Ibid.

21. Simon Parkin, "Zoe Quinn's *Depression Quest*," *New Yorker*, September 9, 2014, http://www.newyorker.com/tech/elements/zoe-quinns-depression-quest.

22. Chris Gayomali, "Anita Sarkeesian Cancels Talk after Anti-Feminism Crusader Threatens Mass Shooting," *Fast Company*, October 15, 2014, http://www.fastcompany.com/3037160/fast-feed/anita-sarkeesian-cancels-talk-after-anti-feminism-crusader-threatens-mass-shooting.

23. Phil Plait, "Shirtstorm," Slate.com, November 17, 2014, http://www.slate.com/blogs/bad_astronomy/2014/11/17/casual_sexism_when_a_shirt_is_more_than_a_shirt.html.

24. Ibid.

25. Sylvia Ann Hewlett, et al. *The Athena Factor: Reversing the Brain Drain in Science, Engineering, and Technology* (Cambridge: Harvard Business Review, 2008), 7–11.

26. Ibid., i.

27. Selena Larson, "White Male 'Allies' Have Surprisingly Little to Say about Fixing Sexist Tech Culture," Readwrite.com, October 9, 2014, http://readwrite.com/2014/10/09/technology-sexism-male-allies-grace-hopper-celebration.

28. Ibid.

29. Ibid (original italics).

30. Ibid.

31. Ibid.

32. Adam K. Raymond, "Why are 23.4 Million People Watching *The Big Bang Theory*," Vulture.com, September 22, 2014, http://www.vulture.com/2014/05/big-bang-theory-ratings.html.

33. *The Big Bang Theory: Cast and Creators Live at PALEYFEST*, directed by The Paley Center for Media, 2013 (Hulu Streaming Video).

References

The Big Bang Theory: Cast and Creators Live at PALEYFEST. Directed by The Paley Center for Media, 2013. Hulu.com.

Bordo, Susan. *The Male Body: A New Look at Men in Public and Private*. New York: Farrar, Straus and Giroux, 1999.

Butler, Judith. *Gender Trouble: Feminism and the Subversion of Identity*. New York: Routledge, 1990.

Butler, Judith. *Undoing Gender*. New York: Routledge, 2004.

Franks, Suzanne E. "Suzy the Computer versus Dr. Sexy." In *She's Such a Geek: Women Write About Science, Technology, and Other Nerdy Stuff*, edited by Annalee Newitz and Charlie Anders, 82–95. Emeryville, CA: Seal, 2006.

Gayomali, Chris. "Anita Sarkeesian Cancels Talk after Anti-Feminism Crusader Threatens Mass Shooting." *Fast Company*, October 15, 2014. http://www.fastcompany.com/3037160/fast-feed/anita-sarkeesian-cancels-talk-after-anti-feminism-crusader-threatens-mass-shooting.

Grosz, Elizabeth. *Volatile Bodies: Toward a Corporeal Feminism*. Bloomington: Indiana University Press, 1994.

Henrion, Claudia. *Women in Mathematics: The Addition of Difference*. Bloomington: Indiana University Press, 1997.

Hewlett, Sylvia Ann, et al. *The Athena Factor: Reversing the Brain Drain in Science, Engineering, and Technology*. Cambridge: Harvard Business Review, 2008.

Kendall, Lori. "Nerd Nation: Images of Nerds in U.S. Popular Culture." *International Journal of Cultural Studies* 2, no. 2 (1999): 260–83.

Larson, Selena. "White Male 'Allies' Have Surprisingly Little to Say about Fixing Sexist Tech Culture." Readwrite.com, October 9, 2014. http://readwrite.com/2014/10/09/technology-sexism-male-allies-grace-hopper-celebration.

Lorre, Chuck, and Bill Prady. "Pilot." *The Big Bang Theory*, season 1, episode 1. Directed by James Burrows. Aired on September 24, 2007, on CBS. *The Bing Bang Theory: The Complete First Season*, DVD. Burbank: Warner Home Video, 2008.

Martinyak, Melissa. "For Nerd Culture, It's Just a Big Bang Bust." *UCSD Guardian*, November 8, 2012. http://ucsdguardian.org/2012/11/08/for-nerd-culture-it%E2%80%99s-just-a-big-bang-bust/.

Molaro, Steven, Jim Reynolds, and Maria Ferrari. "The Contractual Obligation Implementation." *The Big Bang Theory*, season 6, episode 18. Directed by Mark Cendrowski. Aired on March 7, 2013, on CBS. *The Bing Bang Theory: The Complete Sixth Season*, DVD. Burbank: Warner Home Video, 2013.

Molaro, Steven, Eric Kaplan, and Maria Ferrari. "The Egg Salad Equivalency." *The Big Bang Theory*, season 6, episode 12. Directed by Mark Cendrowski. Aired on January 3, 2013, on CBS. *The Bing Bang Theory: The Complete Sixth Season*, DVD. Burbank: Warner Home Video, 2013.

Molaro, Steven, and David Goetsch. "The Jerusalem Duality." *The Big Bang Theory*, season 1, episode 12. Directed by Mark Cendrowski. Aired on April 14, 2008, on CBS. *The Bing Bang Theory: The Complete First Season*, DVD. Burbank: Warner Home Video, 2008.

Parkin, Simon. "Zoe Quinn's *Depression Quest*." *New Yorker*, September 9, 2014. http://www.newyorker.com/tech/elements/zoe-quinns-depression-quest.

Plait, Phil. "Shirtstorm." Slate.com, November 17, 2014. http://www.slate.com/blogs/bad_astronomy/2014/11/17/casual_sexism_when_a_shirt_is_more_than_a_shirt.html.

"The Quantum Mechanics of The Big Bang Theory: Inside Geek Chic." *The Big Bang Theory*, season 1, DVD extra feature. *The Bing Bang Theory: The Complete First Season*, DVD. Burbank: Warner Home Video, 2008.

Raymond, Adam K. "Why are 23.4 Million People Watching *The Big Bang Theory*." Vulture.com, September 22, 2014. http://www.vulture.com/2014/05/big-bang-theory-ratings.html.

Wolf, Naomi. *The Beauty Myth: How Images of Beauty Are Used Against Women*. New York: Wm. Morrow, 1991.

The Genius in the Attic

The Female Technologist in NCIS *and* Criminal Minds

MARIAN R. HJELMGREN *and*
ASHLEY LYNN CARLSON

In 1979 Sandra M. Gilbert and Susan Gubar published their seminal study of nineteenth-century literature, *The Madwoman in the Attic*, in which they discuss the tendency of writers of the period to imagine women as either the idealized "angel in the house" or the vilified "monster-woman."[1] The angel-woman embodies purity and submission—in essence, perfect adherence to nineteenth-century gender ideology. The monster-woman, in contrast, "embodies intransigent female autonomy."[2] In the twenty-first century, representations of women are much less likely to fall squarely along these lines. The angel has moved out of the house, and sex appeal often replaces purity as a central virtue: the new angels are Charlie's, or Victoria's Secret's. But the specter of the monstrous madwoman lingers: she is the woman who will not fit into socially approved categories. Like the madwoman of the nineteenth century, at times she is a positive figure of resistance, yet she is also marginalized and rebuked for daring to step outside of her role.

While women's entry into the workplace is no longer the subject of considerable public debate, social norms today continue to affect the representation of women in the sciences and tech industry. In the United States, fewer than 20% of college degrees in computer and information sciences are awarded to women, and at major research universities, a mere 12% of computer science degree recipients are women.[3] Moreover, multiple studies have demonstrated that women are leaving careers in science, engineering, and technology (SET) due to "hostile macho cultures" within SET companies.[4] Needless to say, women in SET fields are actively combating negative gender stereotypes and patriarchal structures that threaten to disrupt their lives and careers. It may not be surprising, therefore, that televisual representations of women in SET tend to suggest that these women are transgressing prescribed gender roles. In doing so, these representations often hearken back to the nineteenth-century madwoman.

This essay will look at women on two CBS television series, *NCIS* (2003) and *Criminal Minds* (2005), and consider how the female technologists on these programs are contrasted with the other women on each show. Although gender norms have become more fluid in our culture, each of these shows suggests a version of gender normativity within its respective universe through the representations of multiple, conformist female characters. And, in each of these series, the female technologist fails to conform to the show's depiction of normative gender, thus reinforcing the idea that science and tech are in some way "unfeminine." Constructed as madwomen, these characters are both positive portrayals of women asserting themselves in a male-dominated field, and problematic, as they are consistently marginalized.

Abby Sciuto, *NCIS*

NCIS, a show about an elite team of investigators working for the Naval Criminal Investigative Service, has featured a number of women over its twelve seasons. Most of the recurring female characters have been field agents: Caitlin "Kate" Todd (seasons 1–3), Ziva David (seasons 3–11), and Ellie Bishop (seasons 11-present). These female agents are represented as physically strong, intelligent women who work to prove that they are as capable in the field as their male colleagues. For example, in the series pilot, Kate is working for the Secret Service, where she not only is the sole person permitted to carry a gun on Air Force One, but is also in charge of guaranteeing the safety of the president of the United States. When Agent Gibbs, the head of the NCIS team, dismisses her questions about a joint investigation, she tells him, "I earned my jockstrap," and "I grow what I need,"[5] signaling her ability to participate in the masculine culture of investigative work. In later episodes, Ziva makes similar comments to establish herself as an equal member of the team. Their treatment suggests an acceptance of women into the realm of law enforcement, another field in which women are significantly underrepresented. However, this acceptance is achieved through the female characters' ability to conform to the expectations of their male colleagues and the fact that their work does not significantly upend the patriarchal authority established by the male characters. Significantly, although these characters strive to prove themselves as equals, their adherence to normative gender ideology is ultimately reinforced by the show's emphasis on their sexuality.

Agents Todd and David are regularly the object of Agent Anthony "Tony" DiNozzo's sexual advances. DiNozzo, the show's "everyman" character, mirrors the male viewer's gaze by constantly sizing up the physical attractiveness of both of these characters, as well as essentially every other woman he encounters. As such, Tony's interest in these women insists that they are little more than sexual objects. For example, in the episode "The Immortals," Tony is on assignment in Puerto Rico, where he buys souvenirs for Kate and Agent Gibbs. While Gibbs receives a how-to guide on online gaming, Kate reaches into her gift bag and pulls out bikini bottoms and a hat. Tony insists "it's a two-piece" bathing suit, and Gibbs joins in, asking if there is any chance of her trying it on.[6] Moments such as these draw attention to Kate's objectification. DiNozzo also consistently throws out questions about what makes Kate "hot," what she would do if a strange man came into her bedroom, and so on. While the two never have a romantic relationship, Tony's constant banter keeps Kate's sexuality in the forefront of the viewer's mind.

In the first episode of the third season, Kate is shot and killed. However, even her death does not stop Tony and Special Agent McGee, another member of the team, from continuing to sexualize her by imagining her in various sexy outfits: a school-girl uniform with the skirt being blown up, a latex superhero suit, and a dominatrix suit complete with whip. This culmination of Kate as a sexualized character is set alongside the introduction of Ziva David, initially an Israeli military agent before joining NCIS. When we first meet Ziva, she has her hair in a simple ponytail and interrupts Tony's sex-fantasy of Kate. There is immediate chemistry between the two, with flirtation on both sides. Ziva locks eyes with Tony as she very deliberately lets down her rather voluminous hair, and Tony is exasperated by her "slouching provocatively" across from his desk.[7] The entirety of Ziva's introduction to the series is sexually charged, showing her in a flattering bathing suit within the first seven minutes of the second episode she appears in. That charge only gains strength as the series continues, peaking in a passionate kiss with Tony before she leaves the agency permanently.[8] Agent Ellie Bishop, the most recent female agent to be paired with Tony, is married, therefore diminishing Tony's sense of her sexual availability, but nevertheless establishing her as an object of male desire. While Kate, Ziva, and Ellie represent women's entry into a male-dominant sphere, they ultimately do not subvert the patriarchal hierarchy; instead, they reinforce it by always being subject to Gibb's authority and DiNozzo's sexual objectification. They establish the show's version of the angel-woman: she is physically strong, assertive, and capable, but ultimately conforms to men's expectations and submits to what most would consider sexual harassment.

Meanwhile, Abby Sciuto, the lab technician, consistently defies expectations. She is portrayed as the most intelligent female member of the team, and, in her role as a female scientist and technologist, she is marginalized in a variety of ways. When Abby first appears onscreen in the pilot episode, we see her in her lab wearing safety goggles. While she doesn't say much to demonstrate her intellect in this initial scene, she soon sets in with intense scientific jargon; her casual mention of performing a "fibrinogen test" showing the "procoagulate numbers were high" is just one demonstration of this.[9] In the same episode, Abby discovers a toxin which is "almost impossible to detect."[10] This near-miraculous discovery is crucial in allowing the rest of the team to take down a murderous terrorist. Abby's role in most episodes develops in a similar fashion: through a series of (often unbelievable) discoveries in the lab, she is able to provide the team with critical information to save the day. Although her colleagues rarely acknowledge her as such, Abby's impressive abilities suggest that she is a genius. Notably, although Gibbs is Abby's boss, her extensive knowledge and skill position her as superior to the men on the team; while the female agents are directly compared to the men by attempting to perform essentially identical tasks, Abby is able to do things nobody else can. She is therefore able to subvert the hierarchy in ways the female agents cannot.

It is not surprising, therefore, that Abby is constructed as a kind of madwoman in the lab and is marginalized in multiple ways that risk undercutting her power. Most obviously, she is established as a member of Goth subculture through her attire and interests outside of work, and thus is cast as either mad or monstrous, and sometimes both. Abby's behavior at times is both uncouth and childlike. She actively rejects "ladylike" conventions; she often makes crude, unprofessional comments at work and her lab is decorated with art and objects that might be considered both inappropriate and childish. For example, in one episode she discusses photocopying "everything from C-notes to ... butts,"[11] and admits to having photocopied her own backside. As another example, her plush puppet "Bert the Farting Hippo" is featured in multiple episodes. Instances such as these serve to make Abby seem more juvenile and boyish, and to represent her as "mad" in comparison to the "sane" Kate or Ziva. This madness is coupled with the monstrous; Abby's interest in death and her choice of wall decor—extreme close-up photographs of horrible wounds—establish her as such.

That Abby represents a less desirable type of woman is reinforced by the ways in which the male characters react to her. She is noticeably less appealing to "mainstream" men such as DiNozzo. This is made clear, for example, when Agent McGee is first introduced and, having not yet met Abby, asks DiNozzo if she is cute. DiNozzo responds by saying that she is not McGee's "type," and then mentioning Abby's interest in tattoos.[12] At the end of the episode McGee tells DiNozzo that he has a lunch date with Abby, but since he still hasn't actually seen Abby, DiNozzo assumes the date will not go well. This episode emphasizes that Abby is an outsider and not appealing to "normal" men. Her lack of "normal" appeal is also evident in the mere fact that DiNozzo never engages Abby in the kind of sexist banter he frequently volleys towards Kate and Ziva. These constant reminders of female sexuality, specifically through Tony's eyes, are conspicuously lacking with Abby. In fact, the first time we see Tony and Abby share close physical quarters is when Tony asks for help with his computer. Abby leans around him from behind, a typically intimate gesture. However, Tony only comments that her perfume smells like gunpowder, to which she replies, "Sweet, huh?"[13] Rather than sexually objectifying her, as he is wont to do with the show's other female characters, Tony recognizes the monstrous in her and is repulsed. Tony's behavior towards Abby, which is markedly different from his behavior towards other women on the show, firmly establishes her as an outsider.

Abby's tendency to act childishly, despite her immense intellect, contributes to her role as a daughter-figure in *NCIS*, specifically in relation to Agent Gibbs. Gibbs embodies the role of father wholeheartedly when it comes to Abby. His affinity for Abby and tolerance for her often inappropriate behavior are accounted for after it is revealed in the third season that Gibbs' first wife and daughter had been killed prior to the events portrayed on the show. Abby's childlike attitude and appearance seem to have endeared her to a man generally seen as crotchety and unapproachable, but they also contribute to the audience's sense that Abby is abnormal. In "Girls Just Wanna Be Smart?" Kerstin Bergman argues that Abby's childishness feminizes her, and describes her as the "sexy child of the NCIS 'family.'"[14] What is interesting is that Abby is clearly sexualized for the television audience, but less so within the world of the show. While she is certainly more "girly" than Kate or Ziva, who both strive to fit in with the men, this does not draw the gaze of the show's male characters, who appear universally more attracted to the more "adult" women. Thus, audiences can voyeuristically enjoy Abby's school-girl sexuality while the show, through the behavior of the male protagonists, gently reminds viewers that doing so defies cultural norms.

Abby's intelligence and her career choice, while not immediately recognizable as a hindrance to her sex appeal compared to the issues already discussed, nonetheless play a part in portraying her as less traditionally attractive. Goth subculture aside, Abby's defining feature is her intellect, which is demonstrated again and again throughout the show, through her meticulous use of science and technology in carrying out forensic investigations, her ability to use deductive reasoning to provide the rest of the team with insight into various crimes, and her flawless use of scientific and medical language. In fact, the first time we meet Abby, she is wearing a t-shirt proclaiming "I [love] NERDS," which is only partially obscured by her lab coat. She is thus situated not only in Goth subculture but also in "nerd" subculture, again depicting the female technician as outsider. As such, only members of her subcultures recognize her as romantically interesting: the male characters who show interest in Abby are "nerds" as well. This again reinforces the show's message that attraction to an individual such as Abby falls outside mainstream culture's norms. In the episode "Eye Spy," another potential love interest for the Goth lab technician is introduced. Ashton, a satellite technician from NASA, is called via video messaging to help with surveillance for a case. Ashton shares an intellectual connection with Abby, but he also notably does not embody traditional standards of male beauty. He is visibly overweight, wears glasses, and has a receding hairline. Open flirting ensues on both sides until Gibbs asserts his dominance, as a father-figure and as a member of mainstream culture, by moving into Ashton's line of sight while clearing his throat meaningfully to end the flirtation.[15] The action of the scene is reminiscent of a father interrupting a potential suitor's advances towards his daughter, but also puts Abby back in her marginalized place. This flirtation is not allowed.

While Abby's character provides a loveable, positive female role model in a scientific field, the consistent emphasis on her monstrous side-interests and her lack of romantic appeal to "normal" men, especially in contrast to the show's construction of "normal" femininity through other characters, is a major issue. *NCIS* regrettably continues the Hollywood tradition of isolating women who demonstrate their intelligence by denying them romantic involvement; simultaneously, the show also manages to hyper-sexualize women whose career depends on their physical capabilities. In allowing Kate and Ziva to be constantly harassed, their gender becomes a major factor in defining them as little more than sexy gun-toters rather than simply capable crime-fighters. It is commendable that Abby's genius is not affected by her gender, but that her gender and sexuality is downplayed to allow that genius to flourish is problematic.

Penelope Garcia, *Criminal Minds*

Much like *NCIS*, *Criminal Minds* features an elite team of men and women who investigate crimes, but this time as part of the FBI's Behavioral Analysis Unit (BAU). In the pilot episode, "Extreme Aggressor," the team consists of four main field agents, all male, and a female "technical analyst," Penelope Garcia. An additional agent who is not part of the regular team, Elle Greenaway, assists in the case. Like Kate and Ziva in *NCIS*, Elle is immediately established as both physically strong and sexually provocative. In the pilot, she is used as a decoy to ensnare a serial rapist and murderer, thus demonstrating her appeal, and she later shoots a suspect, demonstrating her strength, courage, and most importantly, her capability as a field agent. As a result of her success in this case, she is invited to join the BAU and becomes a regular member of the team in subsequent episodes. In her role as the team's newest member, Elle naturally assumes an inferior position to the team's more experienced male members, much like the female agents on *NCIS*, and thus does not upset the dominant male hierarchy. The second episode of the series, "Compulsion," saw the addition of another female character, J.J. Jareau, who serves as the "unit liaison," whose "specialty is untangling bureaucratic knots"[16] Like Elle, J.J. exudes traditional feminine beauty: she is blonde and lithe. Further J.J. fulfills a typically feminine role as a communicator; one of her primary responsibilities is handling the public's emotional response to a crime so that the rest of the team can focus on reasoning their way to a suspect. Elle and J.J. establish the show's construction of normative femininity as including intelligence, but also a particular body type and conservative wardrobe. Like Abby on *NCIS*, Penelope Garcia does not fit into this construction.

While the other agents, male and female, chase down criminals, Penelope works from the safety of the home office. Like Abby Sciuto's lab, Penelope's office is her domain; it is full of computers and monitors, and from this location she provides the rest of the team with critical information in episode after episode. While Spencer Reid is often cited as the show's main genius, Penelope also demonstrates exceptionally high intelligence. In fact, in the pilot episode, reference is made to both characters' genius. Reid states outright that he is a genius, while Penelope, in her very first moment on screen, answers her phone by saying: "You've reached Penelope Garcia in the FBI's office of supreme genius."[17] Although Penelope's genius is often overshadowed by Reid's savant-like (and ultimately unrealistic) abilities, there are additional markers of her intelligence. For example, we learn that Penelope dropped out of Cal Tech, the same school Reid attended. Moreover, she was directly recruited by the FBI for her extraordinary hacking skills that put her among "only a handful of people on the planet."[18]

Penelope, like Abby, has a unique fashion sense that serves to separate her from mainstream culture and deliberately position her as Other. Her style, based on the style of Kirsten Vangsness, the actress who plays her, is often a blend of bright, clashing colors and patterns, completed with funky glasses, large barrettes, and unnatural hair coloring. Penelope's style also lends a childlike quality to the character, as do her negative reactions to violent images from crime scenes.

Moreover, her style, along with her size (Vangsness is a size 12), is far from the Hollywood standard of beauty.[19] While her unique style seems to assert her autonomy, it is simultaneously construed as monstrous. Early in the series, Penelope is clearly constructed as less sexually appealing than her female colleagues through her failed attempts at romance. Penelope has no love interests until the first season's finale, when she meets a man, "Sir Knafe," while playing on online video game. When J.J. asks about him, Penelope says, "This guy is amazing," and then proceeds to explain why her online encounters (which she likens to dates) are so great: "we meet online at specified times that he is never late to, we spend hours adventuring and chatting during which time I have his undivided attention and he lavishes me with flattery."[20] Penelope's interest in her online suitor reinforces nerd stereotypes, but it also demonstrates that she longs for traditional, even chivalric romance—the game is set in Camelot, where her online interest, a knight in armor, calls her "my lady" and begs to be her "humblest servant."[21] Penelope's online relationship specifically points to her inability to find romance in the real world. As her (much thinner) avatar chats with "Sir Knafe," Penelope comments, "why can't the real world be like this?"[22] Worse yet, it turns out that "Sir Knafe" is only using her to infiltrate the FBI's computers; he is not actually interested in her at all.

Similarly, in the season three episode "Lucky" Garcia seems to have finally met a handsome man who is interested in her, but the episode concludes with her new beau shooting her in the chest.[23] In the following episode it is revealed that the man's interest in Penelope has been feigned all along, and his intention from the beginning was to murder her in order to cover up previous crimes. Thus, both of Penelope's potential romantic relationships in the show's first two and a half years suggest that men only fake interest in her when they want something, and that she is not otherwise sexually desirable. She is the monstrous madwoman, a representation that is particularly troubling given that part of Penelope's "madness" seems to be her willingness to believe that a man is interested in her. As she tells the rest of the team, the shooter seemed "deliciously normal," and she admits in retrospect that she "shouldn't have trusted it"; in other words, she should have known a "normal" man would not ask her out.[24] Nevertheless, Penelope has attracted a significant fan base, and perhaps owing to this in season three the character finally had a romance that was based on attraction rather than criminal intent. However, the romantic interest, Kevin Lynch, is Penelope's doppelganger: a geeky, glasses-wearing FBI technical analyst with a penchant for loud-patterned shirts. Thus, even this relationship reinforces Penelope's outsider status.

Penelope is portrayed as a smart, interesting character with a good sense of humor, yet she is also constructed as the madwoman. Like *NCIS*, *Criminal*

Minds suggests that highly intelligent women, perhaps more specifically those in science and technology fields, are functioning outside of cultural norms. While it is encouraging that both Penelope and Abby disrupt gender norms and offer portrayals of women who are not typically "Hollywood beautiful," it is troubling that these portrayals are specifically overlaid with high intelligence and technical expertise; this suggests an either/or scenario, in which women are either members of the dominant culture and of average intelligence, or they are highly intelligent scientists and technologists who are doubly marginalized by their choice of career and their position outside of mainstream culture.

Conclusion

While shows like *NCIS* and *Criminal Minds* seem to represent cultural progress towards a greater acceptance of women in science and technology fields, these portrayals are flawed in ways that risk deterring other women from pursing similar careers. The physically strong women on each team clearly demonstrate that women can succeed in traditionally male roles, but the women in scientific and technological roles reinforce stereotypes that women who choose these fields are somehow weird, different, or abnormal. On both shows, the ways in which male characters react to their unique qualities—qualities that are not specifically related to their careers—work to establish that they are monstrous. Tellingly, like the madwoman in the attic, both are physically separated from the normative sphere of their agencies through private workspaces (Abby's lab and Penelope's office) that divide them from their team's communal areas. It is hard not to root for them; like the madwomen described by Gilbert and Gubar, they are "fiercely independent characters who seek to destroy all the patriarchal structures."[25] Yet the consequences of their independence, like the consequences for the Victorian madwoman, force viewers to question whether they would like to *be* them. Thus they send problematically mixed messages: yes women can succeed in science and tech, but to do so is not normal. It's laudable that television producers and writers have sought to make television more inclusive, both by representing female characters who fall outside of Hollywood's norms for femininity and beauty and by representing women in science and technology. Still, these characters remain unnecessarily marginalized.

Notes

1. Sandra M. Gilbert and Susan Gubar, *The Madwoman in the Attic*, 2d ed. (New Haven: Yale University Press, 2000[1979]), 20, 28.
2. Ibid., 28.

3. "By the Numbers," *Women and Information Technology*, *NCWIT.org*, February 28, 2014, http://www.ncwit.org/sites/default/files/resources/btn_02282014web.pdf. Based on graduation rates in 2012.

4. Sylvia Ann Hewlett, et al., "The Athena Factor: Reversing the Brain Drain in Science, Engineering, an Technology," *Harvard Business Review Research Report*, June 2008, i, http://documents.library.nsf.gov/edocs/HD6060-.A84–2008-PDF-Athena-factor-Reversing-the-brain-drain-in-science,-engineering,-and-technology.pdf.

5. Donald P. Bellisario and Don McGill, "Yankee White," *NCIS*, season 1, episode 1, directed by Donald P. Bellisario, aired September 23, 2003, on CBS.

6. Darcy Meyers, "The Immortals," *NCIS*, season 1, episode 4, directed by Alan J. Levi, aired October 14, 2003, on CBS.

7. Donald P. Bellisario, "Kill Ari: Part 1," *NCIS*, season 3, episode 1, directed by Dennis Smith, aired September 20, 2005, on CBS.

8. Gary Glasberg, "Past, Present, and Future," *NCIS*, season 11, episode 2, directed by James Whitmore, Jr., aired October 1, 2013, on CBS.

9. Bellisario and McGill, "Yankee White."

10. Ibid.

11. Donald P. Bellisario and Don McGill, "Left for Dead," *NCIS*, season 1, episode 10, directed by James Whitmore, Jr., aired January 6, 2004, on CBS.

12. George Schenck and Frank Cardea, "Sub Rosa," *NCIS*, season , episode 7, directed by Michael Zinberg, aired November 18, 2003, on CBS.

13. John C. Kelley, "Marine Down," *NCIS*, season 1, episode 9, directed by Dennis Smith, aired December 16, 2003, on CBS.

14. Kerstin Bergman, "Girls Just Wanna Be Smart? The Depiction of Women Scientists in Contemporary Crime Fiction," *International Journal of Gender, Science and Technology* 4, no. 3 (2012): 321, http://genderandset.open.ac.uk/index.php/genderandset/article/viewFile/224/438.

15. George Schenck, Frank Cardea, and Dana Coen, "Eye Spy," *NCIS*, season 1, episode 11, directed by Alan J. Levi, aired January 13, 2004, on CBS.

16. Jeff Davis, "Compulsion," *Criminal Minds*, season 1, episode 2, directed by Charles Haid, aired September 28, 2005, on CBS.

17. Jeff Davis, "Extreme Aggressor," *Criminal Minds*, season 1, episode 1, directed by Richard Shepard, aired September 22, 2005, on CBS.

18. Chris Mundy, "Penelope," *Criminal Minds*, season 3, episode 9, directed by Felix Alcala, aired November 21, 2007, on CBS.

19. Diane Anderson-Minshall, "The Lesbian Star of [Criminal Minds] Goes Noir," *Advocate*, October 31, 2011, 2, http://www.advocate.com/arts-entertainment/television/2011/10/31/lesbian-star-criminal-minds-goes-noir.

20. Edward Allen Bernero, "The Fisher King: Part I," *Criminal Minds*, season 1, episode 22, directed by Edward Allen Bernero, aired May 10, 2006, on CBS.

21. Ibid.

22. Ibid.

23. Andrew Wilder, "Lucky," *Criminal Minds*, season 3, episode 8, directed by Steve Boyum, aired November 14, 2007, on CBS.

24. Mundy, "Penelope."

25. Gilbert and Gubar, *The Madwoman in the Attic*, 77–78.

References

Anderson-Minshall, Diane. "The Lesbian Star of [Criminal Minds] Goes Noir." *Advocate*, October 31, 2011. http://www.advocate.com/arts-entertainment/television/2011/10/31/lesbian-star-criminal-minds-goes-noir.

Bellisario, Donald P. "Kill Ari: Part I." *NCIS*, season 3, episode 1. Directed by Dennis Smith. Aired September 20, 2005, on CBS. *NCIS: The Complete Third Season*, DVD. Los Angeles: CBS Paramount Television, 2006.

Bellisario, Donald P., and Don McGill. "Left for Dead." *NCIS*, season 1, episode 10. Directed by James Whitmore, Jr. Aired January 6, 2004. *NCIS: The Complete First Season*, DVD. Los Angeles: CBS Paramount Television, 2004.

____, and ____. "Yankee White." *NCIS*, season 1, episode 1. Directed by Donald P. Bellisario. Aired September 23, 2003, on CBS. *NCIS: The Complete First Season*, DVD. Los Angeles: CBS Paramount Television, 2004.

Bergman, Kerstin. "Girls Just Wanna Be Smart? The Depiction of Women Scientists in Contemporary Crime Fiction." *International Journal of Gender, Science and Technology* 4, no. 3 (2012): 314–329. http://genderandset.open.ac.uk/index.php/genderandset/article/viewFile/224/438.

Bernero, Edward Allen. "The Fisher King: Part I." *Criminal Minds*, season 1, episode 22. Directed by Edward Allen Bernero. Aired May 10, 2006, on CBS. Netflix.com.

"By the Numbers." *Women and Information Technology*, NCWIT.org. February 28, 2014. http://www.ncwit.org/sites/default/files/resources/btn_02282014web.pdf.

Davis, Jeff. "Compulsion." *Criminal Minds*, season 1, episode 2. Directed by Charles Haid. Aired September 28, 2005 on CBS. Netflix.com.

____. "Extreme Aggressor." *Criminal Minds*, season 1, episode 1. Directed by Richard Shepard. Aired September 22, 2005, on CBS. Netflix.com.

Gilbert, Sandra M., and Susan Gubar. *The Madwoman in the Attic*. 2d ed. New Haven: Yale University Press, 2000.

Glasberg, Gary. "Past, Present, and Future." *NCIS*, season 11, episode 2. Directed by James Whitmore, Jr. Aired October 1, 2013, on CBS. *NCIS: The Eleventh Season*, DVD. Los Angeles, CA: CBS Paramount Television 2014.

Hewlett, Sylvia Ann, Carolyn Buck Luce, Lisa J. Servon, Laura Sherbin, Peggy Shiller, Eytan Sosnovich, and Karen Sumberg. "The Athena Factor: Reversing the Brain Drain in Science, Engineering, an Technology." *Harvard Business Review Research Report*, June 2008. http://documents.library.nsf.gov/edocs/HD6060-.A84-2008-PDF-Athena-factor-Reversing-the-brain-drain-in-science,-engineering,-and-technology.pdf.

Kelley, John C. "Marine Down." *NCIS*, season 1, episode 9. Directed by Dennis Smith. Aired December 16, 2003, on CBS. *NCIS: The Complete First Season*, DVD. Los Angeles: CBS Paramount Television, 2004.

Meyers, Darcy. "The Immortals." *NCIS*, season 1, episode 4. Directed by Alan J. Levi. Aired October 14, 2003 on CBS. *NCIS: The Complete First Season*, DVD. Los Angeles: CBS Paramount Television, 2004.

Mundy, Chris. "Penelope." *Criminal Minds*, season 3, episode 9. Directed by Felix Alcala. Aired November 21, 2007, on CBS. Netflix.com.

Schenck, George, and Frank Cardea. "Sub Rosa." *NCIS*, season 1, episode 7. Directed by Michael Zinberg. Aired November 18, 2003, on CBS. *NCIS: The Complete First Season*, DVD. Los Angeles: CBS Paramount Television, 2004.

Schenck, George, Frank Cardea, and Dana Coen. "Eye Spy." *NCIS*, season 1, episode 11. Directed by Alan J. Levi. Aired January 13, 2004, on CBS. *NCIS: The Complete First Season*, DVD. Los Angeles: CBS Paramount Television, 2004.

Wilder, Andrew. "Lucky." *Criminal Minds*, season 3, episode 8. Directed by Steve Boyum. Aired November 14, 2007, on CBS. Netflix.com.

Gladiators in Dresses

Scandal, *Femininity* and Emotional Genius

Jennifer Kirby

Geniuses come in all shapes and sizes, but not all television genres. Highly intelligent characters populate the television landscape across selected genres, including episodic procedurals set in the worlds of crime investigation, forensics, law, or medicine; comedies centered on the figure of the "geek," usually a white, unusually smart but socially inept young man[1]; and fantasy programs featuring witches, prophets, seers or other supernaturally gifted characters. The terrain of the melodrama, however, associates itself less with characters possessing high intelligence than high emotion. Unlike the protagonist of the procedural (whether male or female), who works in the area of solving crimes or mysteries and uses logical reasoning and rational intelligence to deduce facts or solve problems, the melodramatic heroine defines herself traditionally via her excessive emotion[2] and above all her femininity: her concerns are centered around the private sphere of home, love, and family.[3] Both the genre, which traditionally attracts a large female audience, and the characters are subject to a process of emphatic gendering.[4]

Created by the award-winning woman behind the extraordinarily successful medical drama *Grey's Anatomy*, Shonda Rhymes, *Scandal* (2012) crosses these generic boundaries by integrating an ongoing melodramatic narrative about an affair between the fictional Republican President of the United States, Fitzgerald Grant (Tony Goldwyn) and his female, African American campaign advisor, Olivia Pope (Kerry Washington), with narrative strands concerning her political and covert activities as a fixer. The show thus combines the genius figure from the procedural with the melodramatic heroine familiar from more woman-centered emotional genres, as it simultaneously recasts the figure of the genius in terms of both gender and race.

Scandal represents highly intelligent women who use their emotional genius to influence the masculine spheres of politics and public relations. While a man gains the political glory, it is the women behind the scenes whose feminine proficiency in predicting, understanding, and generating emotion ensures their success or downfall. Female emotion has historically been characterized as dangerous and unstable and contrasted with masculine rationality.[5] In *Scandal*, however, two women employ their ability to predict and utilize emotional responses either to serve or oppose the political interests of the male president. Professional "fixer" Olivia Pope is well-known for her incredible intelligence and ability to solve crimes and handle public relations disasters for rich and powerful friends, calling her team "gladiators in suits." In some cases, Olivia is able to resolve scandalous personal situations for her various clients with her ability to negotiate delicate and volatile emotions. She acts both as President Grant's mistress and sometime advisor/advocate, and she is often the cause of the president's success precisely because she is able to advise him on how aspects of his personal life will impact public perception. Her rival and sometime collaborator, First Lady Mellie (Bellamy Young), by contrast, is not a professional woman and has in fact given up her professional life in order to be the First Lady. Nevertheless, she wields enormous power due to her genius in affecting public response through her strategic presentation and revelation of various aspects of her intimate relationship with the President. The show thus equates feminine emotional intelligence (on the part both of Olivia and Mellie) with genius problem-solving and suggests that emotion does not express itself simply in irrational hysteria, but may be directed into controlled strategy.

Just as the show offers a more feminine conception of genius, it also challenges stereotypes surrounding the racial profile of the television genius. The show emphasizes Olivia's beauty and glamour as a black woman and thus differentiates her from more conventional images of intelligence that often center on the white, male "nerd" figure. *Scandal* therefore problematizes the gender, race, and genre biases of television genius.

Not Your Usual Genius: Gender and Race

In *Scandal*, Olivia Pope defies both social and televisual stereotypes of genius. She is a highly skilled woman who wields enormous power, yet she is also immaculately dressed, appearing frequently in elegant coats and even extravagant gowns at official White House functions. Shows as diverse as *Charlie's Angels* and *Scooby-Doo, Where Are You!* depict intellectually gifted women as less attractive than their less intelligent peers, reflecting "a deeply rooted fear of brilliant women."[6] The trope of ugliness thus demonizes intelligent women. Olivia Pope, by contrast, challenges the binary opposition in popular culture between feminine beauty and male intelligence, separating extraordinary intellectual abilities from their corresponding image of the unattractive, white male "nerd."[7] Largely due to the success of high profile geniuses of computing, such as Bill Gates and Steve Jobs, being a nerd has become increasingly "cool" for white men and is now regarded as "a pathway to economic fame and fortune."[8] Both women and African Americans, on the other hand, are largely excluded from this "social identity."[9] Women are generally allowed to only inhabit one persona and are recognized more for their beauty than their intelligence, suggesting that if one is feminine then one cannot inhabit the masculine role of "geek."[10] American television shows, such as *The Big Bang Theory* and *Silicon Valley*, continue to reinforce the association between masculine social awkwardness and genius. Sometimes beautiful women are able to succeed in masculine realms by virtue of their attractiveness, but only so long as "their beauty contains their brilliance, signaling their adherence to conventions of femininity even if they use masculine smarts."[11] Indeed, within computing circles beautiful women grapple with disproportionate media attention to their appearances.[12] While *Scandal* draws attention to actress Kerry Washington's not inconsiderable beauty, this beauty does not preclude her from providing invaluable insights to the President.

Although smart women are sometimes accepted by both subcultures and in popular culture representations, these women are usually demonstrably Caucasian.[13] In television shows that focus on high-powered female lawyers, for example, African American women are generally minor characters and serve little purpose other than adding token diversity.[14] Meanwhile, African American women figure prominently in reality television shows, embodying the stereotype of the "evil black woman" through over-the-top hysterics, quick tempers, and the representation of black contestants as "liars and bitches, but white contestants as smart and shrewd."[15] Olivia Pope dispels the stereotypes associated with sensational and hysterical images of black women in reality shows, instead displaying "the mental and verbal athleticism of a crisis manager."[16] Olivia is poised and capable, demonstrating "the *allure* of black respectability."[17] She runs her own company and wields enormous power over the decision-making process of the leader of the free world. Olivia is hysterical at times, but her visceral responses must eventually be subjugated beneath her professional responsibility and capabilities.

Despite this portrayal of an African American woman as an essential member of the President's team, Olivia nevertheless remains the President's mistress and thus outside of his family: she is on the President's staff, but never quite breaks into the inner sanctum of his home. Her genius serves both the man and the country. In this way, *Scandal* lays itself open to charges of perpetuating the image of the African American woman's sexual attractiveness for the white master, while asking viewers to "focus only on her positive traits of power, both sexual and economic."[18] Her genius supports the white man and his political institutions and yet does not elevate her from a position of servitude. Olivia Pope can thus be interpreted through the notion of the stereotype of the "Black lady."[19] This stereotype distinguishes middle-class African American women from their working class counterparts and "is designed to counter claims of Black women's promiscuity."[20] The Black lady attains her respectability through her participation in the professional workforce.[21] She represents an updating or modernization of "the image of the Mammy, the loyal female servant" because she remains "appropriately subordinate to White and/or male authority."[22] The Black lady requires a certain degree "of ambition and aggressiveness" in order to be competent in her middle-class occupations "within the male-defined ethos of corporations, government, industry, and academia," but must direct this aggressive ambition towards serving the interests of white authority, not towards her own advancement.[23] In the episode "Mama Said Knock You Out,"[24] Olivia attempts to solve a crisis that occurs when the President, Fitz, finds out that his wife has been sleeping with his running mate, Andrew (Jon Tenney). This revelation happens to directly precede an important television interview with the entire Grant family. Olivia advises the couple that they must do the interview because the public speculation as to why the interview was cancelled would damage Fitz's chances at re-election. Fitz and Mellie have a ferocious argument and when Olivia tries to interject, Fitz dismisses her with the exclamation, "I am talking to my wife!"[25] He thus emphasizes his exclusion of Olivia from the family; she must remain an outsider, the perpetual mistress. Hurt, Olivia invokes the language of servitude, asking the President's Chief of Staff Cyrus (Jeff Perry), to tell her "that we're not the help" and that she is more than "the maid" who appears to clean up "when they ring the bell."[26] The racial allusion in her outburst is clear; Olivia openly refers to the history of black women first as slaves and then as domestic servants. She nevertheless resolves this moment of self-awareness and internal conflict by appealing to her own sense of professional duty. Cyrus urges Olivia to return and solve the crisis because "it's not just that family you're putting back together, it's the whole damn country."[27] The black woman is asked to utilize her genius and suppress her personal pride and self-worth to ensure not only the stability of the Grant family, but also that of America. When Olivia returns to Fitz, he apologizes to her, but she rejects his apology, telling him that he should direct his remorse and apologies to his family in order to ensure that the interview is a success. She informs him that she is "at work" and that she needs him to apologize to Mellie instead because Olivia "cannot fail" at the one thing that's working in her life: her job.[28] She therefore disavows her own satisfaction and happiness in order to advance the interests of Fitz and his administration in her professional capacity as a "Black lady."[29] She prioritizes her political genius over personal validation.

Scandal's racial discourses remain complex and problematic. The show does not necessarily encourage the audience to discount these ambiguities, but instead draws attention to them through dialogue such as Olivia's references to acting as "the help" and asks the audience to form their own opinions. Nevertheless, the notion of a black woman as political genius complicates the stereotypical image of the genius in the popular imagination.

Genius and Emotional Literacy

If Olivia Pope challenges conventions surrounding the physical appearance of genius, she also challenges the type of abilities that usually define a genius by possessing an emotional, as well as rational, intelligence.

Philosophical thought has traditionally associated rationality and reason with masculinity, thus, as Karen Jones writes, devaluing women's contributions to society due to their "assumed deficiency in rationality."[30] Genevieve Lloyd argues that women have been excluded from the discourses of rationality not because women are inherently irrational or because there exists "a distinctively female thought-style" but because our conceptions of the "ideals of Reason have historically incorporated an exclusion of the feminine, and that femininity itself has been partly constituted through such processes of exclusion."[31] Philosophy has consistently constructed a binary opposition between reason and emotion, associating masculinity with the former and femininity with the latter.[32] In order to possess rationality, one must transcend all the emotions that fall under the category of the feminine.[33] Indeed, the emotions of a woman are frequently linked to the gendered condition of excessive and "uncontrollable" hysteria.[34] Ironically, in the realm of art men have been considered geniuses for their adoption of supposedly feminine qualities, such as "instinct, emotion, sensibility, intuition, imagination," while these same qualities represent weakness in the biologically female and offer reasons to exclude women from the category of genius.[35]

The opposition between masculine reason and feminine emotion produces a number of problematic feminist responses that attempt to challenge the valorization of masculine qualities.[36] One cannot remedy the historical exclusion of women from the rational public sphere by advocating the position that women should now be recognized as possessing all the same rational characteristics as men, because the cultural ideal of rationality was founded on a specific set of characteristics that were associated with masculinity and thus such a response, Lloyd writes, "seems implicitly to accept the downgrading of the excluded character traits traditionally associated with femininity."[37] By contrast, according to Jones, the "different voice" approach appears to rescue feminine traits by insisting that "available conceptions of rationality" are "either incomplete or accorded an inflated importance."[38] These theorists argue that traditional conceptions of rationality exclude significant human capabilities that "enable us to respond well to our reasons" because these capabilities relate to women and "women's nurturing activities within the private sphere."[39] Alison Jaggar provides one of the key arguments in this perspective, suggesting that the emotions, which are often seen as "impediments to rational choice and to the reliable formation of true belief," in fact "enable us to respond to our reasons."[40] Thus it is clear that "the devaluation of those capacities traditionally viewed as feminine has resulted in a less than adequate conception of rationality."[41] This notion of feminine capabilities remains problematic, however, because it risks falling back into "a deeper, older structure of male norms and female complementation."[42] *Scandal* complicates such binary divisions by emphasizing the degree to which supposedly feminine skills can be recast as aspects of genius and strength not only within the private sphere and/or within art,[43] but within the male-dominated arena of political strategy.

In her work as a professional fixer, Olivia often employs unconventional strategies; she is able to solve public relations disasters by employing emotional nuance to provide solutions that move beyond monetary compensation or legalities. In "The Other Woman," for example, Olivia is hired when a prominent minister in the African American community is found dead on top of his mistress.[44] Although the woman will not accept a pay out to keep quiet, Olivia identifies with her due to her own clandestine relationship with Fitz and the lack of public recognition of this relationship. Appealing to the woman's feelings rather than her bank account, Olivia convinces the minister's wife to allow the mistress a spot at the funeral, eliminating the threat to the minister's reputation by giving the mistress a gesture of acknowledgement of her place in the life of the man she loved. Olivia's empathy with the mistress allows her to predict and capitalize on her emotional needs.

Similarly, Pope possesses qualities that members of President Fitzgerald Grant's campaign team lack and is able to further his political career through her ability to predict how the public will feel, rather than think, about the President. In "The Trail," a series of flashbacks to Fitz's campaign for the presidential nomination demonstrates how Olivia brings her emotional literacy to Fitz's political race.[45] In flashback, a young Fitz asks his staff and volunteers for ideas to beat his opponent, Sally Langston (Kate Burton). A woman stands up and suggests a further right stance on moral issues. Fitz dismisses her suggestion, beginning, "The problem is..."[46] We hear Olivia's voice before we see her as she interrupts, "Your marriage.... It looks like you don't screw your wife, which would be fine except that..."[47] At this point the camera shows Olivia pacing at the back of the room before she continues to elaborate on the importance of "family values" to the Republican Party. Olivia seems to literally appear from nowhere, breaking into Fitz's meeting from the back. In this way, the scene emphasizes the freshness of Olivia's strategy. She moves further up towards Fitz and tells him that his marriage "looks cold, distant, dead."[48] In a later flashback, Olivia has cancelled all of Fitz and Mellie's events for the following fortnight and informs them that the best thing they can do is actually talk to each other at events and present the image of a "believable, loving, dedicated couple."[49] After some disagreement, Fitz convinces Mellie that she needs to "pretend like this isn't a dead marriage" if she intends to be First Lady.[50] In the next scene, a montage begins of Fitz and Mellie exchanging meaningful looks at each other. First, on the steps of their children's elementary school a reporter asks if it is "a little risky" to take time off from campaigning to attend a parent-teacher conference and Fitz replies that "if it's a choice between losing touch with your family and losing a primary [looks lovingly at Mellie and back] it's not really a choice, is it?"[51] In this way, Fitz cements his appeal as dedicated husband and father. The sequence culminates with a campaign event where Fitz and Mellie are handing out ice cream to children. Mellie holds up an ice cream for Fitz, who takes a bite and gets ice cream on his chin. Mellie notices Olivia, who says to Cyrus, "Wait for it, wait..." and Mellie wipes the ice cream off Fitz's chin.[52] He laughs, thanks her and kisses her as the photographers frantically photograph the couple's moment. Olivia declares, "Perfect."[53] Olivia recognizes the power and importance of outward signifiers of emotion and teaches the couple how to communicate emotionally with each other and the public.

In a later episode, Olivia uses a set of feminine social skills usually associated with soap operas to pre-empt a political disaster. Feminist scholarship suggests that the act of watching a soap opera engages a specific set of "social competencies seen as feminine: reading faces, interpreting relationships, contemplating the impact of events on feelings."[54] Olivia uses the skill of interpreting facial expressions and assessing emotional states to identify the President's son, Jerry (Dylan Minnette), as a potential liability to Fitz's public image.[55] Prior to a televised family interview, Olivia coaches Fitz's two children. Jerry appears nervous, agitated and combative, repeatedly asking if the interview is live and whether he can take back "something stupid."[56] Unnerved by her observations of Jerry, Olivia instructs her team to investigate his background further. One of Olivia's employees, Abby, asks if they should be focusing on a teenage boy when they "are in the middle of a war with a top-secret spy organization," but Olivia rules that Jerry is more important today. Jerry's emotional cues indicate to Olivia that his unhinged state should take precedence over superficially more serious issues because, as Olivia tells Fitz and Mellie, the family interview "might be the most important interview of the campaign." The team discovers that Jerry has been running a twitter account under a pseudonym criticizing the government and his father's administration. It is Olivia's intelligence in the area of reading emotional signifiers and expressions that alerts her to the existence of a potentially damaging crisis, which regular campaign staff would have missed.

If Olivia is in the professional business of manipulating and reading emotion, Mellie contributes equally to the political success or failure of her husband, despite her decision to leave behind a professional career as a talented lawyer to fulfill the apparently subservient role of First Lady. In many ways, it is Mellie, in collaboration with Olivia, who safeguards her husband's continued reign in the White House. We learn via flashback that Cyrus convinced Mellie that she could not continue her career and support her husband as First Lady at the same time.[57] The suggestion here is that the wife should support the husband's intelligence and strategy and take a passive role, gaining her satisfaction only from her fulltime position as Fitz's wife. Mellie, however, applies dogged determination to securing her position as First Lady and in fact is involved in a conspiracy to rig the election that puts her husband in office without his knowledge. Although Mellie is disgusted by her husband's affair with Olivia, she knows, as Dreher writes, "that going along with the program would guarantee her sociopolitical status. *Status* is her love—not her husband."[58] In Season One's "Grant: For the People" Fitz's reputation is damaged by the release of a sex tape, seemingly of Fitz with a young intern (although it is later revealed to be with Olivia).[59] Mellie is less hurt by the fact of her husband cheating (as she is aware of his affair with Olivia) than by the failure of Olivia to satisfy Fitz and keep him away from other women,[60] telling Olivia, "I do my job," but telling Olivia on the other hand that she "let down the team" by *not* sleeping with Fitz and allowing him to be tempted by the intern.[61] In an effort to preserve her "job"

Mellie once again comes up with a creative solution, demonstrating her genius in political strategy by maximizing her image as adoring wife and mother and appealing to the public's emotions. Mellie hatches a plan to announce that the sex tape depicts herself and Fitz in the act of conceiving a child. She informs Fitz that they will have to start trying immediately to actually get pregnant and that when she tells the media that it was her on the tape she "will also share my outrage about the replaying of our private moment in such a public, reckless and irresponsible manner ... and how upsetting it has been for our family at such a fragile time, given that I'm newly pregnant."[62] Mellie knows exactly how to spin her explanation of the sex tape to boost the public's sympathy and turn a negative situation into an opportunity for public engagement. When Mellie informs Fitz of her plan she slyly says, "You could look a little bit happier, honey, we did just save your presidency."[63] From the positions of wife and mistress respectively, Mellie and Olivia are able to enhance Fitz's public image using their emotional literacy. Interestingly, Mellie, like Olivia, must suppress her own emotional reaction to Fitz's cheating in order to redirect her emotive capacities into calculated political strategy.

Genre and Intelligence: Finding the Melodramatic Genius

Just as Mellie and Olivia utilize their emotional literacy within the masculine sphere of political strategy, *Scandal* recasts the genius figure within the sphere of melodrama. Genius has traditionally been represented in supposedly masculine genres, such as crime procedurals. As Christine Gledhill writes, melodrama on the other hand, is generally regarded as being primarily targeted towards women because of its "socially mandated feminine concerns: family, domestic life, personal relationships and "feelings" which frequently run to tears."[64] As Jason Mitell points out, certain audience reactions are regarded as masculine even if female viewers also enjoy a show or genre.[65] For example the "analytic puzzle-solving common to mysteries" represents a kind of "forensic fandom" that, regardless of the actual gender of fans, is "culturally coded as masculine ... the same way that sentimental crying is regarded as effeminate."[66] In this way, television genre reinforces "the long-standing stereotypical mapping of rationality as male and emotion as female, or the gendered dichotomy between thinking and feeling."[67] Even when a detective in a procedural is female, as in *Prime Suspect* or *The Killing* for example, her success is largely due to her ability to think along rational lines and focus her energies on the case at hand. In fact *Prime Suspect* gained respect by consciously separating itself from so-called women's genres with even its title suggesting that the show "sees itself first and foremost as a crime drama."[68]

In the contemporary television landscape, prestigious dramas emphasize their serialized elements to reinforce their value over procedurals due to the assumed higher degree of intellectual attention and commitment that serials require from their audiences.[69] Despite this connection between soap operas and prime-time prestigious dramas in terms of their serialized structure, Newman and Levine argue that quality dramas consciously attempt to downplay feminine subject matter, especially romantic narratives, in order to distinguish themselves from culturally debased melodramatic soap operas.[70] These shows do not completely ignore romantic narratives but "the degree of prominence of relationships in their storytelling potentially degrades their Quality status in relation to the most distinguished serials."[71] Jason Mittell invokes Linda Williams' redefinition of melodrama to counter this argument, suggesting that in fact many highly acclaimed shows include more subtle aspects of melodrama.[72] Williams argues that melodrama has been misrepresented by definitions that focus on the aspect of "excess," especially "in terms of degrees of emotion."[73] She claims that melodrama is now "so basic to all forms of popular moving-picture entertainment" that the notion of excess no longer applies as a defining characteristic.[74] Indeed, Williams notes that even a series such as *The Wire*, praised for its gritty realism, includes melodramatic aspects because, for example, it produces an emotional connection between the audience and characters that we see, through the qualities of serial television, continually repeating the same mistakes and being unable to escape their circumstances.[75] Nevertheless, the perception remains that stories that focus on romance and sexuality in particular target women and that this narrowcasting reinforces the separation between trivialized feminine television and the masculine, public sphere.[76]

Tied to this perception around feminine and masculine genres is the notion that television targeted specifically at women minimizes the intelligence of female characters by focusing on their love lives over their professional lives, even when they are in high-powered jobs.[77] In *Scandal*, much like in Shonda Rhymes's previous show *Grey's Anatomy*, which focused on female doctors, Olivia's position as a melodramatic heroine embroiled in a love triangle does not prevent her from being simultaneously represented as a political and public relations genius. Although the show openly embraces its melodramatic conventions and high emotion, refusing to even attempt to replicate the subtlety of quieter, more low-key quality dramas, it nevertheless paints both Olivia and Mellie as highly intelligent women. In this way, it defies genre expectations and locates the genius within the melodrama.

Conclusion: Reinventing the Television Genius?

Scandal complicates stereotypes not only of what a strategic genius on television should look like in terms of gender and race, but also of what capabilities and qualities that genius should embody and in which genres (s)he should appear. The show recasts feminine emotional literacy away from the figure of the hysterical melodramatic heroine and into the role of controlled political strategy, while divorcing the trope of televisual intelligence from the characteristics of the nerd. Although some aspects of its racial discourse merit further attention and debate, the show provocatively suggests that geniuses—like gladiators—do indeed sometimes wear suits, or even dresses.

Notes

1. Karin E. Westman, "Beauty and the Geek: Changing Gender Stereotypes on the *Gilmore Girls*," in *Geek Chic: Smart Women in Popular Culture*, ed. Sherrie A. Inness (New York: Palgrave Macmillan, 2007), 11–16; Sherrie A. Innes, "Introduction. Who Remembers Sabrina? Intelligence, Gender and the Media," in *Geek Chic: Smart Women in Popular Culture*, ed. Sherrie A. Inness (New York: Palgrave Macmillan, 2007), 4.

2. Linda Williams, "Mega-Melodrama! Vertical and Horizontal Suspensions of the 'Classical,'" *Modern Drama* 55, no. 4 (2012): 525.

3. Christine Gledhill, "Speculations on the Relationship Between Soap Opera and Melodrama," in *The Gender and Media Reader*, ed. Mary Celeste Kearney (New York: Routledge, 2012), 466.

4. Ibid.

5. Genevieve Lloyd, *The Man of Reason: "Male" and "Female" in Western Philosophy* (London: Routledge, 1993), 32, 104.

6. Innes, 1–2.

7. Westman, 11–16.

8. Innes, 4.

9. Ibid.

10. Westman, 11.

11. Ibid. 16.

12. Ibid. 16–18.

13. Deborah Caslav Covino, *Amending the Abject Body: Aesthetic Makeovers in Medicine and Popular Culture* (Albany: State University of New York Press, 2004), 46–50, 109, cited in Westman, 16.

14. Sharon Sutherland and Sarah Swan, "Raising the Bar: Brilliant Women Lawyers from Ann Kelsey to Miranda Hobbes," in *Geek Chic: Smart Women in Popular Culture*, ed. Sherrie A. Inness (New York: Palgrave Macmillan, 2007), 140.

15. Kimberley Springer, "Divas, Evil Black Bitches, and Bitter Black Women African-American Women in Postfeminist and Post-Civil Rights Popular Culture," in *Feminist Television Criticism A Reader*, 2d ed, ed. Charlotte Brunsdon and Lynn Spigel (New York: Open University Press, 2008), 81–82.

16. Kwakiutl L. Dreher, "*Scandal* and Black Women in Television," in *African Americans on Television Race-ing for Ratings*, ed. David J. Leonard and Lisa A. Guerrero (Santa Barbara: Praeger, 2013), 396.

17. Nina Cartier, "Black Women On-Screen as Future Texts: A Look at Black Pop Culture Representations," *Cinema Journal* 53, no. 4 (2014): 154.
18. Cartier, 144–155.
19. Patricia Hill Collins, *Black Sexual Politics African Americans, Gender and the New Racism* (New York: Routledge, 2004), 139.
20. Ibid.
21. Ibid.
22. Ibid., 140.
23. Ibid.
24. Zahir McGhee, "Mama Said Knock You Out," *Scandal*, season 3, episode 15, directed by Tony Goldwyn, aired March 27, 2014, on ABC. Broadcast television.
25. Ibid.
26. Ibid.
27. Ibid.
28. Ibid.
29. Collins, 140.
30. Karen Jones, "Gender and Rationality," in *The Oxford Handbook of Rationality*, ed. Alfred R. Mele and Piers Rawling (Oxford: Oxford University Press, 2004), 301.
31. Lloyd, xix.
32. Lloyd, 104; Jones, 302.
33. Lloyd, 104.
34. Sander L. Gilman et al., introduction to *Hysteria Beyond Freud*, ed. Sander L. Gilman et al. (Berkeley: University of California Press, 1993), xv.
35. Christine Battersby, *Gender and Genius Towards a Feminist Aesthetics* (London: The Women's Press, 1989), 3.
36. Lloyd, 104.
37. Ibid.
38. Jones, 302.
39. Ibid, 304.
40. Alison Jaggar, "Love and Knowledge: Emotion in Feminist Epistemology," in *Women, Knowledge, and Reality*, ed. A. Garry and M. Pearsall (New York: Routledge, 1996), cited in Jones, 304.
41. Ibid.
42. Lloyd, 105.
43. Battersby, 3.
44. Heather Mitchell, "The Other Woman," *Scandal*, season 2, episode 2, directed by Stephen Craig, aired October 4, 2012, on ABC. *Scandal the Complete Second Season* (New York: ABC Studios, 2014), DVD.
45. Jenna Bans, "The Trail," *Scandal*, season 1, episode 6, directed by Tom Verica, aired May 10, 2012, on ABC. *Scandal the Complete First Season* (New York: ABC Studios, 2013), DVD.
46. Ibid.
47. Ibid.
48. Ibid.
49. Ibid.
50. Ibid.
51. Ibid.
52. Ibid.
53. Ibid.
54. Tania Modelski, *Loving with a Vengeance: Mass Produced Fantasies for Women* (New York: Routledge, 2008) and Charlotte Brunsdon, "*Crossroads:* Notes on a Soap Opera," in *Regarding Television*, ed. E. Ann Kaplan (Los Angeles: American Film Institute, 1983), 95–

113, cited in Micheal Z. Newman and Elana Levine, *Legitimating Television Media Convergnece and Cultural Status* (New York and London: Routledge 2012), 91.
	55. McGhee, "Mama Said Knock You Out."
	56. Ibid.
	57. Peter Nowalk, "Everything's Coming Up Mellie," *Scandal,* season 3, episode 7, directed by Michael Katleman, aired November 14, 2013, on ABC. Broadcast television.
	58. Dreher, 394.
	59. Shonda Rhymes, "Grant: For the People," *Scandal,* season 1, episode 7, directed by Roxann Dawson, aired May 17, 2012, on ABC. *Scandal the Complete First Season* (New York: ABC Studios, 2013), DVD.
	60. Dreher, 395.
	61. Rhymes, "Grant: For the People."
	62. Ibid.
	63. Ibid.
	64. Gledhill, 466.
	65. Jason Mittell, "Serial Melodrama," in *Complex TV: The Poetics of Contemporary Television Storytelling*, pre-publication edition (MediaCommons Press, 2012–13), paragraph 25.
	66. Ibid.
	67. Ibid.
	68. Deborah Jermyn, "Women with a Mission: Lynda La Plante, DCI Jane Tennison and the reconfiguration of TV crime drama," in *Feminist Television Criticism A Reader,* 2d ed., ed. Charlotte Brunsdon and Lynn Spigel (New York: Open University Press, 2008), 59.
	69. Michael Z. Newman and Elana Levine, *Legitimating Television Media and Cultural Status* (New York: Routledge, 2012), 80–81.
	70. Ibid., 81–82, 94–98.
	71. Ibid., 97.
	72. Mittell, paragraphs 20–21.
	73. Williams, 525.
	74. Ibid., 526.
	75. Ibid., 534–537.
	76. Christine Scodari, "Sex and the Sitcom: Gender and Genre in Millennial Television," in *The Sitcom Reader: America Viewed and Skewed*, ed. Mary M. Dalton and Laura R. Linder (New York: State University of New York Press, 2005), 241–242.
	77. Ibid., 244.

References

Bans, Jenna. "The Trail." *Scandal*, season 1 episode 6. Directed by Tom Verica. Aired May 10, 2012, on ABC. *Scandal the Complete First Season,* DVD. New York: ABC Studios, 2013.
Battersby, Christine. *Gender and Genius Towards a Feminist Aesthetics*. London: The Women's Press, 1989.
Cartier, Nina. "Black Women On-Screen as Future Texts: A Look at Black Pop Culture Representations." *Cinema Journal* 53, no. 4 (2014): 150–157.
Collins, Patricia Hill. *Black Sexual Politics African Americans, Gender and the New Racism*. New York: Routledge, 2004.
Dreher, Kwakiutl L. "*Scandal* and Black Women in Television." In *African Americans on Television Race-ing for Ratings*, edited by David J. Leonard and Lisa A. Guerrero, 390–401. Santa Barbara: Praeger, 2013.
Gledhill, Christine. "Speculations on the Relationship Between Soap Opera and Melo-

drama." In *The Gender and Media Reader*, edited by Mary Celeste Kearney, 464–479. New York: Routledge, 2012.

Innes, Sherrie A. "Introduction. Who Remembers Sabrina? Intelligence, Gender and the Media." In *Geek Chic: Smart Women in Popular Culture*, edited by Sherrie A. Inness, 1–10. New York: Palgrave Macmillan, 2007.

Jermyn, Deborah. "Women with a Mission: Lynda La Plante, DCI Jane Tennison and the Reconfiguration of TV Crime Drama." In *Feminist Television Criticism A Reader*, 2d ed. edited by Charlotte Brunsdon and Lynn Spigel, 57–71. New York: Open University Press, 2008.

Jones, Karen. "Gender and Rationality." In *The Oxford Handbook of Rationality*. edited by Alfred R. Mele and Piers Rawling, 301–319. Oxford: Oxford University Press, 2004

Lloyd, Genevieve. *The Man of Reason":Male" and "Female" in Western Philosophy*. London: Routledge, 1993.

McGhee, Zahir. "Mama Said Knock You Out." *Scandal*, season 3, episode 15. Directed by Tony Goldwyn. Aired March 27, 2014, on ABC. Broadcast Television.

Mitchell, Heather. "The Other Woman." *Scandal*, season 2, episode 2. Directed by Stephen Craig. Aired October 4, 2012, on ABC. *Scandal the Complete Second Season,* DVD. New York: ABC Studios, 2014.

Mittell, Jason. *Complex TV: The Poetics of Contemporary Television Storytelling*, pre-publication edition. MediaCommons Press, 2012–13.

Nowalk, Peter. "Everything's Coming Up Mellie." *Scandal*, season 3, episode 7. Directed by Michael Katleman. Aired November 14, 2013, on ABC. Broadcast television.

Rhymes, Shonda. "Grant: For the People." *Scandal*, season 1, episode 7. Directed by Roxann Dawson. Aired May 17, 2012, on ABC. *Scandal the Complete First Season*, DVD. New York: ABC Studios, 2013.

Sander L. Gilman, Helen King, Roy Porter, G. S. Rousseau and Elaine Showalter. Introduction to *Hysteria Beyond Freud*, edited by Sander L. Gilman, Helen King, Roy Porter, G. S. Rousseau and Elaine Showalter. Berkeley: University of California Press, 1993.

Scodari, Christine. "Sex and the Sitcom: Gender and Genre in Millennial Television." In *The Sitcom Reader: America Viewed and Skewed*, edited by Mary M. Dalton and Laura R. Linder, 241–252. New York: State University of New York Press, 2005.

Springer, Kimberley. "Divas, Evil Black Bitches, and Bitter Black Women African-American Women in Postfeminist and Post-Civil Rights Popular Culture.' In *Feminist Television Criticism A Reader*, 2d ed. edited by Charlotte Brunsdon and Lynn Spigel, 72–91. New York: Open University Press, 2008.

Sutherland, Sharon, and Sarah Swan. "Raising the Bar: Brilliant Women Lawyers from Ann Kelsey to Miranda Hobbes." In *Geek Chic: Smart Women in Popular Culture,* edited by Sherrie A. Inness, 137–152. New York: Palgrave Macmillan, 2007.

Westman, Karin E. "Beauty and the Geek: Changing Gender Stereotypes on the *Gilmore Girls*." In *Geek Chic: Smart Women in Popular Culture*, edited by Sherrie A. Inness, 11–30. New York: Palgrave Macmillan, 2007.

Williams, Linda. "Mega-Melodrama! Vertical and Horizontal Suspensions of the 'Classical.'" *Modern Drama* 55, no. 4 (2012): 523–543.

"I'm not a girl, I'm a genius"[1]

The Creative Souls of Brenda Leigh Johnson and Cristina Yang

Cecilia J. Pang

In Oscar Wilde's *The Picture of Dorian Gray*, Lord Henry proclaims, "No woman is a genius."[2] Indeed, throughout history, there has been scant mention of women geniuses; there is no recognized woman genius classical composer, only one woman (Marie Curie) is cited on the *Ranker's* list of genius thinkers in history,[3] and until very recently no woman had ever won a Fields Medal, the highest honor in mathematics.[4] Nevertheless, according to Pope John Paul II, "our time in particular awaits the manifestation of that 'genius' which belongs to women, and which can ensure sensitivity for human beings in every circumstance: because they are human."[5] Likewise, the time has come for contemporary television to create more full-blooded female characters, which are not entirely subjugated, sexualized, or stereotyped. The characters Brenda Leigh Johnson from *The Closer* and Cristina Yang from *Grey's Anatomy* are two rare examples that exemplify intelligence incarnate: Brenda is known as the closer because she is a master of deduction, brilliant in cajoling confessions from criminals. Cristina, on the other hand, is a remarkable, respectable researcher and cardio-thoracic surgeon, and a walking encyclopedia of medical knowledge. Although they do not fit into a conventional definition of genius, that is, those who possess superhuman abilities or hyper-extraordinary accomplishments, I consider Brenda and Cristina female geniuses because they fully embody the extrinsic personality profile of female creative genius, as summarized by Gene N. Landrum in his book, *Profiles of Female Genius*:

> An obsessively driven, intuitive thinking Promethean spirit who has a renegade mentality and is comfortable with ambiguity and risk-taking. She has an awesome self-esteem, which empowers her to be independent and self-reliant. Because of her excessive energy and work ethic her peers label her "workaholic," and an optimistic "will-to-power" attitude gives her a unique charismatic persona that attracts numerous disciples who assist her in her maniacal drive to the top.[6]

Brenda and Cristina have a similar compulsion to excel, "type A" work ethic, rebellious personality against the establishment, risk-taking temperament, intuitive disposition, and charismatic magnetism, and they are both driven and competitive to a fault, operating with innovative styles not normally found on television. All these traits make them exceptional and memorable.

Analysis of these two characters is particularly useful because *The Closer* has completed its entire run of seven seasons (2005–2012), and even though *Grey's Anatomy* continues to air (2005-present), the storyline of Cristina Yang is finished due to the recent exit of actress Sandra Oh. This allows us to evaluate the entire character arcs of Brenda Leigh Johnson and Cristina Yang from their arrivals, as Deputy Chief at Los Angeles Police Department (LAPD) and Surgical Intern at the Seattle Grace Hospital, respectively, to their departures. Moreover, while Brenda and Cristina differ in backgrounds (southern belle vs. Korean American), journeys, and narratives, they both demonstrate a devotion to their professions that seems deeply rooted in masculinity, as well as an allegiance to femininity in their pursuit of romantic relationships. This chapter seeks, through textual analysis, to compare their professional development against their personal experiences, and to identify if and how intelligence factors in their handling of work-life balance, especially in relation to gender concerns such as sexuality, beauty, marriage, and motherhood. In conclusion, I will suggest that the phenomenon of the female genius also appears in other well-known TV shows, indicative of a trend that in twenty-first century United States culture, more and more women seek self-fulfillment through the pursuit of individualistic success in careers, without having to renounce relationships or families.

The Closer is a police procedural created by James Duff that delineates a morally ambiguous middle-aged brainiac white divorcee running a racially diverse, mostly male, squad. In contrast, *Grey's Anatomy* is a medical drama created by Shonda Rhimes that depicts the growth and development of a group of highly competitive and slightly dysfunctional surgical interns and residents. Both shows are character driven ensemble dramas featuring strong female characters whose professional lives intersect with their personal struggles. Both are also considered products of the post-feminist era where the presumption of equality for women is taken for granted, and success beyond that is a result of individual initiative.[7] Therefore, even though both *The Closer* and *Grey's Anatomy* follow the formulaic prime time television series structure, they are unique in their portrayals of strong women characters that are smart and beautiful, proper and flawed, serious and funny. In an interview with the *New York Times*, Kyra Sedgwick described her attraction and empathy to Brenda's contradictions: "She was just totally flawed and yet extremely capable, and the dichotomy of being someone incredibly intuitive about others while completely clueless about herself appealed to me. I could relate."[8]

Historically, TV medical dramas have progressed from idealism to realism; the characters in the earliest TV medical dramas reinforce positive stereotypes, while those in later examples of the genre demonstrate both fallible behaviors and moral ambiguity.[9] *Dr. Kildare* is a representative of the former, whereas *ER* is an example of the latter. Crime procedurals have followed a similar track where *Police Woman* is a model of idealism and *Cagney & Lacey* is emblematic of realism. Nevertheless, according to Rebecca Collins, the portrayal of women in prime time television in the twenty-first century remains mostly stereotyped and sexualized,[10] which makes *The Closer* and *Grey's Anatomy* particularly refreshing. The audience's warm welcome of the former show helped position TNT as one of the top providers of basic cable programming and the success of *Grey's Anatomy* has led its creator, Shonda Rhimes, to rule Thursday night with multiple shows running on ABC (*Grey's Anatomy*, *Scandal*, and *Private Practice*).

Although James Duff and Shonda Rhimes did not set out to portray these Brenda and Cristina as geniuses, it is important to note that in the fictional world these types of characters have popped up repeatedly in cultural media. According to the TV Tropes Wiki, a website created by fans for fans, Brenda Leigh Johnson is considered a representative of the *Southern Fried Genius* whereby the character "may have the same down-home sensibilities or otherwise act like a good ol' southerner, but is very, very smart."[11] Indeed, her southern drawls of the saccharine expression "Thank yew, thank yew very much" might induce occasional mimicry from her crew but they are actually her manipulative devices to disarm/command someone with kindness.

In contrast, Cristina is a classic example of the "*Insufferable Genius*'" trope, whose prototype is one who's "very talented, knows he's very talented, and doesn't mind telling you repeatedly what a talented person he is."[12] Cristina not only boasts incessantly that she's the one with the answers, but she also insists on winning every competition and bet. Her encounter with the examiner at the oral board in "Let the Bad Times Roll" is the perfect illustration of her unbearable precocious arrogance:

CRISTINA: You know what? Oh, God. I can answer these questions anyway you want using medical techniques from any era. So how about if we just ... you know, pick a decade you are comfortable with and go from there.

DR. THOMAS: Well then, it's been a pleasure being witness to such a genius. I can now finally retire knowing that such advanced and creative minds work in the surgical field.[13]

Despite these conventional conceits, ultimately, it is the smartness, complexity, capability, and character flaws of Brenda and Cristina, conceived and crafted by their creators, that compel our interest to stay tuned. Shonda Rhimes asserts, "I think for me the excitement or the interest is that it feels like one of the few times on a big scale we are celebrating smart. We are making stars out of people because they are brainiacs, not athletic or pretty."[14] Empowering women and exalting intelligence are main points of attraction in *The Closer* and *Grey's Anatomy*.

Undeniably, both Brenda Leigh Johnson and Cristina Yang are highly intelligent characters with outstanding achievements. In addition to having worked at the CIA and the Atlanta Police Department prior to LAPD, Brenda is also a polyglot who speaks German, Russian, and Czech (although her language skills are rendered useless in the Hispanic-dominated Los Angeles). Interestingly, she usually cloaks her smartness behind the persona of a sweet savory southern belle. Cristina, on the other hand, appears to be the sour snarky Dragon Lady who loves nothing more than parading her precocity and boasting of her brilliance. A graduate of Smith College, she earned her Ph.D. in Biochemistry from the University of California, Berkeley, and her M.D. from Stanford University, where she graduated first of her class. Both characters realize Landrum's depiction of an "obsessively driven" career woman who would do anything to achieve her goals. Brenda is devoted to probing and penetrating until she solves her cases, whereas Cristina is determined to become a successful cardiothoracic surgeon.

"Trading the familiar for the unfamiliar"[15]

Traditionally many people equate genius with extremely high verbal and mathematical intelligence; however, Lewis M. Terman, who developed the revised "Stanford-Binet" IQ test, proved that having a high Intelligence Quotient does not necessarily equate to being a genius. Robert W. Weisberg proposes expanding the concept of genius to include creativity and posits the idea of "ordinary thinking to produce extraordinary outcomes."[16] In order to assess creativity, Weisberg believes one should develop skills in *divergent thinking*, which uses "fluency, flexibility, and originality to 'diverge' from what we know, to produce many original ideas" instead of *convergent thinking*, which uses "information to 'converge' on a single solution or idea."[17] This coincides with Landrum's thesis that creativity emanates from within, from an inner driving force, an inner knowing or intuition, which has its foundation in an unwavering self-image.[18]

According to Nancy Andreasen, the original ideas of divergent thinking are often developed during a REST state: when one is doing one thing and not thinking about what the mind is doing.[19] Brenda's character in *The Closer* exemplifies this concept as she often solves her murder cases while she is multi-tasking or doing something else entirely unrelated to the case; often an 'eureka' moment strikes and she hears something that helps her make the association. Her creative process is based mostly on her intuition and on listening, through which she connects the divergent dots. Moreover, she often conducts interrogations by relying on her instincts and following on glimmers of clues. She disarms the suspects first with sweet courtesy and charm, and then pounds with threats and intimidation. She is brilliant in running the gamut of emotional tactics to flatter, beguile, entrap, wheedle, coerce, scare, badger, or deceive a suspect to achieve her objective. In addition, she is facile with perceiving non-verbal signals, such as body language and facial expressions, and is deft at responding to the emotions of others. Above all, Brenda is first and foremost an intuitive thinker, whose strength lies in her rational approach to solving cases.

Cristina Yang also relies on intrinsic thinking to solve problems. For example, in "The Becoming," when Preston Burke suffers from a hand injury, Cristina understands his lashing out at her is misplaced anger arising from his own frustrations, so she responds by devising plans to help him rehabilitate. She schemes for him to operate first on chickens, then on corpses, and finally suggests acting as his surrogate hand in the Operating Room to perform the surgeries. Unlike Brenda however, her creativity leans more toward accidental than intuitive, through trial and error, rather befitting for a scientist. For example, in "Deny, Deny, Deny," she accidentally observes a patient downing non-prescription pills, and smartly diagnoses the patient as having Munchhausen Syndrome; or in "Perfect Storm," due to a power outage in the hospital, Cristina has to learn how to operate on a patient by listening to his heart, which also demonstrates that Cristina thrives in crisis-mode. Even her greatest achievement with the heart conduit research arrives by accident. Nevertheless, even though Cristina's creativity might have been exhibited in accidental discoveries, because of her single-mindedness toward her goal, she is able to overcome difficulties to arrive at innovative diagnoses.

Furthermore, both Brenda and Cristina excel in regulating their emotions, possibly because their jobs involve life and death situations so they must be able to keep their emotions under control. And as high achievers, they are confident and self-motivated, so they understand how to direct their emotions to optimal advantage. Most importantly, they simply prefer to employ a "thinking" strategy to problem resolution, which echoes Landrum's analyses of female geniuses, the majority of whom utilize the more "male-like," thinking approach to decision-making.[20]

"Step forward into the unknown and assume it will be brilliant"[21]

Unquestionably, Brenda and Cristina meet the qualifications of what Landrum terms "creative renegades," who "go where others fear to tread."[22] They are driven by a potent self-confidence, which in turn is propelled by passion in whatever they do. Brenda is fearless when it comes to tearing down the bureaucratic walls with her artless and unbending lines of inquiries. Above all, she smartly solves problems by thinking outside the box. However, sometimes Brenda's creativity leads her to take some license with the law, as seen in her unorthodox interrogative methods, including discouraging a suspect's right to counsel. At other times, she releases suspects into hostile environments, knowing they will be killed. In "Tijuana Brass," she even puts a corrupt Mexican police officer in jail under a false identity because she knows there is a hit on the alleged murderer. Nevertheless, her risk-taking and come-what-may attitude do occasionally put her and her division at risk. The final season's storyline is rife with legal complications because she frees a killer in gang territory, again knowing he would be murdered. Ultimately, she pays a huge price and loses her job over this act of defiance, which also leads the series to its inevitable end. James Duff, the show's creator, argues, "She may violate a rule or two, but she doesn't break the law."[23] Indeed, she perhaps pushes legal boundaries, but arguably does not cross those lines. She merely seeks ways to creatively use legal ambiguities to her advantage.

Likewise, Cristina Yang is a brazen risk-taker who loves breaking the rules, and operates through a macro-vision lens. In "Who's Zoomin' Who?" she and Izzy, a fellow surgical intern, decide to perform an unauthorized autopsy in search of the cause of death. Dr. Bailey, their supervisor, is furious to catch them in action and admonishes them harshly: "You broke the law, you could be arrested for assault. Do you like jail? The hospital could be sued. I could lose my license, my job. I like my job. Did you think about any of this before you started cutting the poor man's body?" Cristina's reaction to Bailey's tirade is simply, "we want to run some tests," because "at this point, what could it hurt?"[24] Bailey has to concede because as always, Cristina is right. Cristina's rebellious mentality and resilient attitude stems from an incomparable self-esteem that forms her fierceness and fearlessness, especially towards authority. Interestingly, later on, in "Putting on the Ritz," when she catches her intern Shane perform a complex procedure on his own in the ER, Cristina compliments Shane by calling him a shark because all good surgeons, like her, are sharks—they see what they want and do whatever it takes to get it. She even encourages him to decide on how to continue the unauthorized surgery and helps him complete it. Cristina's receptivity to Shane not only veers diametrically opposite from her reply to Bailey, but it further reflects her abhorrence of old dogma and proclivity for the road less traveled.

Furthermore, neither Brenda nor Cristina is a born leader. They become transformative leaders through their intelligence, inventiveness, and inspiration. Brenda has to prove her mettle to earn the trust of her squad. In the pilot of *The Closer,* shortly after the arrival of Chief Brenda Leigh Johnson, all the members of Priority Homicide squad submit requests to be transferred to other departments. Brenda simply responds, "They may dislike me because I'm new [but] once I get to work and they see me in action, they will have a whole list of reasons to hate my guts."[25] Throughout season one, we see how she earns the squad's respect and settles in her leadership position. Despite her unorthodox policing, her leadership qualities are summed up in Sergeant Gabriel's celebratory victory toast in the season three finale: "For keeping the team together despite some pretty hefty pressure, and for trusting her instincts, about us too, by the way, and for how she always works so hard to get her man: I say, Hail to the Chief."[26] In short, Brenda not only excels in collaboration and team building, she also fights for her brood like a mother hen; above all, she is a role model to her squad in how she goes after the perpetrator relentlessly and creatively.

In *Grey's Anatomy*, Cristina Yang started as "a grunt, a nobody, the lowest at the bottom of the surgical food chain," whose sole purpose in life is to get ahead: "I'd rip your face off if it meant I got to scrub in."[27] She will do anything to achieve her goals—steal patients from another department to bolster her surgical skills, threaten a roommate in exchange for a professional favor, and even offer her boyfriend Owen to her mentor Dr. Teddy Altman just so Teddy would stay on in Seattle to continue training her. As the series progresses, she grows to become a "brutal but effective" resident who both terrorizes and inspires her interns. As her last mentor Dr. Thomas prophesizes:

> Mediocre surgeons will see you and feel themselves wilting in your shadow. Do not shrink to console them. Do not look for friends here. You won't find them. None of these people has the capacity to understand you. They never will. If you're lucky, one day when you're old and shriveled like me, you'll find a young surgeon

with little regard for anything but their craft, and you'll train them like I trained you. Until then, read a good book. You have greatness in you, Cristina. Don't disappoint.[28]

Her leadership journey brings to mind the Chinese idiom 'the blue comes from the indigo plant but is bluer than the plant itself" which figuratively refers to how a student surpasses the master.

Renegades as they might be, Brenda and Cristina are two of the television's most beloved and incomparable characters because they remain their own women, at whatever cost. According to Weisberg, the characteristics for a creative individual include "broad interests, independence of judgment, self-confidence, intuition, and a firm sense of self."[29] Both Brenda and Cristina embody self-confidence and independence of judgment. Brenda probably has an edge over Cristina with intuition, but Cristina definitely leads with her firm sense of self. However, interestingly, neither displays broad interests, as they are always steadfast with their tasks at hand, and their sight on how to transform the world.

"Life is about making choices"[30]

In addition to having a vision for change, the road to genius requires exceptional effort. Malcolm Gladwell contends in his book *Outliers* that the key to any success is 10,000 hours of practice. Statistics reveal that most geniuses are indeed workaholics, but they are mostly men because "women tend to choose work life balance rather than the pursuit of eminence.[31] Indisputably, both Brenda and Cristina are workaholics.

However, unlike their predecessors Murphy Brown or Ally McBeal, who are also driven career women but who are single, Brenda and Cristina show that they can *choose* to have both career and family, embrace traditional womanhood, and maintain high-powered jobs. In fact, it is James Duff's intent to show how Brenda handles her work-life balance by crafting a central theme around each season that juxtaposes the criminal case with Brenda's personal story. To that end, Brenda's relationship with Fritz is possibly one of the healthiest relationships in television programming, as their characters are from friendship to courtship to live-in partnership to marriage. Nevertheless, Fritz's high tolerance and indulgence of Brenda's compulsive obsession with her work is not an acknowledgment that her job is more important than his, an FBI special agent, rather, it is an acceptance of her weathered individualism. Occasionally, he does run out of patience when she delays personal matters in favor of her cases, or especially when their work divisions cross lines. In "Live Wire," Fritz confronts

Brenda with her unconventional sleuthing after being sent on a needless and expensive stakeout that compromises three years of his work as an undercover agent:

> BRENDA: *(chases after Fritz until he stops)* Now, wait a minute! All I did—all I did was try to get the justice system to work for my victim! That is all I did!
> FRITZ: That is bullshit! You didn't do it for the justice system! You didn't do it for the victim! You did it to close your case! That's it! It's obviously the most important thing to you. It's clearly not me, and you know, maybe that's fine, but Brenda for once in your life, be honest with yourself!![32]

While Fritz accepts that Brenda's fixation on work might come before him, he never asks Brenda to change. His hope is for her to hold a mirror to face her nature.

Structurally, *Grey's Anatomy* also intersects the characters' public versus private spheres, but when it comes to work-life balance, Cristina has always maintained that surgery is her priority. *New York Magazine* wrote of the character: "There's probably no woman on TV right now more single-mindedly dedicated to her career than Cristina. It has long been her defining characteristic."[33] Therefore, it is not surprising that when Preston Burke proposes to her in "Wishin' and Hoping," she is hugely hesitant, taking eight days to decide, and even runs to Ellis Grey, mother of Meredith and a world famous surgeon, to ask if she can be a great surgeon and have a life. And when Burke leaves her at the altar because he realizes he's been trying to make Cristina into the woman he wants her to be, she feels humiliated but also relieved. Later, Cristina succumbs to marrying Owen Hunt because she is deeply in love with him even though Owen, too, expects Cristina to change, which reflects an old-fashioned patriarchal way of thinking. Ultimately, Cristina's marriage to Owen fails, not because of her enslavement to work but because of their varied values towards parenthood.

From the start, Cristina has always been abundantly clear about her position of not wanting to be a mother, though she is happy to be godmother to Meredith's and Callie's children. Twice she gets pregnant and twice she wants abortions. The first time turns out to be an ectopic pregnancy, but the second time she did terminate the birth—on screen. Her course of action not only reflects her staying true to her character, but also illustrates the psychological dichotomy a woman inevitably faces with such a controversial issue. In "Free Falling," when Meredith questions if she wanted to be a mom because she didn't go through with the abortion the first time, Cristina's reply profoundly articulates her struggle:

> I wish I wanted a kid. I wish I wanted one so bad because then this would be easy. I would be happy. I'd have Owen and my life wouldn't be a mess, but I don't. I don't want a kid. I don't wanna make jam, I don't wanna carpool, and I really, really,

don't wanna be a mother. I wanna be a surgeon. And please, get it. I need someone to get it. And I wish that person was Owen and that any minute he'd get it and show up for me. But that's not gonna happen. And you're my person, and I need you to be there at six o'clock tonight to hold my hand because I am scared, Mer, and sad because my husband doesn't get that. So, I need you to.[34]

Cristina's unapologetic resoluteness to exercise her right to choose as a woman is a reflection of how she stays strong and true to herself as well as her dedication to the path of genius. it is also what made her a revolutionary character in the TV landscape.

On the other hand, it is not entirely clear how Brenda Leigh Johnson feels about motherhood other than her showing maternal instincts through the caretaking of a stray cat whose gender she does not know. In "Head Over Heels," Fritz inquires if she has any interest in having kids; her evasive response that children should follow marriage not only reflects her stance on traditional values but also suggests she does want children, but only when she is ready and in her own time. However, when she is diagnosed with perimenopause and may not be able to have children, she is visibly distraught because the choice is taken away from her. Later she learns that what she actually suffers is Polycystic Syndrome, which can be reversible through surgery, thus suggesting she will be able to have children, if she so chooses.

Choice is central to the character make-up of Brenda Leigh Johnson and Cristina Yang in regards to work-life balance. In spite of their workaholic mentality, they prove that they can have both career and family, so long as it remains their choice to have or have not, even though in both their cases, they remain childless when their story lines end.

"Male brains confront challenges differently than female brains"[35]

Another common conception is that most geniuses, for all their brilliance, do not lead well-adjusted lives and are often slovenly in their personal lives. Interestingly, both Brenda and Cristina display similar genius/slob characteristics, which further reflect their priorities toward work over household commitments. In early episodes of *The Closer*, Brenda is often seen shuffling chaotic piles of clothes or candies or dirty dishes in drawers or closets. Still, her messiness pales in comparison to Cristina's slovenliness. The extreme clutter in Cristina's apartment resembles a hoarder's home. Unlike Brenda, who tries to hide her mess, Cristina proudly owns up to her grunginess in "Much Too Much": "I don't do laundry, I buy new underwear. See and uh, under the table? Six months of magazines I know I'll never read but I won't throw out. I don't wash dishes, vacuum, or put the toilet paper on the holder. I hired a maid once, she ran away crying. Uh ... the only things in my fridge are water, vodka, and diet soda. And I don't care."[36] Interestingly, messiness and poor cooking skills are commonly attributed, albeit somewhat cliché, masculine idiosyncrasies.

Yet Brenda and Cristina also maintain their femininity. Brenda Leigh Johnson is both a fragile flower and an action girl who bravely trots murder to scenes in heels and skirts. She has no sense of direction and cannot navigate the complicated maze of Los Angeles, is constantly looking for personal items such as keys or phone, and worries about getting older, turning forty, gaining weight, or putting together a decent outfit. She also enjoys her occasional big glass of Merlot; above all, she is a sugar junkie who likes her ding-dongs and always keeps a stash of candies and sweets in her drawer. Notably, all of the flaws (lack of sense of direction, obsession with body image, and addiction to sweets) align with stereotypical gendered feminine characteristics. More remarkable is how she employs femininity to play to her strengths as an interrogator. She uses her gender, as Jill Dolan maintains, "to catch her suspects. Her femininity is a tool in her box, rather than something defining. She can turn her feminine wiles on when she needs them to make progress, but the script makes sure the audience knows that she's making a choice, not falling back on biological destiny."[37] For instance, in "Till Death Do Us Part One," upon entering the interviewing room, she lets her hair down, drops a pen to exhibit her behind to the suspect, aping the dumb blonde game; or, in "About Face," in order to lure a suspect she dyes her hair blond and has a complete make-over so as to emulate the victim's look. Her transformation from her usual unflattering wardrobe of oversized sweaters and floral skirts into a skin tight dress even draws jeering and overt attention from her own squad, which not only creates fodder for comedy, but also serves as a sexist mockery of the gentlemen-prefer-blondes convention.

On the other hand, the way Brenda goes after her prey relentlessly, ruthlessly, and remorselessly while ruffling the regulative powers-that-be appears to be a stereotyped masculine approach. Notwithstanding, Brenda never tries to masculinize herself in order to appear strong and equal even when she is wielding a gun or braving potential rapists and murderers. According to James Duff, "We worked very hard at not making a woman succeed because she could act like a man, but making a woman succeed because she could be a woman."[38]

Unlike Brenda, Cristina does not know how to turn on her feminine wiles or 'speak girl.' Her feeble attempt to inquire how her fellow interns feel in "Piece of My Heart" only draws sneers and laughter because it is out of the norm for her. However, she is supremely confident with both her looks and her brains. In "Let It Be," as she gets ready for her first date with Preston Burke, she proudly proclaims she looks hot not only in scrubs, but also in her sleep. Later, in "This is How We Do It," Owen compliments the way she looks; her response, "Oh screw beautiful. I'm brilliant If you want to appease me compliment my brain,"[39] is not a refusal to be objectified physically as much as a preference to be honored intellectually as well. She is completely comfortable in her own skin.

Furthermore, in order to be taken seriously as a genius, Cristina feels she has to masculinize herself, for instance, by riding a motorcycle. As Kaela Jubas maintains, even her choice for surgery becomes a gendered identity.[40] In the pilot episode "A Hard Day's Night," her assertion that "surgery is hot. It's the marines. It's macho, it's hostile, it's hard work," reveals an inclination to compete and thrive in a man's profession.[41] Furthermore, Cristina's blatant use of sexuality as release is also more typically stereotyped as a masculine habit. Cristina's relationships with Preston Burke and Owen Hunt both start as sexual hookups. After the divorce from Owen, she has sex with her intern Shane purely for the physical release of tension and later with Dr. Parker at the Mayo Clinic just so she can fit into the new environment. She fully demonstrates the capability to separate emotions from sexuality, another commonly attributed masculine characteristic.

In spite of her penchant towards masculine gendered identification, Cristina is never portrayed as a tomboy; instead, "her femininity is emblazoned upon her body through lingerie."[42] It is also expressed through her soft, receptive, generous support in relationships. Her relationship with Meredith, her best friend and her "person," in particular reveals the doubleness that highlights her *feminine* quality as well as the predominant *masculine* energy in Cristina, which makes her protective of Meredith. Cristina has no qualms confronting Derek whenever she feels he makes Meredith miserable. The relationship between Derek, Meredith, and Cristina functions at times like a sexless love triangle. In her final episode, her parting words to Meredith, "He is very dreamy, but he is not the sun—you are,"[43] is particularly illuminating, and gives Meredith strength to stand up and fight for herself.

Both Brenda and Cristina triumphantly debunk the various gender myths of slovenliness versus neatness, beauty versus brain, and work versus domesticity and prove that they are entirely capable of competing, succeeding, and even leading in deeply macho worlds, without necessarily sacrificing their femininity.

"The end is the beginning is the end"[44]

As the above analysis illustrates, Brenda Leigh Johnson and Cristina Yang might not fit the myth of conventional geniuses who are renowned for their extreme IQs, extraordinary achievements, superior intellectual performances, or hyperactive minds; instead, they represent a more rounded definition of modern genius where creativity, intuition, self-esteem, and leadership matter as well as the drive to succeed. The phenomenon of this kind of female genius also appears in other well-known TV shows such as the forensic anthropologist Dr. Temperance Brennan in *Bones,* the crisis-manager Olivia Pope in *Scandal,* and Carrie Matthison, a CIA officer with bipolar disorder, in *Homeland.* This is indicative of a progressive movement towards a greater recognition of other visionary women, who seek self-actualizations through work, and whose successes are based on their will to excellence, personal empowerment, and work ethic—not their gender.

Brenda Leigh Johnson and Cristina Yang represent the kind of three-dimensional woman characters we want to see more of on television, women who are neither sexualized nor stereotyped, women who are both masculine and feminine, creative and risk-taking, assertive but vulnerable, self-determining but collaborative, devout workaholics, and who, on their own terms, choose or reject marriage and motherhood. In short, they are legacies in television programming because they prove that they can and do have it all.

Notes

1. Joanna Russ, *The Female Male* (Boston: Beacon Press, 1975), 65.
2. Oscar Wilde, *The Picture of Dorian Gray: An Annotated, Uncensored Edition* (Cambridge: Belknap Press of Harvard University Press, 2011), 114.
3. Walter Graves, "The Greatest Minds of All Time," *Ranker,* http://www.ranker.com/list/greatest-minds-of-all-time/walter-graves.
4. In July 2014, Maryam Mirzakhani became the first woman Fields medalist.
5. John Paul II, Apostolic letter Mulieris Dignitatem of the Supreme Pontiff John Paul II on the dignity and vocation of Women on the occasion of the Marian year (August 15, 1988), http://www.vatican.va/holy_father/john_paul_ii/apost_letters/documents/hf_jp-ii_apl_15081988_mulieris-dignitatem_en.html.
6. Gene N. Landrum, *Profiles of Female Geniuses: Thirteen Creative Women Who Changed the World* (New York: Prometheus, 1994), 396–7.
7. Bonnie J. Dow, *Prime-Time Feminism: Television, Media Culture, and the Women's Movement Since 1970* (Philadelphia: University of Philadelphia Press, 1996), 87–88.
8. Katherine Shattuck, "Playing it more Marlowe than Marple," *The New York Times,* November 26, 2010, http://www.nytimes.com/2010/11/28/arts/television/28kyra.html?pagewanted=all&_r=0.
9. Elena Strauman and Bethany Crandell Goodier, "Not Your Grandmother's Doctor Show: A Review of Grey's Anatomy, House, and Nip/Tuck," *Journal of Medical Humanities* (2008): 128, doi:10.1007/s10912-008-9055.3.
10. Rebecca L. Collins, "Content analysis of gender roles in media: where are we now and where should we go?" *Sex Roles* 64 (2011): 290, doi:10.1007/11199-010-9929-5.
11. "Southern Fried Genius," *TV Tropes Wiki,* accessed June 10, 2014, http://tvtropes.org/pmwiki/pmwiki.php/Main/SouthernFriedGenius.

12. "Insufferable Genius," *TV Tropes Wiki*, accessed June 10, 2014, http://tvtropes.org/pmwiki/pmwiki.php/Main/InsufferableGenius.

13. Matt Byrne, "Let the Bad Times Roll," *Grey's Anatomy*, season 8, episode 22, directed by Kevin McKidd, aired May 3, 2012, on ABC.

14. Katie Leone, "2014 Scripps Spelling Bee: 'Scandal,' 'Grey's Anatomy' creator Shonda Rhimes talks Bee love," ABC15.com, accessed June 12, 2014, http://www.abc15.com/nct/national/2014-scripps-spelling-bee-scandal-greys-anatomy-creator-shonda-rhimes-talks-bee-love.

15. Zoanne Clark, "Break on Through," *Grey's Anatomy*, season 2, episode 15, directed by David Paymer, aired January 29, 2006, on ABC.

16. Robert W. Weisberg, "Case Studies of Innovation: Ordinary Thinking Extraordinary Results," in *The International Handbook of Innovation*, edited by Larisa V. Shavinina (Oxford: Elsevier Science, 2003), 204.

17. Robert W. Weisberg, *Creativity: Beyond the Myth of Genius* (New York: W.H. Freeman, 1993), 60.

18. Landrum, *Profiles of Female Geniuses*, 41.

19. Nancy C. Andreasen, "Secrets of the Creative Brain," *The Atlantic Monthly*, June 25, 2014, http://www.theatlantic.com/features/archive/2014/06/secrets-of-the-creative-brain/372299/.

20. Landrum, *Profiles of Female Geniuses*, 128.

21. William Harper, "Fear (of the Unknown)," *Grey's Anatomy*, season 10, episode 24, directed by Tony Phelan, aired May 15, 2014, on ABC.

22. Landrum, *Profiles of Female Geniuses*, 86–106.

23. Sandra Gonzalez, "'The Closer' final season: Kyra Sedgwick and creator James Duff on the last six episodes," *Entertainment Weekly*, July 9, 2012, http://insidetv.ew.com/2012/07/09/the-closer-final-season-kyra-sedgwick.

24. Gabrielle Stanton and Harry Werksman, Jr., "Who's Zoomin Who?," *Grey's Anatomy*, season 1, episode 9, directed by Wendez Stanzler, aired May 22, 2005, on ABC.

25. James Duff, "Pilot," *The Closer*, season 1, episode 1, directed by Michael M. Robin, aired June 13, 2005, on ABC.

26. Mike Berchem, Story and Teleplay by Adam Belanoff and James Duff, "Next of Kin, Part 2," *The Closer*, season 3, episode 15, directed by James Duff, aired December 3, 2007, on ABC.

27. Shonda Rhimes, "The First Cut is the Deepest," *Grey's Anatomy*, season 1, episode 2, directed by Peter Orton, aired April 3, 2005, on ABC.

28. Jeannie Renshaw, "Beautiful Doom," *Grey's Anatomy*, season 9, episode 5, directed by Stephen Cragg, aired November 8, 2012, on ABC.

29. Weisberg, *Creativity: Beyond the Myth of Genius*, 72–73.

30. Mimi Schmir, "Let It Be," *Grey's Anatomy*, season 2, episode 8, directed by Lesli Linka Glatter, aired November 13, 2005, on ABC.

31. Sandra Upson and Laura Friedman, "Where are all the Female Geniuses?" *Scientific American Mind* 23, no. 5 (November 2012): 63–65, http://www.scientificamerican.com/article/where-are-all-the-female-geniuses/.

32. Steven Kane, "Live Wire," *The Closer*, season 4, episode 4, directed by Elodie Keene, aired August 4, 2008, on ABC.

33. Willa Paskin, "A Character on Grey's Anatomy Actually Had an Abortion on Prime-Time Television Last Night," *New York Magazine*, September 23, 2011, http://www.vulture.com/2011/09/someone_actually_had_an_aborti.html.

34. Tony Phalen and Joan Rater, "Free Falling," *Grey's Anatomy*, season 8, episode 1, directed by Rob Corn, aired September 22, 2011, on ABC.

35. Stacy Mckee, "What Is It About Men," *Grey's Anatomy*, season 8, episode 4, directed by Tom Verica, aired October 6, 2011, on ABC.

152   Part II. Gender and Genius

36. Gabrielle Stanton and Harry Werksman, Jr., "Much too Much," *Grey's Anatomy*, season 2, episode 10, directed by Wendy Stanzler, aired November 27, 2005, on ABC.

37. Jill Dolan, "Rise and Shine and The Closer," *The Feminist Spectator* (blog), September 25, 2006, http://www.thefeministspectator.com/2006/09/25/rise-and-shine-and-the-closer/.

38. Adam Bryant, "The Closer Finale Postmortem: Creator James Duff Talks Brenda's Final Confession," *TV Guide.com*, August 13, 2012, http://www.tvguide.com/news/closer-finale-postmortem-james-duff-1051943.aspx.

39. Peter Nowalk, "This is How We Do It," *Grey's Anatomy*, season 2, episode 8, directed by Ed Ornelas, aired March 24, 2011, on ABC.

40. Kaela Jubas, "Grey('s) Identity: Complications of Learning and Becoming a Popular Television Show," *Review of Education, Pedagogy, and Cultural Studies*, 35:2 (2013):135, doi:10.1080/10714413.2013.778653.

41. Shonda Rhimes, "A Hard Day's Night," *Grey's Anatomy*, season 1, episode 1, directed by Peter Horton, aired March 27, 2005, on ABC.

42. Claudia Mitchell and Jacqueline Weid-Walsh, eds., *Girl Culture: An Encyclopedia Volume 1* (Westport, CT: Greenwood Press, 2008), 8.

43. William Harper, "Fear (of the Unknown)."

44. Joan Rater, "The End is the Beginning is the End," *Grey's Anatomy*, season 9, episode 11, directed by Cherie Nowlan, aired January 17, 2013, on ABC.

References

Andreasen, Nancy C. "Secrets of the Creative Brain." *The Atlantic Monthly*. June 25, 2014. http://www.theatlantic.com/features/archive/2014/06/secrets-of-the-creative-brain/372299/.

Belanoff, Adam, James Duff, Mike Berchem. "Next of Kin, Part 2." *The Closer*, season 3, episode 15. Directed by James Duff. Aired December 3, 2007, on ABC. Netflix.com.

Bryant, Adam. "The Closer Finale Postmortem: Creator James Duff Talks Brenda's Final Confession." *TV Guide.com*, August 13, 2012. http://www.tvguide.com/news/closer-finale-postmortem-james-duff-1051943.aspx.

Byrne, Matt. "Let the Bad Times Roll." *Grey's Anatomy*, season 8, episode 22. Directed by Kevin McKidd. Aired May 3, 2012, on ABC. Netflix.com.

Clark, Zoanne. "Break on Through." *Grey's Anatomy*, season 2, episode 15. Directed by David Paymer. Aired January 29, 2006, on ABC. Netflix.com.

Collins, Rebecca L. "Content analysis of *gender* roles in media: Where are we now and where should we go?" *Sex Roles* 64, 3/4 (2011): 290–298. doi:10.1007/11199–010–9929–5.

Dolan, Jill. "Rise and Shine and The Closer." *The Feminist Spectator*. September 25, 2006. http://www.thefeministspectator.com/2006/09/25/rise-and-shine-and-the-closer/.

Dow, Bonnie J. *Prime-Time Feminism: Television, Media Culture, and the Women's Movement Since 1970*. Philadelphia: University of Pennsylvania Press, 1996.

Duff, James. "Pilot." *The Closer*, season 1, episode 1. Directed by Michael M. Robin. Aired June 13, 2005, on ABC. Netflix.com.

Gonzalez, Sandra. "'The Closer' final season: Kyra Sedgwick and creator James Duff on the last six episodes." *Entertainment Weekly*, July 9, 2012. http://insidetv.ew.com/2012/07/09/the-closer-final-season-kyra-sedgwick.

Harper, William. "Fear (of the Unknown)." *Grey's Anatomy*, season 10, episode 24. Directed by Tony Phelan. Aired May 15, 2014. Netflix.com.

John Paul II. Apostolic letter *Mulieris Dignitatem* of the Supreme Pontiff John Paul II on the dignity and vocation of Women on the occasion of the Marian year. August 15, 1988.

http://www.vatican.va/holy_father/john_paul_ii/apost_letters/documents/hf_jp-ii_apl_15081988_mulieris-dignitatem_en.html.

Jubas, Kaela. "Grey('s) Identity: Complications of Learning and Becoming a Popular Television Show." *Review of Education, Pedagogy, and Cultural Studies* 35:2 (2013): 127–143. doi:10.1080/10714413.2013.778653.

Kane, Steven. "Live Wire." *The Closer*, season 4, episode 4. Directed by Elodie Keene. Aired August 4, 2008, on ABC. Netflix.com

Landrum, Gene N. *Profiles of Female Geniuses: Thirteen Creative Women Who Changed the World*. New York: Prometheus, 1994.

Leone, Katie. "2014 Scripps Spelling Bee: 'Scandal,' 'Grey's Anatomy' creator Shonda Rhimes talks Bee love." ABC15.com. Accessed June 10, 2014. http://www.abc15.com/nct/national/2014-scripps-spelling-bee-scandal-greys-anatomy-creator-shonda-rhimes-talks-bee-love.

Levine, Elana. "Grey's Anatomy: Feminism." In *How To Watch Television*, edited by Ethan Thompson and Jason Mitchell, 139–147. New York: New York University Press, 2013.

Mckee, Stacy. "What Is It About Men." *Grey's Anatomy*, season 8, episode 4. Directed by Tom Verica. Aired October 6, 2011, on ABC. Netflix.com.

Mitchell, Claudia A., and Jacqueline Weid-Walsh, eds. *Girl Culture: An Encyclopedia Volume 1*. Westport, CT: Greenwood Press, 2008.

Nowalk, Peter. "This is How We Do It." *Grey's Anatomy*, season 2, episode 8. Directed by Ed Ornelas. Aired March 24, 2011, on ABC. Netflix.com.

Paskin, Willa. "A Character on Grey's Anatomy Actually Had an Abortion on Prime-Time Television Last Night." *New York Magazine*, September 23, 2011. http://www.vulture.com/2011/09/someone_actually_had_an_aborti.html.

Phalen, Tony, and Joan Rater. "Free Falling." *Grey's Anatomy*, season 8, episode 1. Directed by Rob Corn. Aired September 22, 2011. Netflix.com.

Rater, Joan. "The End is the Beginning is the End." *Grey's Anatomy*, season 9 episode 11. Directed by Cherie Nowlan. Aired January 17, 2013, on ABC. Netflix.com.

Renshaw, Jeannie. "Beautiful Doom." *Grey's Anatomy*, season 9 episode 5. Directed by Stephen Cragg. Aired November 8, 2012, on ABC. Netflix.com.

Rhimes, Shonda. "The First Cut is the Deepest." *Grey's Anatomy*, season 1, episode 2. Directed by Peter Orton. Aired April 3, 2005, on ABC. Netflix.com.

_____."A Hard Day's Night." *Grey's Anatomy*, season 1, episode 1. Directed by Peter Horton. Aired March 27, 2005, on ABC. Netflix.com.

Russ, Joanna. *The Female Male*. Boston: Beacon Press, 1975.

Schmir, Mimi. "Let It Be." *Grey's Anatomy*, season 2, episode 8. Directed by Lesli Linka Glatter. Aired November 13, 2005, on ABC. Netflix.com.

Shattuck, Katherine. "Playing it more Marlowe than Marple." *The New York Times*, November 26, 2010. http://www.nytimes.com/2010/11/28/arts/television/28kyra.html?pagewanted=all&_r=0.

Stanton, Gabrielle, and Harry Werksman, Jr. "Much too Much." *Grey's Anatomy*, season 2, episode 10. Directed by Wendy Stanzler. Aired November 27, 2005, on ABC. Netflix.com

_____, and _____. "Who's Zoomin' Who?" *Grey's Anatomy*, season 1, episode 9. Directed by Wendez Stanzler. Aired May 22, 2005, on ABC. Netflix.com.

Strauman, Elaine, and Bethany Crandell Goodier. "Not Your Grandmother's Doctor Show: A Review of Grey's Anatomy, House, and Nip/Tuck." *Journal of Medical Humanities* 29 (2008): 127–131. doi:10.1007/s10912-008-9055.3.

TV Tropes Wiki. Accessed June 10, 2014. http://tvtropes.org/pmwiki/pmwiki.php/Main/HomePage.

Upson, Sandra, and Laura Friedman. "Where are all the Female Geniuses?" *Scientific American Mind* 23, no. 5 (November 2012): 63–65. http://www.scientificamerican.com/article/where-are-all-the-female-geniuses/.

Weisberg, Robert W. "Case Studies of Innovation: Ordinary Thinking Extraordinary Results." In *The International Handbook of Innovation*, edited by Larisa V. Shavinina, 204–237. Oxford: Elsevier Science, 2003.

_____. *Creativity: Beyond the Myth of Genius*. New York: W.H. Freeman, 1993.

Wilde, Oscar. *The Picture of Dorian Gray: An Annotated, Uncensored Edition*. Cambridge: Belknap Press of Harvard University Press, 2011.

Part III

Genius, Difference and Deviance

What's the Difference?

Pathologizing Genius and Neurodiversity in Popular Television Series

Carol-Ann Farkas

> SHERLOCK: It has its costs ... learning to see the puzzle in everything. They're everywhere—once you start looking—it's impossible to stop.... It just so happens that people, and all the deceits and delusions that inform everything they do, tend to be the most fascinating puzzles of all. Of course they don't always appreciate being seen as such...
> WATSON: Seems like a lonely way to live...
> SHERLOCK: As I said, it has its costs.—*Elementary,* "The Rat Race"[1]

College students, detectives, theoretical physicists, fixers, and secret agents: characters whose minds function in a radically different way from those of everyone around them have become central to the plots of many popular North American television shows. These characters all possess extraordinary intelligence, even genius, and this brilliance, insight, and creativity is often portrayed as only one of many traits associated with non-specific eccentricity, or with very-specific diagnoses, such as autism spectrum disorders (ASD), bipolar disorder, and post-traumatic stress disorder (PTSD). Intelligence alone does not make these characters sufficiently interesting—their intellectual power must be complicated, tempered, even undercut, by unconventional, atypical behavior. The resulting portrayal of cognitive and psychological *difference* offers television producers considerable narrative flexibility: characters' intelligence is useful fuel for a variety of comedic and dramatic plots; they can be made to act as conventionally or unconventionally as the plot demands. Their difference, particularly when framed as illness, can also be used metaphorically, usually to question the sanity of the society which labels them as insane or unstable.

Because these characters are so central to their respective narratives—becoming, by virtue of their intellect and behavior, the main source and target of jokes, the focus for social cohesion, the embodiment of sensationalized nonconformity, even the super-hero or savior—it is possible to argue that their popularity and visibility can potentially improve societal acceptance of psychological and cognitive difference. However, as I will explain in this chapter, the demand to create entertaining television leads producers to pick and choose from available diagnostic criteria with unrealistic, distorting results. Programs such as *Community*, *The Big Bang Theory*, *Scandal*, *Homeland*, and current and recent iterations of Sherlock Holmes (*Elementary*, *Sherlock*, *House*) reinforce negative stereotypes about "difference" and "normalcy"—namely, that intelligence and creativity must equate with instability and pathology, and that *difference* marks individuals, allowing them to contribute meaningfully to society without being able to integrate fully into it.[2] Difference is exploited as much as, if not more than, it is celebrated.

"Difference": Defining the Deliberately Indefinite

In the context in which I use the term here, "difference," can potentially mean everything and nothing; it is a catch-all for the varied traits we see in many popular television characters which set them apart, strikingly, from both the other, "normal" characters on a given show, as well as from the "typical" viewer. Difference generally encompasses some form of exceptional intellect—the encyclopedic, the creative, the savant—made inseparable from the implied or explicit presence of mental disorders. Importantly, difference is a product of connections which are often incomplete, inconsistent, and inexpert; the television version of difference relies heavily on un-interrogated assumptions about just what establishes characters and viewers as the "normal" or "typical" baseline with which the "different" characters can be so strikingly juxtaposed. Difference is often a product of indifference—to the nature of intelligence, to specific diagnostic criteria, to behaviors and conditions which are poorly understood, and to an emerging political and cultural movement which seeks to challenge our notions of "different" and "normal" with a model of *neurodiversity*. That latter concept has become a meaningful way for people with cognitive and psychological differences, originally autism spectrum disorders, now encompassing a range of neurodevelopmental, perceptual, and cognitive traits, to assert identity, competence, and autonomy rather than diagnosis, deficit, and dependence.³ "Neurodiversity" has significant social and political dimensions that do not factor into the construction of characters on the television shows I consider here. It is, in fact, because many of these programs have evolved with seeming indifference to recognizing either specific diagnostic criteria or the claims of the neurodiversity movement, while simultaneously pathologizing intelligence—that their treatment of "difference" is so problematic.

Characters such as Sheldon (*The Big Bang Theory*), Abed (*Community*), Huck (*Scandal*), Carrie (*Homeland*), House, and Sherlock Homes (BBC's *Sherlock,* CBS's *Elementary*) are constructed through a mix-and-match process, combining above-average intelligence with non-specific behaviors such as social backwardness, oddity, obsessiveness, violence, and instability; the assemblage of traits implies specific disorders, but the only characters assigned diagnoses are Holmes (addiction) and Carrie (bipolar disorder). Setting aside concerns for strict realism, having a range of behaviors or symptoms to play with gives television writers the ability to endow the genius character with skills or deficits that someone with a specific diagnosis or identity might not typically have, minimizing certain traits and challenges while blowing others out of proportion. Often, when characters are not assigned any particular diagnosis, other characters will apply specific symptoms, assessments, and identities. Sometimes, one character's diagnosis of another is, in the context of the fictional relationship, part of a well-intentioned effort towards understanding; or, a symptom or disorder is tossed out casually, derogatorily, as part of a dynamic where the "different" character's behavior is being corrected, excused, dismissed, or mocked. As the fuel for ability, difference allows the genius characters to do work and interact with others in ways that complicate and enliven the plot; when cast as deficit, difference creates needs and vulnerabilities, which in turn evoke empathetic, communal friendship, or judgment and teasing, or all of the above, from the other characters. In all of the cases that I consider here, each character's rare intellect is folded in with traits and behaviors which are, implicitly, different from the norm, familiar enough that the audience can recognize them, unfamiliar enough that writers can take whatever liberties they need in service of an engaging story.

For example, while Sheldon and Abed exhibit many behaviors that viewers associate with ASD, producers have always decided against assigning these characters any particular diagnosis or identity within their respective narratives. Leaving their behavior undefined allows the characters to range from brilliant to naive, from the glue that holds their social group together, to barely able to look after themselves on their own—whatever will be most funny, or touching, or both. *Scandal*'s Huck is a savant in the realms of hacking and torture, he seems to have been on the autism spectrum before he was recruited by B6–13, and his training and his time in solitary confinement seem to have left him with PTSD. But, we do not really know, nor are we meant to. What matters to the narrative of *Scandal* is that Huck is conveniently *just as* intelligent, sadistic, tender, loyal, and/or sexually perverse as a given plot line requires. Our contemporary Sherlocks are self-consciously aware of their difference, and use it as justification to defy rules, laws, and ethical principles as needed, though not without consequences, particularly in their relationships. House is nothing but miserable, possibly on the autism spectrum, or possibly even sociopathic; *Elementary*'s Holmes is a recovering addict, with symptoms of OCD or Asperger's; the BBC's Sherlock openly declares himself a high-functioning sociopath, although his associates jokingly suggest that Asperger's is a more accurate descriptor. And on *Homeland*, Carrie's bipolar disorder is the key to her brilliant, uncanny insight; when it is convenient, she can be allowed to lapse off her medication, sliding into erratic, reckless, sometimes sexually promiscuous behavior.[4] Her instability facilities instability in the plot, which enhances risk, conflict, and suspense in ways we viewers love, but which might have little to do with the real, individual experience of life with this condition.

Characters' differences have an additional narrative function: mental disorder and eccentricity have a long and varied history of being employed by authors to add metaphorical complexity to narrative. The "mad genius" is often accorded "heightened creativity or clairvoyance," able to see truths or patterns that elude others mired in the complacency of their sane ordinariness.[5] Think of *One Flew Over the Cuckoo's Nest*, *American Psycho*, or *Fight Club*, where the characters' pathology is meant to be a product, a reflection, and an indictment of a pathological society. Similarly, the instability of Carrie's bipolar disorder can stand in for the instability of meaning, knowledge, identity, and allegiance in post–9/11 intelligence and politics. As Rohr has found, the character whose "madness" marks them as different can then be freed from the constraints of convention to function as the "wise fool" who "embod[ies] some kind of wisdom or deep knowledge of eternal human truths" or behavior; or as a representation of a "paradigmatic normal individual" trying to make sense of the shifting boundaries of contemporary social relations.[6] In such characters, Draaisma suggests, the lack of social skills also "eliminates much that is artificial, phony, or plainly dishonest in normal social communication."[7] For example, Sheldon's inability to understand certain kinds of social cues is made the subject of mockery, but in the process, his point of view often underlines the irrationality of the "normal" behaviors that cause conflict in his friends' lives.[8] Similarly, Abed's character on *Community* is able to openly question social norms and assumptions (such as the centrality of drunkenness as a rite of passage for college students). His perception of a reality that fluidly integrates dreams, imagination, and alternate timelines challenges our narrower, limited view of the world. And, according to creator Dan Harmon, Abed's difference, and his frustration at trying to fit in with so-called "normal" social relationships, represents "our fear of being alone and alienated from others."[9]

Role Models or Commodities? Co-Constructing Difference

In creating Abed, Harmon did not anticipate how either viewers or his own understanding of the character would evolve.[10] The character took on a polysemic life of his own, generating multiple meanings for viewers, which exceeded the original vision of his creators; indeed, all of the characters considered here have become co-constructions, whose literal and figurative meanings reflect the needs and values of networks, producers, writers, and the range of the viewing public. Consequently, while my concern in this analysis is to focus on the potential harm of this process, it is important to acknowledge that, for many of the people involved in the co-construction of any given character, it is both possible, and completely valid, to find positive, beneficial meaning.

In particular, it can be argued that the different character does vital cultural work, rendering visible forms of experience that have been hitherto marginalized and stigmatized, using the genre of fictional television to endow "difference" with positive figurative associations, and to model a vision of integration, where the neurodiverse and neurotypical are able to form communities of friendship, respect, and care. For example, as Harmon suggests, no matter where we might situate ourselves in relation to the autism spectrum, we can all relate to Abed on a figurative level, identifying with his difficulty in establishing and negotiating social relationships.[11] When viewers laugh at and with Sheldon, Abed, and their neurotypical friends, they experience what Walters terms the "comic corrective," where they "are invited to understand ways in which traditionally 'abnormal' characters are not as abnormal as they seem and more frequently connect other characters and social groups rather than collapse them."[12] Or, as actor Jim Parsons has said of Sheldon, "This is who this person is; he's just another human."[13] Such characters, explicitly located on the autism spectrum, or less specifically rendered as different, become "essential to social cohesion and even work to resist the assumption that cognitive difference separates neurotypical and autistic characters into categories of 'normal' and 'abnormal.'"[14] The different characters are often identifiable—diagnosable—to viewers as having one disorder or another. But their ability to work, study, and connect in a variety of social situations offers an important rebuttal to prevalent stereotypes about cognitive difference, lumped in indiscriminately with all forms of mental disorder, including those most associated with dysfunction, delusion, and violence. Sheldon and Abed, along with Huck, Carrie, and our Sherlock Holmeses, make us laugh; they keep us in suspense; we're captivated by their intelligence; we care about what happens to them; they have our attention. Given the ways in which mental disorders have historically been pushed to the margins of social visibility because of the discomfort that they evoke, the fact that this set of characters collectively arrests our gaze marks a significant cultural shift.

But, what I find problematic here is inherent in my use of the concept of gaze, which, in the field of cultural studies, signals a relationship not of guaranteed subjectivity, but of potential objectification, exploitation, and misrepresentation. Intelligent, unconventional difference makes for television that is clever, entertaining, stimulating, sometimes artistically or philosophically challenging, very popular, and very lucrative. Difference thus becomes a product, a commodity: if eccentric, pathologized genius sells, then producers and writers will continue to sell it, with multiple narratives dependent on characters constructed as "different," "brilliant," and "interesting" without much fidelity to specific diagnostic categories (or efforts to defy diagnoses), and without much concern for cultural response to the resulting portrayals.

The Function of Difference in Shaping and Constraining TV Narrative

According to *The Big Bang Theory* creator Bill Prady, Sheldon Cooper was not initially intended to have a specific diagnosis of Asperger's—Sheldon was based on people that Prady knew, "programmer types," with Sheldon's extreme intelligence combined with idiosyncratic behaviors and difficulty in social situations.[15] Prady and co-creator Chuck Lorre did not want to diagnose Sheldon, or any of the other characters on the show, with anything in particular because they recognize that they would be constrained by that diagnosis; they claim not to want the responsibility and also acknowledge that making fun of someone with a named disorder might repel viewers, while someone who is simply "unusual" can be the subject of unlimited humor.[16] In interviews, Prady demurs from being too specific about what he calls Sheldon's "quirks," saying: "I just think of his actions as 'Sheldony.' Some things feel instinctively correct for his character.... Are these things Asperger's? ... I don't know."[17] In a similar vein, Harmon has said, "I don't know that the character [of Abed] is representative of anything. I wouldn't want to do that because I'd rather he be a unique thing than some kind of symbol for people to write letters about. I just think that he's a very unique guy with a strange social mannerisms."[18]

Harmon and Prady are right that specific diagnoses would affect character and plot development, both logistically and ethically. To explicitly impose a diagnosis or identity on characters—to treat them with strict realism—is to risk potentially limiting what writers can have them do, in what circumstances they could do it, and how other characters would interact with them in response. Quite simply, as long as Sheldon and Abed are not labeled in any way, as long as they are simply "unique" with "strange social mannerisms," the other characters, and by extension viewers, can enjoy mocking their strangeness. If that strangeness becomes a named condition or disorder, the jokes are no longer harmless, but bigoted and cruel.[19] Viewers might get offended and, as Harmon fears, "write letters." Indeed, committing to specific diagnoses would invoke responsibilities—ethical decisions—which would make certain kinds of plots impossible. If House's Vicodin addiction, egotism, and regular disregard for patient rights were treated realistically, he would have had his license suspended after the first episode. Once Sherlock announces his own sociopathy, viewers are put on alert to expect further evidence of it, and find themselves assessing his behavior through that lens: is this how a sociopath acts? Does Sherlock care too much in this instance and not enough in that? As long as Huck exhibits traits of this or that disorder, but is never diagnosed with anything in particular, he can be treated more like a pet monster: barely tamed, sometimes pathetically dependent, at other times usefully ferocious.

And if a character "has" a condition, the plot is required to be *about* that condition to some degree—a narrative choice which strains the conventions of genres employing a frame of verisimilitude to contain what are, essentially, fantasies: the hyperbolic extremes of comedy, the suspense and titillation of melodrama. For example, when *Elementary* creator Robert Doherty gave Sherlock Holmes' infamous drug use a more responsible and realistic treatment, turning it into explicit addiction, Holmes was suddenly a less compelling version of the character—now he is dependent on Watson as his recovery companion. He makes sympathetic speeches at 12-step meetings, where he expresses mature and healthy insights about his own psychosocial development, and he admits to needing both emotional and physical connection to other people. In a different genre, with different characters, this characterization could be extremely affecting. But a Sherlock Holmes with ordinary "issues," "relatable attachments," and a realistically-rendered inner emotional life, is a weakened and less interesting iteration of himself: the appeal of Holmes has always been that he is not meant to be *like* us. Holmes is meant to be the embodiment of flawless, logical problem-solving, of ratiocination, of decryption, of pattern recognition, and as such, his character takes on something of the fantastical: encyclopedic, arcane knowledge, a seemingly-eidetic memory, indifference or even aversion to the distraction of emotional response, and drug use which calms his over-powered mind. While Holmes is capable of behaving "typically," his intelligence and unconventional behavior exempt him from the dependencies, rules, and ethics which delimit our own lives.

Packaging a character's brilliance with a specific disorder requires the writers to follow through, or when they discover that consistent realism presents an obstacle to narrative excitement and suspense, the parameters of the disorder have to be forcibly manipulated, or occasionally swept aside. *Homeland*'s co-creator, Alex Gansa, the show's writers (including Meredith Stiehm, whose sister has bipolar disorder), and actor Claire Danes have described attempting careful research for the portrayal of Carrie's illness. Gansa has also maintained that it would be "dangerous" to equate Carrie's mental disorder with her brilliance, saying that the show itself is "agnostic" on the relationship. Nevertheless, many viewers and critics have responded to the show with some dismay, finding "Carrie's latest manic state to be more about advancing the plot than about accurately portraying [bipolar disorder]."[20] This deployment of symptoms, particularly mania, has been very selective over the course of the series; the character of Carrie is never allowed to escape her diagnosis, and that diagnosis is frequently pressed into service in the machinery of the plot. This is most evident in the third season when Carrie and Saul harness (unleash?) her bipolar symptoms to create a devious mousetrap, fictions within fictions. Mania and delusion come to suffuse the whole storyline in a way which simultaneously enthralls, employs madness as metaphor, and reinforces stereotypes of the inextricability of mental illness, instability, and brilliance. This is a great deal of meaning to ask of one diagnostic label.

It is easier to exploit the eccentric genius character, giving him or her symptoms, than to take on the encumbrance of a confining diagnosis. Nevertheless, while many programs deliberately avoid labels, both viewers and actors identify the combination of unconventional behavior with exceptional intelligence as a "difference" which must be accounted for; indeed, "it doesn't seem OK anymore to just be eccentric—it has to be pathologized in some way."[21] Our cultural knowledge has accumulated to the point that we cannot observe certain behaviors without subsuming them within a diagnostic category; our geniuses' quirks become medicalized into symptoms. Actor Jim Parsons has said that his portrayal of Sheldon is strongly influenced by John Elder Robison' memoir of living with autism, *Look Me in the Eye,* a work recommended by *The Big Bang Theory* co-star Johnny Galecki.[22]

More recently, Parsons has expressed some ambivalence about the lack of specificity surrounding Sheldon's identity: "I asked the writers ... '[reporters] are asking me if Sheldon has Asperger's,' and they were like, 'No.' And I said, 'OK.' And I went back and I said, 'No.' And then I read some more about it and I went, OK, well, if the writers say he doesn't, then he doesn't, but he certainly shares some qualities with those who do. I like the way it's handled."[23] While *Community* creator Dan Harmon originally resisted labeling Abed— and still does within the show itself—he found that after a certain point, the character's identity was being read, and constituted, by viewers as being on the autism spectrum. Harmon was led to do research on ASD, and retrospectively found that he and his writers had created a profile of Asperger's somewhat by accident, or through cultural osmosis.[24] As Draaisma has found, extreme intelligence often ends up equated with autism and other mental disorders in fictional media; no matter how good the intention, creators cannot seem to escape the pull of stereotyped thinking:

> Actors insist that they invest months of preparation to study the movements and reactions of autistic persons; script writers read scientific articles on autism; directors call on consultants, they all want an *absolutely* sincere and truthful rendition of autism; what they come up with is an autistic character with freak-like savant skills, unlike anything resembling a normal autistic person.[25]

In other words, while many programs are not about characters "with" particular conditions, the awareness of conditions and identities suffuses the construction and reception of the character. Moreover, no matter how specifically or vaguely a character's behavior is accounted for, there is enough medicalized (mis)information circulating in popular culture now that viewers will impose a diagnosis if one is not explicitly provided. It is simply disingenuous for producers to claim otherwise, and (Frankenstein-like) to deny responsibility for what they create. And yet, whether consciously or otherwise, that is what is happening.

While many viewers welcome Abed and Sheldon as representatives of neurodiversity on prime-time television, neither character can fully embody the range of abilities and challenges encompassed by the autism spectrum. Rather, both characters serve as "aspirational" portrayals, because of their close social networks, the esteem that others have for their respective forms of intellectual brilliance, and in Sheldon's case in particular, professional success.[26] Sheldon and Abed might represent idealized extremes at one end of a broad spectrum; elsewhere on that spectrum, the challenges of acquiring coping skills while also negotiating externally-imposed "societal limitations"[27] and stigma mean that a significant number of people with ASD struggle to live independently.[28]

The depiction of Carrie's bipolar disorder might be a realistic representation, but of the experience of a highly educated white woman who has the support of a knowledgeable and caring upper-middle class family, and who is employed by a government agency that may not be exempt from biased attitudes about mental illness, but which does offer excellent health insurance. Similarly, Holmes' situation is hardly typical, as he has access to financial, social, therapeutic, and professional resources which are far beyond the reach of the average addict whose life has been gutted by his illness. But these particular characters, are, after all, in works of *fiction*, where brilliance and privilege are made more compelling and complex with the addition of a mental health issue. Getting along—as a student, researcher, detective, spy, or fixer—because, *and in spite of*, this difference is an effective ingredient for the creation of a television hero; but as a way for the public to learn more about the bio-psycho-social reality of living with ASD, addiction, or bipolar disorder, these portrayals are, if not inaccurate per se, very selective and limited.

Brilliance and Disorder: Blurring the Lines Between Stereotype, Stigma, Exploitation and Entertainment

Moreover, our television geniuses cannot be allowed to succumb to any of the more debilitating symptoms to which they might realistically be prone, if their difference were written with greater consistency or accuracy. Severe or poorly controlled (particularly chronic) symptoms of the disordered mind defy the generic conventions of episodic television, and would deprive the characters of the level of focus necessary to drive the action: Sheldon and Abed *must* be capable of odd social gaffes, charmingly baroque schemes (the blanket fort colony), and clever banter; each Sherlock Holmes must manage to work with others, avoiding self-sabotaging behavior such as cruel manipulation, reminding himself to occasionally follow scripts for acceptable social behavior. Carrie must keep herself medicated and stable most of the time: viewers enjoy the unpredictability of a well-scripted manic episode, but the paralysis of severe depression or heavy sedation can only be featured sparingly.

At the same time, if chronic disability might make for ineffective televisual storytelling, chronic ability poses the same problem: our characters cannot be allowed to be too functional, admirable, or aspirational. Like good, complex protagonists, they must have weaknesses and vulnerabilities, but because these characters are *different*, so must their flaws be. It is often the characters' flaws and vulnerabilities that prompt important developments in their relationships: Sheldon's intractability in dealing with others, Huck's and Abed's breakdowns and retreats into dissociative states, Watson or Wilson pushed too far by the self-centeredness of a Holmes or a House, or Carrie's instability undermining Saul's trust.

But the genius character's flaws function on an additional level: for them, disturbingly, not only is difference regularly cast as a pathology, it is also harmfully burdened with stigmatizing views of *madness,* deeply rooted in social and moral judgment, and highly resistant to corrective education: "The common [public] perception is that those afflicted with MD [mental disorders] are dangerous; developmentally disabled, of low intelligence, have communication disorders, or all of these; are dysfunctional; and do not contribute as workers as they lack desire or are lazy."[29] Researchers have found that the lay public generally misunderstands the causes, manifestation, and management of cognitive and psychological difference. In particular, neurodiversity is not yet a mainstream concept; meanwhile, lay people's "knowledge" of mental disorders is a patchwork of beliefs and assumptions gathered largely, and lopsidedly, from "sketchy or generic depictions" in the media.[30] In this cultural climate then, neither producers nor viewers are able to provide informed, critical thinking to their conception of characters' difference. As the most benign example, whether viewers think that Sheldon or Abed have Asperger's or are "merely" eccentric, they are not necessarily applying some set of diagnostic criteria to assess the characters; they are categorizing the characters according to the same hazy ideas about those "engineering guys" that the shows' producers are drawing from, a portrayal that does little to overturn lay beliefs that intelligent "nerds" or "geeks" must necessarily be odd, socially backward, and helpless outside of their area of savant-like expertise.[31]

Stereotype-fueled inaccuracy paves the way for exploitation; as a result, difference becomes a convenient justification for titillating behavior that viewers might not accept in more conventional characters. The character whose genius makes her different is not simply authorized to violate social, ethical, and legal rules; the confused association of brilliant and disordered thinking recapitulates lay assumptions that the different individual is not as capable of adhering to positive social norms as a neurotypical person.[32]

Most troubling is the way in which difference functions to underwrite violence.[33] It is certainly the case that there are some correlations between specific mental disorders and particular kinds of (self) destructive behavior; un- or poorly-treated conditions sometimes do result in dysfunctional, impulsive, or compulsive acts, ranging from difficulties with social interactions to violence. It is also certainly the case that "only a minority of those afflicted with MDs [mental disorders] commit severe crimes and that the percentage of general violence associated with MD is low, indeed not above 14 percent."[34] And yet, public perception is skewed by sensationalistic news coverage which often "emphasi[zes] the violent, delusional, and irrational behavior of people with a mental illnes ... to attract attention."[35] The information circulating in popular discourse conflates "knowledge" about health and crime, priming lay audiences to accept stereotypes in both non-fictional and fictional sources. The so-called "factual evidence" provided in one genre reproduces and reinforces the tendency in our culture to equate mental and cognitive difference not just with disability, but with frightening criminality: moreover, the over-representation of 'dysfunctional behavior ... generate[s] intense emotional responses [which can] exert exceptional power over audiences and are even capable of overriding positive personal experiences, corrective information, and positive news."[36]

Thus, every time the plot of *Homeland* requires Carrie to slip into mania, paranoia, mistrust, and alienation, the story gets more intense and interesting—and risks reinforcing unproductive beliefs about mental disorders: that unmedicated symptoms heighten insight (and being medicated comes at the expense of creativity), and that it is difficult to control the symptoms, and hence to control and regulate the behavior of the person who has them. As a far more harmful example, Huck's unnamed psychological and cognitive issues are often exploited for mawkish effect, meant to draw on viewer sympathy for the veteran whose service for his country has been repaid with trauma and isolation. These same issues are somehow used to provide a rationale for his, by turns, cheerful, compulsive, or sexualized practice of interrogation and execution. This is one of the most egregious examples, exploiting the fear and ignorance we have about the "different" individual in the name of entertainment. It is necessary to point out, since *Scandal* will not, that it is not PTSD or Asperger's which make Huck a terrorist or torturer, it is his screenwriters.

Tinkering with the Diagnosis: The Exploitation and Isolation of Difference and Brilliance

Tinkering with symptoms and characteristics makes our television geniuses more engaging, but "treat[ing] psychological disorders as a professional asset [and] turning a diagnosis into a magic tool for crime solving [are] simpler than writing a complicated, fully realized character."[37] We end up with caricatures, not characters, and while these characters do elicit sympathy, it is not empathy. On the one hand, we might find these characters compelling, even likable. We might relate to their position as outsiders, appreciate the diversity of experience they bring to the television landscape, and fantasize about having their intelligence and their ability to exist beyond the pale of social conventions. But on the other hand, insofar as they have difficulty interacting with others, are the butt of jokes, occasionally lose control of their judgment, or are the perpetrators of extreme violence, we don't feel *with* them or have any desire to *be* them in a lasting way.

The appeal of these characters is not that we consistently see ourselves in them. Rather than minimizing stereotypes of normalcy and difference, these shows reinforce them; the character who is different is generally the only one of his kind (or, as with Huck, has unenviable company), whose social and coping skills are set in marked contrast to those around him. The different characters often do enjoy a community of good friends, and earn the respect of their colleagues, but that is as much in spite of their difference as because of it; often, the bond is based on a mix of exceptional skill and exceptional vulnerability on one side, and long-suffering patience and grudging dependence on the other. Putting up with the abrasive arrogance of House and Sherlock is the price paid by their colleagues for their brilliance. *Elementary*'s Sherlock depends on Watson as his sobriety coach; Huck would be homeless if it weren't for Olivia; Sheldon has to be driven everywhere, his tastes pandered to, his good behavior rewarded with ice cream; Abed occasionally has breakdowns that require elaborate interventions from his friends to get him back to *his* normal; Carrie's and House's colleagues have to risk their own careers and reputations to compensate for procedural and ethical transgressions.

The trust and friendship that we see evolving between these characters is heartening but it is not entirely realistic, and it has an unnerving transactional quality, where each side has a lack that the other supplies. The relationship is not commensurate: while the "ordinary" characters benefit from the different characters' talent, they could get along on without it, but the different character needs, even relies on, her friends for figurative, and sometime literal, survival. When it comes to the character of exceptional intellectual difference, "it is mostly the savantism that constitutes [their] 'worth.' … Without their savant skills there would not be much of a plot, or a social life for them either."[38]

The focus of this collection is the television genius, and yet my analysis has tended to concentrate on the traits, or symptoms, which mark these characters as different, rather than merely brilliant—arguably, intelligence is their least interesting, because least exploitable, attribute. And this leads me to my final point: what I find particularly problematic about these characters is the very consistent conflation of exceptional and pathologized thinking, arising not from evidence, but from romanticized, essentializing stereotypes about cognitive and psychological difference.

Researchers have found some correlation between traits associated with creative genius and certain mental disorders such as depression, bipolar disorder, schizophrenia.[39] Comparable studies have found that the "restrictive and intense interest" that is common in ASD is "associated with a hyper systematizing cognitive style leading to talent in scientific endeavors."[40] However, we must remember the dictum that correlation is not causation: genius is not a guaranteed product of cognitive or mental difference. And while certain disorders do correlate with genius, there is a kind of symptomatic sweet-spot, where individuals on the mild end of the bipolar or autism spectrums are able to cultivate the positive ones without being prohibitively afflicted by others: more severe conditions "may limit the nature of occupational and social opportunities that would contribute to creative accomplishments, and repeated experiences of these lost opportunities may suppress the motivation, self-confidence, and hope needed to pursue accomplishments."[41]

Similarly, while there may be some basis for associating genius with mental disorders, genius can occur independently of diagnosable pathology. Sometimes, exceptional intellectual achievement depends on hard work as much as innate talents and/or disorders. Nevertheless, legends of creative brilliance, in the form of the mad or eccentric artist or scientist, continue to have a strong influence in popular culture[42]; such figures have become ingredients in formulaic storytelling, particularly on television.[43] Critics have noted that our popular narratives tend to construct extreme intelligence and inventive creativity as, variously, a kind of autistic savantism, or a super-power, or, somehow, both. In the first case, as Draaisma observes, "even if savantism mostly comes with autism, the majority of cases of autism do not have savantism."[44] In fact, the incidence of savantism is perhaps 10%, and often arises where other skills necessary to independent living are not well-developed at all.[45] Both fictional and non-fictional portrayals of savantism "enfreak" extreme skill or talent in one specific area as markedly abnormal.[46] If a character possesses genius, such intelligence is, technically, not normal, yet somehow we cannot allow "not normal" to be extra-normal, or simply different, nor can we extend our definition of normal to include a greater variation in human accomplishment. Rather what is not normal—different—must be made abnormal, and folded in with other "abnormal" traits associated with disorder or pathology.

Even when genius is made a super-power, where the character's brilliance gives him or her powers of insight and creative pattern recognition that others lack, that power is made to be less a gift or endowment, and more a burden or disability. On the one hand, superheroes can "take care of situations with which normal people cannot deal"; being endowed with powers that exceed what is "normal" authorizes them with a concomitant indifference to "hierarchical models of authority."[47] This combined ability to perform the role of savior while being unconstrained by the banal rules of quotidian existence is enormously appealing in storytelling. But as DuBose observes, extraordinary powers require "a separation of realities, an 'our world' and 'their world' dichotomy"[48] that refuses the superhero the privileges of the "normal" life that we need them to save. While we love to watch characters like Sherlock Holmes, House, Carrie, or Huck use their minds to perform near-miraculous problem-solving for the benefit of others, we accept (or demand) that their genius also come at great cost, as though anyone who dares lay claim to heightened intellect may only do so through a reciprocal sacrifice of sanity, stability, contentment, "normal" feeling, and the capacity (or right) to maintain healthy relationships.

In thus representing intelligence as inseparable from the larger, non-specific, but very-definitely pathologized syndrome of "difference," the television programs examined here run the risk of teaching (because we *do* learn from our stories) some unproductive lessons about how the human mind works. Namely, these programs imply that there is some well-established "normal"— of behavior, intelligence, perception, cognition—wherein healthy roles are performed, transactions conducted, and ordinary problems solved. Extraordinary problems require the intervention of the abnormal, but how one gets assigned to the abnormal realm is unclear: is intelligence caused by some disorder? Does being different make someone a genius? Does genius create pathologized difference? Sheldon, Abed, Sherlock Holmes, Huck, and Carrie exhibit skills and behaviors that are arguably well within the expansive, inclusive normal of neurodiversity. But it would take a conscious, considered argument on the part of television producers to reframe "difference" in this way. Instead, producers exploit existing stereotypes—stigmas—about cognitive and psychological difference, and pathologize intelligence, taking it out of the realm of attainability or even desirability for "neurotypical" characters and viewers alike.

But what difference does this "difference" make? We all know that these are just sitcoms, just melodramas, just silly diversions: how much harm (or good) can they really do? As researchers have found, literacy about physical and mental health is quite poor amongst the general public. In particular, while awareness of the prevalence of mental and cognitive disorders has increased in recent decades, lay beliefs about how disorders manifest themselves, how they are managed, and how they both limit ability and fuel adaptation, are stubbornly resistant to modification. Deeply-ingrained, stigmatizing attitudes prevail.[49]

That lay people have a poor understanding of cognitive and psychological difference is not surprising, as general levels of literacy, as well as knowledge of culture and science, are also surprisingly low despite the amount of information that envelopes us all.[50] Importantly, however, lay people *want* to know more about science, medicine, health, and behavior.[51] Our desire for knowledge is reflected in our obsessive research about our own health, and it is certainly responsible for at least some of our fascination with fictional geniuses. We enjoy watching them do research, make clever connections and allusions, solve puzzles; we enjoy watching them *think*.

Consequently, television producers and writers are letting us all down when they merely exploit traits of cognitive and psychological difference, when they pick and choose symptoms, when they portray the intelligent character as also always "having" disorders that make them dangerous or "the source of humor and ridicule,"[52] and when they "enfreak" the fictional genius's behavior and abilities. This stigmatization marginalizes the lay viewers who themselves are different in some way,[33] and reinforces suspicion and ignorance, not only about the nature of disordered thought, but exceptional, creative thought as well. Such ignorance is neither willful nor inevitable, While "people often find it difficult to recognize 'mental disorders' [...] and generally do not understand the meaning of psychiatric terminology,"[54] they make meaningful use of the information they are given, whatever its quality. Lay people "try to explain conditions by piecing together 'bits' of information that are socially influenced and constructed."[55] Thus, regardless of what the producers of any given show claim to be doing, whether earnestly raising awareness of a particular issue, or cynically or heedlessly playing with character for the sake of entertainment, they are educating the public one way or another. All the "bits" and pieces that viewers pick up *in the aggregate* contribute to our knowledge of brilliance and difference. Audiences *could* be learning more, and more positively, about difference and neurodiversity, if only they were given better material to work with.

Notes

1. Craig Sweeny, "Rat Race," *Elementary*, season 1, episode 4, directed by Rosemary Rodriguez, aired October 25, 2012 on CBS.

2. There are, of course, many other eccentric geniuses in past and current television programs who fit the criteria for difference which I use here. My sample has been determined by the mix of genres, implied or explicit diagnoses, and—full disclosure—personal viewing habits.

3. Joseph Straus, "Idiots Savants, Talented Aments, Mono-Savants, Autistic Savants, Just Plain Savants, People with Savant Syndrome, and Autistic People Who Are Good at Things: A View From Disability Studies," *Disability Studies Quarterly* 34, no. 3 (2014), http://dsq-sds.org/article/view/3407/3640.

4. Constructing these television characters as "different" allows them to push the boundaries of heteronromative sexuality: "difference" is made to correlate with the unconventional, the hyper-sexual, the asexual, the risqué, the titillating, and the kinky.

5. Susanne Rohr, "Screening Madness in American Culture," *Journal of Medical Humanities*, June 2014, doi: 10.1007/s10912-014-9287-3.

6. Ibid.

7. Douwe Draaisma, "Stereotypes of Autism," *Philosophical Transactions of the Royal Society* 364 (2009): 1478.

8. Shannon Walters, "Cool Aspie Humor: Cognitive Difference and Kenneth Burke's Comic Corrective in *The Big Bang Theory* and *Community*," *Journal of Literary and Cultural Disability Studies* 7, no. 3 (2013): 271–288.

9. Dan Harmon, interview by Kevin Pollack, *Kevin Pollack Chat Show* #150, February 14, 2014, http://www.youtube.com/watch?v=QXGjRkjAXrM.

10. Ibid.
11. Ibid.
12. Walters, "Cool Aspie Humor," 272.
13. Sam Thielman, "Jim Parsons Hits the Stratosphere: The Star of TV's Biggest Show Talks About *The Big Bang Theory*, Emmy Awards and Larry Kramer," *Adweek,* September 1, 2014, http://www.adweek.com/news/television/jim-parsons-hits-stratosphere-159809.
14. Walters, "Cool Aspie Humor," 274.
15. Alan Sepinwall, "Reader Mail: Reader Mail: Does Sheldon from 'Big Bang Theory' have Asperger's?," *The Star Ledger,* August 13, 2009, http://www.nj.com/entertainment/tv/index.ssf/2009/08/reader_mail_does_sheldon_from.html.
16. Ibid.
17. Paul Collins, "Must-Geek TV: Is the World Ready for an Asperger's Sitcom?" *Slate,* February 6, 2009, http://www.slate.com/articles/arts/television/2009/02/mustgeek_tv.html.
18. Sepinwall, "Reader Mail."
19. And Prady's writers demonstrate their capacity for bigoted cruelty on a regular basis, targeting Walowitz's mother. By keeping her partly imaginary—she is never seen, only heard—and thus not fully humanized, the writers are free to conjure her as a grotesque, whose monstrous body can be the fuel for running jokes.
20. Nolan Feeney, "*Homeland:* The Case Against Calling Carrie a Bipolar 'Superhero,'" *The Atlantic,* October 7, 2013, http://www.theatlantic.com/entertainment/archive/2013/10/-em-homeland-em-the-case-against-calling-carrie-a-bipolar-superhero/280321/2/.
21. Nick Patch, "Autism in Pop Culture: Characters on Autism Spectrum on TV, But Do They Get It Right?," *Huffington Post—Canada,* December 27, 2012, http://www.huffingtonpost.ca/2012/12/27/autism-in-pop-culture_n_2369681.html.
22. Jim Parsons, interview by Noel Murray, *AV Club,* May 1, 2009, http://www.avclub.com/article/jim-parsons-27415.
23. Thielman, "Jim Parsons Hits the Stratosphere."
24. Dan Harmon, Interview by Kevin Pollack, *Kevin Pollack Chat Show* #150, February 14, 2014, http://www.youtube.com/watch?v=QXGjRkjAXrM.
25. Draaisma, "Stereotypes of Autism," 1478.
26. Patch, "Autism in Pop Culture."
27. J.C. Huws and R.S.P. Jones, "'They Just Seem to Live Their Lives in Their Own Little World': Lay Perceptions of Autism," *Disability and Society* 25, no. 3 (2010): 341.
28. Natalie A. Henninger and Julie Lounds Taylor, "Outcomes in Adults with Austism Spectrum Disorders: A Historical Perspective," *Autism* 17, no. 1 (January 2013): 6.
29. Anat Klin and Dafna Lemish, "Mental Disorders Stigma in the Media: Review of Studies on Production, Content, and Influences," *Journal of Health Communication* 13, no. 5 (2008): 435
30. Huws and Jones, "'They Just Seem to Live Their Lives in Their Own Little World," #336"; A.F. Jorm, "Mental Health Literacy: Public Knowledge and Beliefs About Mental Disorders," *The British Journal of Psychiatry* 177 (2000): 398; Heather Stuart, "Media Portrayal of Mental Illness and Its Treatments: What Effect Does It Have on People with Mental Illness?," *CNS Drugs* 20, no. 2 (2006): 101.
31. Monika Bednarek, "Constructing 'Nerdiness': Characterisation in *The Big Bang Theory*," *Multilingua* 31 (2012): 203.
32. There is an additional, gendered component to these assumptions. The instability and hypersexuality of Carrie's bi-polar disorder might be, diagnostically, realistic; but I would argue that its televisual presentation also draws uncomfortably on gendered stereotypes of "female" hysteria.
33. Klin and Lemish, "Mental Disorders Stigma in the Media," 435; Stuart, "Media Portrayal of Mental Illness and Its Treatments," 102.
34. Klin and Lemish, "Mental Disorders Stigma in the Media," 438.

35. Stuart, "Media Portrayal of Mental Illness and Its Treatments," 101.
36. Ibid., 102.
37. Esther Breger, "TV Needs to Stop Treating Mental Illness Like a Superpower," *New Republic*, April 24, 2014, http://www.newrepublic.com/article/117515/black-box-abc-and-tvs-mental-illness-problem.
38. Draaisma, "Stereotypes of Autism," 1478.
39. Sheri L. Johnson, et al., "Creativity and Bipolar Disorder: Touched by Fire or Burning with Questions?," *Clinical Psychology Review* 32 (2012): 7; Kay Redfield Jamison, "Great Wits and Madness: More Nearly Allied?," *The British Journal of Psychiatry* 199 (2011): 352.
40. Simon Kyaga, et al., "Mental Illness, Suicide, and Creativity: 40-Year Prospective Population Study," *Journal of Psychiatric Research* 47 (2013): 89.
41. Johnson et al., "Creativity and Bipolar Disorder," 2.
42. Rohr, "Screening Madness in American Culture."
43. Breger, "TV Needs to Stop Treating Mental Illness Like a Superpower," 3.
44. Draaisma, "Stereotypes of Autism," 1477.
45. Huws and Jones, "'They Just Seem to Live Their Lives in Their Own Little World,'" 341.
46. Straus, "Idiots Savants, Talented Aments, Mono-Savants, Autistic Savants, Just Plain Savants, People with Savant Syndrome, and Autistic People Who Are Good at Things."
47. Mike DuBose, "Morality, Complexity, Experts, and Systems of Authority in *House* MD: Or, 'My Big Brain is My Superpower,'" *Television and New Media* 11, no. 1 (2010): 24.
48. Ibid.
49. Otto F. Wahl, "Stigma as a Barrier to Recovery from Mental Illness," *Trends in Cognitive Sciences* 16, no. 1 (2012): 9.
50. Michigan State University, "Scientific Literacy: How Do Americans Stack Up?," *ScienceDaily*, February 7, 2007, www.sciencedaily.com/releases/2007/02/070218134322.htm.
51. Pew Research Center for the People and the Press, "Public's Knowledge of Science and Technology," April 22, 2013, http://www.people-press.org/2013/04/22/publics-knowledge-of-science-and-technology.
52. Wahl, "Stigma as a Barrier to Recovery from Mental Illness," 9.
53. Ibid.
54. Jorm, "Mental Health Literacy," 396.
55. Huws and Jones, "'They Just Seem to Live Their Lives in Their Own Little World,'" 341.

REFERENCES

Bednarek, Monika. "Constructing 'Nerdiness': Characterisation in *The Big Bang Theory*." *Multilingua* 31 (2012): 199–229.
Breger, Esther. "TV Needs to Stop Treating Mental Illness Like a Superpower." *New Republic*, April 24, 2014. http://www.newrepublic.com/article/117515/black-box-abc-and-tvs-mental-illness-problem.
Collins, Paul. "Must-Geek TV: Is the World Ready for an Asperger's Sitcom?" *Slate*, February 6, 2009. http://www.slate.com/articles/arts/television/2009/02/mustgeek_tv.html.
Draaisma, Douwe. "Stereotypes of Autism." *Philosophical Transactions of the Royal Society* 364 (2009): 1475–1480.
DuBose, Mike. "Morality, Complexity, Experts, and Systems of Authority in *House* MD: Or, 'My Big Brain is My Superpower.'" *Television and New Media* 11, no. 1 (2010): 20–36.
Feeney, Nolan. "*Homeland:* The Case Against Calling Carrie a Bipolar 'Superhero.'" *The Atlantic*, October 7, 2013. http://www.theatlantic.com/entertainment/archive/2013/10/-em-homeland-em-the-case-against-calling-carrie-a-bipolar-superhero/280321/2/.

Harmon, Dan. Interview by Kevin Pollack. *Kevin Pollack Chat Show* #150. February 14, 2014. http://www.youtube.com/watch?v=QXGjRkjAXrM.
Henninger, Natalie A., and Julie Lounds Taylor. "Outcomes in Adults with Austism Spectrum Disorders: A Historical Perspective." *Autism* 17, no. 1 (January 2013): 103–116.
Huws, J.C. and R.S.P. Jones. "'They Just Seem to Live Their Lives in Their Own Little World': Lay Perceptions of Autism." *Disability and Society* 25, no. 3 (2010): 331–44.
Jamison, Kay Redfield. "Great Wits and Madness: More Nearly Allied?" *The British Journal of Psychiatry* 199 (2011): 351–52.
Johnson, Sheri L., et al. "Creativity and Bipolar Disorder: Touched by Fire or Burning with Questions?" *Clinical Psychology Review* 32 (2012): 1–12.
Jorm, A.F. "Mental Health Literacy: Public Knowledge and Beliefs About Mental Disorders." *The British Journal of Psychiatry* 177 (2000): 396–401.
Klin, Anat, and Dafna Lemish. "Mental Disorders Stigma in the Media: Review of Studies on Production, Content, and Influences." *Journal of Health Communication* 13, no. 5 (2008): 434–49.
Kyaga, Simon, et al. "Mental Illness, Suicide, and Creativity: 40-Year Prospective Population Study." *Journal of Psychiatric Research* 47 (2013): 83–90.
Michigan State University. "Scientific Literacy: How Do Americans Stack Up?" *ScienceDaily,* February 7, 2007. www.sciencedaily.com/releases/2007/02/070218134322.htm.
Parsons, Jim. Interview by Noel Murray. *AV Club.* May 1, 2009. www.avclub.com/article/jim-parsons-27415.
Patch, Nick. "Autism in Pop Culture: Characters on Autism Spectrum on TV, But Do They Get It Right?" *Huffington Post—Canada*, December 27, 2012. http://www.huffingtonpost.ca/2012/12/27/autism-in-pop-culture_n_2369681.html.
Pew Research Center for the People and the Press. "Public's Knowledge of Science and Technology." April 22, 2013. http://www.people-press.org/2013/04/22/publics-knowledge-of-science-and-technology.
Rohr, Susanne. "Screening Madness in American Culture." *Journal of Medical Humanities,* June 2014. doi: 10.1007/s10912-014-9287-3.
Sepinwall, Alan. "Reader Mail: Reader Mail: Does Sheldon from 'Big Bang Theory' have Asperger's?" *The Star Ledger,* August 13, 2009. www.nj.com/entertainment/tv/index.ssf/2009/08/reader_mail_does_sheldon_from.html.
Straus, Joseph. "Idiots Savants, Talented Aments, Mono-Savants, Autistic Savants, Just Plain Savants, People with Savant Syndrome, and Autistic People Who Are Good at Things: A View From Disability Studies." *Disability Studies Quarterly* 34, no. 3 (2014). http://dsq-sds.org/article/view/3407/3640.
Stuart, Heather. "Media Portrayal of Mental Illness and Its Treatments: What Effect Does It Have on People with Mental Illness?" *CNS Drugs* 20, no. 2 (2006): 99–106.
Sweeny, Craig. "Rat Race." *Elementary*, season 1, episode 4. Directed by Rosemary Rodriguez. Aired October 25, 2012, on CBS. Amazon.com.
Thielman, Sam. "Jim Parsons Hits the Stratosphere: The Star of TV's Biggest Show Talks About *The Big Bang Theory,* Emmy Awards and Larry Kramer." *Adweek,* September 1, 2014. http://www.adweek.com/news/television/jim-parsons-hits-stratosphere-159809.
Wahl, Otto. "Stigma as a Barrier to Recovery from Mental Illness." *Trends in Cognitive Sciences* 16, no. 1 (2012): 9–10.
Walters, Shannon. "Cool Aspie Humor: Cognitive Difference and Kenneth Burke's Comic Corrective in *The Big Bang Theory* and *Community." Journal of Literary and Cultural Disability Studies* 7, no. 3 (2013): 271–288.

Temperance Brennan

A Case Study in Genius and Autism Spectrum Disorder

Kristin Larson

When intellectual superiority is portrayed on television, it is often infused with quirky personality features that allow for engaging character development and humor. This is true for Temperance Brennan, the female protagonist in the series *Bones*, whose genius is implied and whose social skills are lacking. She is a forensic anthropologist employed at the Jeffersonian Institute in Washington, D.C. (a fictional research and educational institute, based on the Smithsonian Institute), and she works with the FBI to assist in solving murders. Brennan is portrayed as a genius both implicitly in her scientific achievements and competence, as well as explicitly, in that she informs other characters of her status as a genius. She claims, quite bluntly, that she is the best forensic anthropologist in the world, and those around her seem to agree; her partner, FBI special agent Seeley Booth, refers to her as a "forensic genius"[1] and her boss, Camille Saroyan, acquiesces to her demands because of her brilliance. If genius is a judgment based on exceptional intelligence, creativity, and influence, then Brennan qualifies.[2]

Brennan is a complex character, whose personality is dominated by rationality and social deficits. Her intellectualism is set in contrast to Booth's gut instinct and emotional intelligence. However, her superior intellect is coupled with a level of direct communication that violates social rules for appropriate discourse. While her bluntness can be interpreted as warranted arrogance or a scientist's commitment to factual declaration, it can also be interpreted as a severe deficit in social skills that is indicative of mental illness. Brennan's tendency toward awkward social interaction, literal interpretation of sarcasm and metaphors, and expert skill in one area of expertise has led some viewers to conclude that Brennan has Asperger's Disorder. Conversely, the trauma she experienced in childhood complicates her relationships and development. Is it psychopathology or insecurity? The following is a case study, investigating the relationship between Brennan's genius and mental illness. Specifically, this study interrogates the idea, popular among Autism and Asperger communities, that Brennan has High Functioning Autism (HFA).

Evidence of High Functioning Autism

While there is no mention in the series of Brennan having a diagnosis of any mental illness, there is no shortage of conjecture on the subject in online forums (i.e., Wrongplanet.net, an online community for Autism and Asperger's), blogs, and even some published literature.[3] In many ways, Brennan's behavior is consistent with HFA. Individuals whose behavior is characterized by social impairment, difficulty with non-verbal communication and restricted interests or behavior, with no cognitive or language delays, were diagnosed with Asperger's Disorder until recently. With the release of the fifth edition of the Diagnostic and Statistical Manual of Mental Disorders in May of 2013, this disorder was subsumed under Autism Spectrum Disorder.[4] Now, this combination of symptoms is most often referred to as HFA. The *International Classification of Disorders*, tenth edition (*ICD-10*), recognizes this disorder and adds the feature of specialized skills in narrow or abnormal fields of interest.[5] Popular representations of HFA are so common in crime dramas that viewers become superficially familiar with the disorder and feel free to speculate about diagnoses.[6]

Brennan is portrayed as having a restricted, almost obsessive interest and superior skill in forensic anthropology. For example, this is strongly suggested when, on her honeymoon in Buenos Aires, she abandons her vacation plans with her new husband, Booth, and happily volunteers her services to help identify a skeletonized murder victim.[7] Similarly, she demonstrates a lack of familiarity with pop culture that may be further evidence of her restricted interests. As per the *ICD-10*, this can be seen as indicative of HFA.

Those with HFA are also likely to have difficulty making friends and maintaining friendships. This is most likely due to the inability to understand social rules rather than a desire to withdraw from social contact.[8] Brennan's social interactions are awkward, sometimes offensive, and often to humorous or dramatic effect. Contributing to interpersonal difficulties, she shares very little about herself but will talk in minute, clinical detail about her interests, specifically her knowledge about skeleton anatomy.[9] Her conversations indicate HFA in that they are pedantic and fail to acknowledge the listener's lack of engagement or understanding.[10] For instance, in one episode she entertains a baby by waving her hands and chanting, "dancing phalanges."[11] From this perspective, her use of technical jargon and formal style of speech may be more indicative of HFA than simply a consequence of her intelligence.[12]

Also consistent with HFA, Brennan's social deficits are exacerbated by difficulty in interpreting figurative language and non-verbal aspects of communication, including sarcasm, metaphors, jokes, and facial expressions.[13] When Booth describes making love as when two people become one, Brennan ignores (or misinterprets) the emotional reference saying, "It is scientifically impossible for two objects to occupy the same space."[14] On several occasions, Brennan has been asked to speak from her heart, to which she responds that she will, instead, speak from her mouth. When approached by a woman who wanted to engage in a personal conversation saying, "I wanted to talk to you, woman to woman, if that is possible," Brennan responds, "It is possible, because we are both women."[15] Each of these instances demonstrates a limited ability to understand common figurative expressions.

Brennan also demonstrates restricted emotional intelligence that is associated with HFA. This impairs her ability to express herself and interpret others' emotions. In season four, FBI psychologist Lance Sweets offers to give her skills training, stating, "We'll start with a simple exercise um, to recognize emotions from facial expressions. Then I'll give you skills to deal with those emotions.[16] This scene ultimately suggests that Sweets interprets her behavior as HFA. On one hand, the series suggests that this is a virtuous deficit, in that it makes her bad at lying. However, she acknowledges frustration in her inability to deceive and manipulate suspects during interrogation, a skill at which Booth excels. Clearly there are enough symptoms to justify speculation regarding her mental health. Nevertheless, the show's creator has resisted making an explicit diagnosis. Still, the actress who portrays Brennan, Emily Deschanel, states, "Hart Hanson, the creator of the show, and I discuss, you know, that my character almost has Asperger syndrome, and, you know, if maybe if it was a film, that I maybe specifically would have Asperger's."[17]

Interestingly, despite a lack of explicit diagnosis on the show, Brennan's seeming HFA has had an impact on the Asperger's and HFA community. The popular conception of an "Aspie," a name embraced by those diagnosed with Asperger's Disorder or HFA, is becoming more acceptable if not desirable. Young people see the label as a valid explanation for their difficulties in socializing as well as an indication of intelligence and a path to belonging to a growing group.[18] One online discussion on Wrongplanet.net describes this label as "cool" specifically because of its representation in popular culture and shows such as "Bones."

Although the show's depiction of aspects of mental illness is intentional, in reality, their association with genius is questionable. Genius and prodigy are separate from savantism, which is to say that not all highly gifted persons have HFA.[19] Being highly intelligent and having social deficits does not implicitly warrant a diagnosis of HFA. More importantly, in Brennan, the features of HFA are inconsistent and the writers have provided enough back-story to warrant considering a differential diagnosis.

Evidence for an Alternative Diagnosis

In spite of the series creator stating that the elements of HFA are integral to Brennan's character, there are qualities of her behavior that are contrary to that diagnosis. Brennan has close relationships and describes Angela as her best friend.[20] Further, she sometimes demonstrates particular empathy and compassion, such as when she offers money to save the life of a pig to which Angela has become attached.[21] Throughout the seasons, Brennan also develops the capacity for romance and intimacy with her partner, Booth. Early in season six, she describes the idea of having sex with Booth as potentially satisfying, yet she states that a relationship would never work. However, by season seven, she tells him, "I love you." These character developments seem to contradict an HFA diagnosis.

Further, her early childhood experiences and restricted emotional expression suggest a well-defended psyche. Brennan describes her parents abandoning her as a child, leaving her in the care of her teenage brother. Her brother also eventually leaves her and she is then placed in the foster care system. She also describes abuse at the hands of a foster family, who locked her in the trunk of a car for two days because she had broken a dish.[22] Her adult behavior is rife with unconscious motivations in response to the threat of re-experiencing her childhood pain. This is representative of classic Freudian defense mechanisms.[23]

Intellectualization is Brennan's defense of choice and it allows her to avoid dealing with the deep wounds caused by this abandonment and abuse. Intellectualization is a means of controlling affect,[24] meaning that it suppresses a normal emotional response to an event through the excessive use of cognitive processes.[25] Bones can be seen suppressing emotional responses by focusing on her work in numerous episodes. Her stoic response to brutalized, decomposing corpses may be attributed to experience and professionalism, but may also be a manifestation of her denial of emotional reactions and her safe retreat to the cognitive realm. Perhaps she is at risk for feeling too much if she reaches out even a little. Her exchange with Angela in the pilot episode suggests as much:

Angela: Honey, ever think you come off a little distant because you connect too much?

>BRENNAN: I hate psychology, it's a soft science.
>ANGELA: I know, but people are mostly soft.
>BRENNAN: Except for their bones.[26]

Her defense mechanism of intellectualization is further entrenched when it is revealed that her mother's final advice before disappearing was to "stop following her heart and use her brain."[27]

It has been theorized that intellectual superiority and competency in an occupation are related to the loss of one's parents.[28] When the child "becomes their own parent" they resolve the loss through outstanding accomplishment. Overcoming the instability of orphanhood is translated into strivings for achievement and power. Brennan's desire to control her destiny is seen in her rejection of changeable emotions in favor of the security of her intellect. Even her choice of career can be described as the defense mechanism of sublimation. Sublimation transforms internal conflicts and negative emotions by channeling them into socially acceptable pursuits.[29] She attempts to resolve her unconscious wounds through a career of finding and "rescuing" the identities of murder victims, and she advocates for these abandoned bodies in a way that no one advocated for her.

Brennan also uses rationalization, using the appearance of a valid explanation for behaviors or feelings, when the true motivation is too painful or conflicted to acknowledge.[30] Her ego believes that she is making conscious choices, yet she overlooks her unconscious motives.[31] She uses her occupation as an excuse to avoid uncomfortable or threatening situations. For example, when she thinks that Booth has been killed, she attempts to avoid the funeral, stating that she has a skeleton to identify. Her friend Angela exposes her pretense, reminding her that the corpse was 500 years old and that its family could wait.[32] She may be a genius, but she is unable to understand or even acknowledge the impact of her childhood experiences.

This insecurity is unveiled in her egotism and super-hero complex. Her extensive training in martial arts, her readiness to engage in hand to hand combat, and her affinity for the super-hero Wonder Woman, can be interpreted as classic overcompensation for her sense of powerlessness as a child.[33] Further, her willingness to engage in sexual relationships that are devoid of meaning may be an attempt to cope with her existential isolation as well as a reaction formation to her fear of abandonment.[34] While she would claim to be independent, confident and dispassionate, her behavior screams 'Notice me! Pay attention to how smart I am!' Her need for reassurance is illustrated by her tendency to remind others of her intellectual superiority. Rather than representing true genius, Alfred Adler would describe this behavior as a defense mechanism referred to as a Superiority Complex, which reveals her true feeling of inferiority.[35] In essence, she does not feel capable of competing with other individuals in the arena of self-worth. This seems to be supported in season five, when a psychic states "The world scares you. So you wrap it up neatly in bonds of reason, education, and proof."[36]

Brennan's childhood trauma, and subsequent denial of its import, is so central to her characterization that other characters directly point it out, such as when Dr. Sweets, the FBI psychologist, states, "You have an irrational prejudice against psychology, probably because of some emotions so complicated for you to deal with.... And I poked and prodded them which makes them real and painful."[37] Further, Brennan rejects the field of psychology, quite boldly, while interacting with Sweets. She rationalizes her dismissive attitude as being based in her loyalty to the scientific method. In the pilot episode, she says, "I hate psychology. My most meaningful relationships are with dead people." She goes on to say, "Dr. Sweets is not a real scientist as he bases his life on the vagaries of psychology and emotion.[38]

If these symptoms were indicative of HFA, she might learn to cope with them, but she would be helpless to eliminate them. Conversely, as the series progresses, Brennan intentionally challenges her inclination to avoid social interaction and emotional expression. She develops an intimate friendship with Angela and risks emotional vulnerability. It is a significant moment when, during a surgery in season eight, she has a vision of her dead mother and her mother encourages her to "follow her heart."[39] Irrational experiences are no longer summarily rejected. Shortly thereafter, Brennan proposes to Booth.[40] At this point in her emotional development, she states, "When Booth and I first met, I didn't believe that such a thing as love existed. I maintained that it was simply brain chemistry, but perhaps Booth is correct. Perhaps love comes first and then creates the reaction. I have no tangible proof, but I'm willing to accept Booth's premise."[41]

From the psychodynamic perspective, both her genius and HFA could be called into question. Ultimately, her rationality, superiority, obsessive work ethic, stunted social interactions, and avoidance of intimacy all serve to protect her fragile self-concept from exposure and vulnerability. She is a brilliant but damaged woman, whose healing is central to the drama.

Conclusions

While it is left unclear whether Brennan's social deficits are the result of mental illness or coping with childhood trauma, it is undeniable that the portrayal of her superior intellect is associated with unusual behavior. Genius is wedded with abnormality. Although abnormal behavior is in no way part of the definition of genius, there is a long history of the association. In dramatic depictions of genius, it seems that our collective understanding requires fairness: for the gift of intelligence, the genius must pay the price in the form of awkwardness, naiveté, or emotional isolation. In the case of Brennan, her deficits appear to be both the evidence and the cost of her intellect. In fiction, the cost of genius is often the human experience. Brennan discovers that it is her genius that separates her from others and, ultimately, herself.

Does genius excuse egotism and condescension? Would viewers accept and embrace this character if she were simply a smart but very rude anthropologist with serious personal issues? Brennan's coworkers not only tolerate her patronizing superiority, they love her in spite of it. The "golden rule" has shifted to "treat others as you treat yourself, unless you are a genius." It appears that genius, in this case, allows us to qualify her behavior as eccentric rather than ill-mannered and her social deficits as quirky. Her giftedness and naiveté engender compassion rather than disdain.

The suggestion of HFA also contributes to a sympathetic character. It has the potential to increase awareness of a disorder that is increasing in prevalence, yet the inconsistent depiction of the traits of HFA may lead to a misunderstanding of the true nature of the disorder. Although many "Aspies" have embraced Brennan, she is not really representative. Even more concerning is the use of deficits consistent with this implied diagnosis for humorous effect. We all share a collective laugh at her expense as she struggles with the most basic relationship and communication skills.

Thus, viewers embrace a model of genius that is inextricably tethered to arrogance, social deficits, and eccentricity. The genius must be mentally ill for us to accept her superiority and forgive her faults. Although *Bones* aims at framing Brennan's deficits as Asperger's Disorder, it doesn't commit to presenting a complete and accurate portrayal of the diagnosis. In spite of this, the character is intriguing in her complexity and rich with layers of deeply rooted motivations. Viewers empathize with her struggles and celebrate her triumphs: developing identity in the midst of genius, overcoming mortal emotional wounds, and developing a heart in the midst of bones.

Notes

1. Josh Berman, "The Wannabe in the Weeds," *Bones*, season 3, episode 14, directed by Gordon C. Lonsdale, aired May 12, 2008, on Fox.
2. Robert S. Albert, "Toward a Behavioral Definition of Genius," *American Psychologist* 30, no. 2 (1975): 140.
3. David C. Giles, "DSM-V Is Taking Away Our Identity: The reaction of the online community to the proposed changes in the diagnosis of Asperger's disorder," *Health* 18, no. 2 (2014): 179.
4. American Psychiatric Association, *Diagnostic and Statistical Manual of Mental Disorders: DSM-V* (Washington, D.C.: American Psychiatric Association, 2013), 50.
5. World Health Organization, *The ICD-10 Classification of Mental and Behavioural disorders: Clinical descriptions and diagnostic guidelines* (Geneva: World Health Organization, 1992), 203.
6. Giles, "DSM-V Is Taking Away Our Identity: The reaction of the online community to the proposed changes in the diagnosis of Asperger's disorder," 179.
7. Dave Thomas, "The Nazi on the Honeymoon," *Bones*, season 9, episode 7, directed by Jeannot Szwarc, aired November 4, 2013, on Fox.
8. Lorna Wing, "Asperger's Syndrome: A clinical account," *Psychological Medicine* 11 (1981): 115.
9. Mohammad Ghaziuddin and Leonore Gerstein, "Pedantic Speaking Style Differentiates Asperger Syndrome from High-Functioning Autism," *Journal of Autism and Developmental Disorders* 26 (1996): 585.
10. Mohammad Ghaziuddin, "Brief Report: Should the DSM V drop Asperger's Syndrome?" *Journal of Autism and Developmental Disorders* 40 (2010): 1146.
11. Karine Rosenthal, "The Baby in the Bough," *Bones*, season 3, episode 12, directed by Ian Toynton, aired April 28, 2008, on Fox.
12. Benjamin Saddock and Virginia Saddock, *Kaplan and Saddock's Synopsis of Psychiatry: Behavioral Sciences Clinical Psychiatry,* 10th ed. (Baltimore: Williams & Wilkins, 2007), 1201.
13. Ibid.
14. Josh Berman, "Death in the Saddle," *Bones*, season 3, episode 3, directed by Craig Ross, Jr., aired October 9, 2007, on Fox.
15. Janet Tamaro, "The Man in the Mud," *Bones*, season 3, episode 10, directed by Scott Lautanen, aired September 14, 2008, on Fox.
16. Elizabeth Benjamin, "The Bones that Foam," *Bones*, season 4, episode 16, directed by David Boreanaz, aired March 12, 2009, on Fox.
17. Ellen Gray, "Boreanaz Says 'Bones' Is Not Procedural," *Philadelphia Daily News*, January 31, 2007, http://www.philly.com/philly/columnists/ellen_gray/20070131_Ellen_Gray__Boreanaz_says__Bones__is_not_procedural.html.
18. Giles, "DSM-V Is Taking Away Our Identity: The reaction of the online community to the proposed changes in the diagnosis of Asperger's disorder," 179.
19. David A. Treffert, "Savant Syndrome: Realities, Myths and Misconceptions," *Journal of Autism and Developmental Disorders* 44 (2014): 564.
20. Josh Berman, "The Perfect Pieces in the Purple Pond," *Bones*, season 4, episode 5, directed by Jeannot Szwarc, aired September 24, 2008, on Fox.
21. Dean Lopata, "The Tough Man in the Tender Chicken," *Bones*, season 5, episode 6, directed by Dwight H. Little, aired November 5, 2009, on Fox.
22. Dean Lopata, "Mayhem on a Cross," *Bones*, season 4, episode 21, directed by Jeff Woolnough, aired April 16, 2009, on Fox.
23. Sigmund Freud, *Inhibitions, Symptoms and Anxiety* (New York: W. W. Norton, 1990), 97.

24. Siegfried Zepf, "About Rationalization and Intellectualization," *International Forum of Psychoanalysis* 20 (2011): 148.
25. Brad Bowins, "Psychological Defense Mechanisms: A new perspective," *The American Journal of Psychoanalysis* 64, no. 1 (2004): 1.
26. Hart Hanson, "Pilot," *Bones* season 1, episode 1, directed by Greg Yaitanes, aired September 13, 2005, on Fox.
27. Michael Peterson, "The Doll in the Derby," *Bones*, season 8, episode 14, directed by Tawnia McKiernan, aired February 4, 2013, on Fox.
28. J. Marvin Eisenstadt, "Parental Loss and Genius," *American Psychologist* 33, no. 3 (1978): 211
29. Saddock and Saddock, *Kaplan and Saddock's Synopsis of psychiatry: Behavioral Sciences clinical psychiatry*, 1201.
30. Ibid.
31. Zepf, "About Rationalization and Intellectualization," 148.
32. Hart Hanson and Stephen Nathan, "The Pain in the Heart," *Bones*, season 3, episode 15, directed by Allan Kroeker, aired May 19, 2008, on Fox.
33. Scott Williams, "Mummy in the Maze," *Bones*, season 3, episode 5, directed by Marita Grabiak, aired October 30, 2007, on Fox.
34. Carla Kettner and Mark Lisson, "Man in the Outhouse," *Bones*, season 4, episode 3, directed by Steven DePaul, aired September 10, 2008, on Fox.
35. Alfred Adler, *Understanding Human Nature* (New York: Greenberg, 1946), 61.
36. Hart Hanson, "Harbingers in the Fountain," *Bones*, season 5, episode 1, directed by Ian Toynton, aired September 17, 2009, on Fox.
37. Berman, "Wannabe in the Weeds."
38. Karina Csolty, "The He in the She," *Bones*, season 1, episode 1, directed by Craig Ross, Jr., aired October 8, 2008, on Fox.
39. Dave Thomas, "The Shot in the Dark," *Bones*, season 8 episode 15, directed by François Velle, aired February 11, 2013, on Fox.
40. Stephen Nathan and Jonathan Collier, "The Secret in the Siege," *Bones*, season 8, episode 24, directed by David Boreanaz, aired April 29, 2013, on Fox.
41. Pat Charles and Josh Berman, "The Dentist in the Ditch," *Bones*, season 8, episode 15, directed by Dwight Little, aired January 28, 2010, on Fox.

References

Adler, Alfred. *Understanding Human Nature*. New York: Greenberg,1946.Albert, Robert S. "Toward a behavioral definition of Genius." *American Psychologist* 30, no. 2 (1975): 140–151.
American Psychiatric Association. *Diagnostic and Statistical Manual of Mental Disorders: DSM-V* Washington, D.C.: American Psychiatric Association, 2013.
Benjamin, Elizabeth. "The Bones that Foam." *Bones*, season 4, episode 16. Directed by David Boreanaz. Aired March 12, 2009, on Fox. Netflix.com.
Berman, Josh. "Death in the Saddle." *Bones*, season 3, episode 3. Directed by Craig Ross, Jr. Aired October 9, 2007, on Fox. Netflix.com.
_____. "The Perfect Pieces in the Purple Pond." *Bones*, season 4, episode 5. Directed by Jeannot Szwarc. Aired September 24, 2008, on Fox. Netflix.com.
_____. "The Wannabe in the Weeds." *Bones*, season 3, episode 14. Directed by Gordon C. Lonsdale. Aired May 12, 2008, on Fox. Netflix.com.
Bowins, Brad. "Psychological Defense Mechanisms: A new perspective." *The American Journal of Psychoanalysis* 64, no. 1 (2004) 1–26.
Charles, Pat, and Josh Berman. "The Dentist in the Ditch." *Bones*, season 8, episode 15. Directed by Dwight Little. Aired January 28, 2010, on Fox. Netflix.com.

Csolty, Karina. "The He in the She." *Bones*, season 1, episode 1. Directed by Craig Ross, Jr. Aired October 8, 2008, on Fox. Netflix.com.
Eisenstadt, J. Marvin. "Parental Loss and Genius." *American Psychologist* 33, no. 3 (1978): 211–223.
Freud, Sigmund. *Inhibitions, Symptoms and Anxiety*. New York: W. W. Norton, 1990.
Ghaziuddin, Mohammad. "Brief report: Should the DSM V Drop Asperger's Syndrome?" *Journal of Autism and Developmental Disorders* 40 (2010): 1146–1148.
Ghaziuddin, Mohammad, and Leonore Gerstein. "Pedantic speaking style differentiates Asperger syndrome from high-functioning autism," *Journal of Autism and Developmental Disorders* 26 (1996): 585–595.
Giles, David C. "DSM-V Is Taking Away Our Identity: The reaction of the online community to the proposed changes in the diagnosis of Asperger's disorder." *Health* 18, no. 2 (2014): 179–195.
Gray, Ellen, "Boreanaz says 'Bones' is not procedural," *Philadelphia Daily News*. January 31, 2007. http://www.philly.com/philly/columnists/ellen_gray/20070131_Ellen_Gray__Boreanaz_says__Bones__is_not_procedural.html.
Hanson, Hart, "Harbingers in the Fountain." *Bones*, season 5, episode 1. Directed by Ian Toynton. Aired September 17, 2009, on Fox. Netflix.com.
_____."Pilot." *Bones*, season 1, episode 1. Directed by Greg Yaitanes. Aired September 13, 2005, on Fox. Netflix.com.
Hanson, Hart, and Stephen Nathan. "The Pain in the Heart." *Bones*, season 3, episode 15. Directed by Allan Kroeker. Aired May 19, 2008, on Fox. Netflix.com.
Kettner, Carla, and Mark Lisson. "Man in the Outhouse." *Bones*, season 4, episode 3. Directed by Steven DePaul. Aired September 10, 2008, on Fox. Netflix.com.
Lopata, Dean. "Mayhem on a Cross." *Bones*, season 4, episode 21. Directed by Jeff Woolnough. Aired April 16, 2009, on Fox. Netflix.com.
_____. "The Tough Man in the Tender Chicken." *Bones*, season 5, episode 6. Directed by Dwight H. Little. Aired November 5, 2009, on Fox. Netflix.com.
Nathan, Stephen, and Jonathan Collier. "The Secret in the Siege." *Bones*, season 8, episode 24. Directed by David Boreanaz. Aired April 29, 2013, on Fox. Netflix.com.
Peterson, Michael. "The Doll in the Derby." *Bones*, season 8, episode 14. Directed by Tawnia McKiernan. Aired February 4, 2013, on Fox. Netflix.com.
Rosenthal, Karine. "The Baby in the Bough." *Bones*, season 3, episode 12. Directed by Ian Toynton. Aired April 28, 2008, on Fox. Netflix.com.
Saddock, Benjamin, and Virginia Saddock, *Kaplan and Saddock's Synopsis of Psychiatry: Behavioral Sciences Clinical Psychiatry*, 10th ed. Baltimore: Williams & Wilkins, 2007.
Tamaro, Janet. "The Man in the Mud." *Bones*, season 3, episode 10. Directed by Scott Lautanen. Aired September 14, 2008, on Fox. Netflix.com.
Thomas, Dave, "The Nazi on the Honeymoon." *Bones*, season 9, episode 7. Directed by Jeannot Szwarc. Aired November 4, 2013, on Fox. Netflix.com
_____. "The Shot in the Dark." *Bones*, season 8, episode 15. Directed by François Velle. Aired February 11, 2013, on Fox. Netflix.com.
Treffert, David A. "Savant Syndrome: Realities, Myths and Misconceptions." *Journal of Autism and Developmental Disorders* 44 (2014): 564–571.
Williams, Scott. "Mummy in the Maze." *Bones*, season 3, episode 5. Directed by Marita Grabiak. Aired October 30, 2007, on Fox. Netflix.com.
Wing, Lorna. "Asperger's Syndrome: A clinical account." *Psychological Medicine* 11 (1981): 115–129.
World Health Organization. *The ICD-10 Classification of Mental and Behavioural Disorders: Clinical descriptions and diagnostic guidelines*. Geneva: World Health Organization, 1992.
Zepf, Siegfried. "About Rationalization and Intellectualization," *International Forum of Psychoanalysis* 20 (2011): 148–158.

True Detective or Smooth Criminal?

The (Dys)functional Genius in Contemporary Detective Shows

Laura-Marie von Czarnowsky *and* Annette Schimmelpfennig

While the genius has become a staple character on television, it seems nowhere more at home than in medical or detective shows. The reason for this is simple: because both doctors and detectives are in the business of answering exceedingly difficult questions, these kinds of shows provide the geniuses with a platform to showcase their talent. The viewer accompanies the geniuses on their hunt, for as Torben Grodal notes, "the dominant emotion activated in [...] detective fictions is the dopamine-supported emotion of seeking."[1] Yet the motivation for "seeking" in these shows may vary, since not all geniuses are seeking to solve a case; some are also seeking redemption. Ingenuity is not only limited to their work life, and, thus, in contemporary detective shows, the genius is a complex personality for whom brilliance is both a blessing and a burden.

This chapter focuses on the current trend of male genius detectives on screen, drawing on four recent examples: BBC's *Sherlock* (2010), NBC's *Hannibal* (2013), HBO's *True Detective* (2013), and Showtime's *Dexter* (2006).[2] Examining how the genius is positioned between highly functional expert and dysfunctional outlaw, we also analyze his loyal and essential companion: the compulsory sidekick, who is often an underestimated moral influence. The ingenuity of the detectives, which can save as well as endanger lives, also appeals to both female characters and equally ingenious adversaries. In keeping with this, we will illustrate the extent to which the genius crosses legal boundaries while continuously emphasizing the intellectual differences between himself and ordinary mortals. These legal and intellectual boundaries are often markedly fluid, and thus allow the genius to appear even more complex, thereby making him even more fascinating both to other characters in his fictional world and to television audiences.

Genius, Julia Kristeva writes, "is quite simply creativity."[3] Yet on television, it seems to be more than this. If we dispute that genius is creativity, we must identify other factors that define genius. Marjorie Garber, in an insightful analysis of the term, explains that the "thinkers of antiquity suggested that every person had two geniuses, one good and one evil, which competed for influence."[4] This certainly applies to all examples discussed here: each genius is torn between good and bad, constantly forced to decide how to use his powers. In the shows discussed in this chapter, the factor that determines this choice is not intrinsic, but externalized. Every genius is accompanied by a sidekick who serves as the straight man to his eccentricity, to highlight his intellect and epiphanies by not exhibiting the same abilities, and to guide the genius beyond strictly intellectual exercises back into the fold of social interactions.

The latter constitutes an area where the genius is not a master, but a novice, for it seems that television insinuates that the price for exceptional brilliance is a severe lack of social competence. Ashley Polasek analyzes *House* (2004) as one of the modern TV iterations of Sherlock Holmes, and finds that "House is a genius without any social graces."[5] Garber too pinpoints the genius's inability to fit in and acknowledges not only a lack of social graces, but an often repeated relationship between genius and eccentricity (especially) in crime fiction. Here, she draws on *House*'s role model Holmes as an example, and calls him "a classic embodiment of the genius."[6] The classic genius then is obviously both bright *and* eccentric, accompanied by a trusty sidekick, and more concerned with the hunt than the after-effects of a puzzle's solution. As Kathleen Belin Owen argues, the postmodern genius shares all of these characteristics; "the postmodern detective story seeks not to evade or eliminate echoes of its genre's traditions; rather, it embraces the traditional, then turns it right on its head."[7] From the beginning, the genius is established as a character that refuses to be either black or white, but moves within a grey area. Thus, as Stephen Cooper writes, "the detective does maintain a position, both professional and moral, which is precariously marginal to either camp."[8] This is because he is never exclusively good or evil, but fluctuates between the restrictions of the law and the temptations of illegality.

The Genius Detectives

Undeniably, the most prominent example of a genius detective is Arthur Conan Doyle's Sherlock Holmes, who in the eponymous BBC production investigates crimes in present-day London. Sherlock is the epitome of the eccentric genius who combines a multitude of stereotypes: he is a quick, analytical thinker, has a vivid imagination, and has precise powers of observation; at the same time, he is unable to pursue healthy relationships. Sherlock is downright rude to everybody. He knows quite well that he is smarter than his colleagues and lets them feel it at any given opportunity, although it seems as if he is unable to channel his output and how he appeals to other people. Impassively, he exposes an affair between two co-workers in "A Study in Pink," yet wonders why he is frequently described as "freak" and "psychopath"[9] by them. Characterizing himself as a "high-functioning sociopath,"[10] Sherlock tries to establish how he is seen by the people around him. He is a prime example of a genius with outstandingly advanced mental capabilities and child-like manners, such as brutal honesty, the constant seeking of endorsement, and stubborn perseverance. Coincidentally, the rational appearance he manically tries to maintain is yet a façade to hide another, darker aspect of his personality: Sherlock is a drug addict who unsuccessfully tries to hide his habit. He cannot fathom that the drugs destroy his brilliant mind and thus reveals the boundaries of his otherwise rational thinking. Geniality, it seems, comes with a price.

ABC's *Hannibal* provides the audience with two men of extraordinary intellectual capacity. On the one hand there is Hannibal Lecter himself, a practicing psychiatrist with a highly developed sense of taste in every aspect. He is witty, suave, and articulate, hence it does not come as a surprise that people encounter him with benevolence. On the other hand there is Will Graham, Hannibal's counterpart. Will, a criminal profiler with endearing characteristics such as a heightened sensibility, a distinctive love for his dogs, and a strong imagination, employs a mental strategy not unlike Sherlock's "mind palace." The genius seems to have an alternative, mental world at his disposal. His intellect affords him the option to retreat from society and to fully stimulate himself intellectually. Hannibal's demeanor resembles that of a sophisticated entrepreneur while Will is humble and reserved, yet they are united in the destructive disorders they suffer from. Hannibal, as a result of childhood trauma, has turned to cannibalism to overcome the demons haunting him. Strikingly, the anthropophagy he practices is marked by his creativity as well. He does not simply kill and eat his victims; Hannibal celebrates every single one and manufactures them into either gourmet dishes, artworks, or both. His ingenuity is multi-layered and reflected in his double life as connoisseur of human nature and ruthless killer. Will, by contrast, suffers from severe paranoid-schizoid episodes. It is unclear whether they are the result of his work or whether they facilitate it, but either way they interfere with his life to a point where he is barely able to function and hide his illness. Hannibal, surprisingly, is more functional, at least on the surface. As a master manipulator he manages to turn his adversaries, such as Mason Verger, into helpless puppets. Yet it is remarkable that it is Will, who constantly has to negotiate what is real and what is not, who sees through Hannibal's game. Both geniuses are, although differently talented, evenly matched. Nevertheless, what they have in common with Sherlock is their eccentric tendencies and lack of social skills. What at the beginning appear to be endearing peculiarities, namely the dog hoarding and the neat over the top-meals, are at second glance indications of personality disorders. Contrary to Sherlock, they mastered the art of hiding their true personalities behind a mask of normality, at least with regard to the first season. They are both respected in their professional fields, which is also their main area of interaction and so serves to hide the fact that they only function in the workplace. In private, both are not only bachelors, but also friendless. The genius, as can be concluded from *Sherlock*, *Hannibal*, and also the following examples, is not meant to be a family man for a reason, as close emotional attachments jeopardize his own safety and that of others.

While Sherlock and Will Graham very obviously fall into the genius category, the case is less clear cut with Dexter Morgan. Dexter, a blood spatter analyst for Miami Metro by day and a vigilante killer with an unquenchable thirst for blood by night, goes to great lengths not to appear as anything but ordinary, thus deliberately subverting Garber's assessment that one of the genius's most significant characteristics is eccentricity.[11] Dexter creates an illusion of perfect conventionality, causing Green to ponder that "[i]n a way, nothing about Dexter is strange."[12] Dexter's genius is located in his ability to kill and remain undetected while blending in and hiding his "Dark Passenger," the part of him that is addicted to murder. This is a significant point of departure from both Conan Doyle's and the BBC's Sherlock, as these iterations fully and visibly inhabit the category of the socially inept genius. Santalauria further finds that Dexter "is not even an archetypal sublime and atrocious Gothic villain like Hannibal Lecter. Dexter's originality lies in the 'normality' of the serial killer. Even though Dexter is a vocational killer, he is only a man who blunders, makes mistakes and tries to do the right things."[13] While all of this is perfectly true, Dexter's power of concealment and his ability to multitask two discrete and contradictory lives marks him not only as an ordinary man, but as a (criminal) genius with good intentions. Both Green and Santaularia connect Dexter with the superhero genre because of the vigilante aspect of *Dexter*'s narrative and his ability to do what others cannot.[14] Unlike most superheroes, Dexter is not a typical knight in shining armor; instead, he reinforces the postmodern detective's stock trait of moral ambiguity. In the series' finale, Dexter, in an act of self-punishment, flees Miami for Oregon, where he works as a normal lumberjack. In his new profession, Dexter's genius is suppressed, thus once more indicating that Dexter needs both crime and punishment to shine. However, for the seven previous seasons, his facade is so perfect that the whole homicide department falls prey to it, with the single exception of Sergeant Doakes, who repeatedly informs Dexter, "You give me the fucking creeps, you know that, Dexter?"[15] In turn, Dexter muses that "There are no secrets in life, just hidden truths, and I beneath the surface."[16] Dexter, positioning himself underneath the surface, elevates his position intellectually: he is the only one who can see the world as it really is, and much like Will Graham, has the ability to see crimes from the killers' perspective and catch or play mouse with them, depending on his current agenda. One can argue that his genius manifests itself in perfectly realizing what kind of image he needs to create in order to pass for normal while being anything but, and more importantly, while sharing none of the emotional bonds that otherwise tie society together. Dexter's voice-over narrative continuously iterates his inability to comprehend basic human emotions such as love or grief. Sexual desire can only be raised in Dexter when it is accompanied by what he considers the supreme intellectual challenge: the perfect murder. This is made clear as early as the pilot when Dexter's admiration of the Ice Truck Killer's technique culminates in Dexter finally making a pass at his girlfriend Rita even though he previously characterized their relationship as mutually asexual. His inner lack of social graces is one key feature of the genius, even though Dexter manages to hide it well.

True Detective plays the genius trope straight. While *Sherlock*, *Hannibal*, and *Dexter* occasionally veer into camp via gunshot fire dialogue, eccentric costuming, or an overabundance of bright colors, *True Detective* takes its story and its genius very (and as some critics have suggested, overly) seriously.[17] Orr admires the quality of the "hyper-literate dialogue by writer/creator Nic Pizzolatto," much of which is given to detective Rust Cohle, "a brilliant misfit prone to rococo outpourings of evangelical nihilism."[18] Cohle inhabits the stereotype, highlighting his ingenuity not only by suddenly bursting into Nietzsche, but also by carrying a black notebook in which he records insights that none of the other characters, including his partner Marty, are able to fathom. In the spirit of Sherlock and Will Graham, Rust's brilliant mind comes at the price of complete social ignorance: he manages to alienate his whole department on his very first day.[19] In the show's frame narrative set in 2012, in which Cohle is interviewed by two policemen on an old case of his, he is depicted as just as aloof, mysterious, brilliant, and unpredictable as he was in 1995, even though he has since left the police force and instead trails criminals on his own. *True Detective,* like *Hannibal, Dexter,* and *Sherlock,* insinuates that the righteous genius cannot be contained by the bonds of the law it is set to uphold.

The Sidekicks

Although the genius is unarguably the center of attention in contemporary detective fiction, the sidekick is equally compulsory. It shall be noted here that "sidekick" may be an understatement, as he is much more than a simple additional character; he is a mirror to the (literally) unreflecting genius and presents an undervalued influence as the possible restorer of jeopardized morality.

Just as Sherlock is the prototype of the genius, John Watson is the prototypical sidekick. Recently returned from the war in Afghanistan, *Sherlock*'s Watson suffers from PTSD. The sidekick, similar to the genius, is established as a character with a troubled past, although he appears far more capable of mastering the challenges of normal life. Watson is aware of his problems and seeks help in the form of psychiatric treatment. While the genius is resistant to any kind of help and critique from the outside world, the sidekick is insightful and considerate. However, he bears a striking resemblance to the supposedly matchless genius. When Watson encounters Sherlock's plain-spoken brother, Mycroft Holmes, in the very first episode, Mycroft assesses him quickly, saying, "you don't seem the kind to make friends easily,"[20] which is utterly true. Like Sherlock's, Watson's social environment is restricted, although it seems by circumstances and not by choice. As different as Watson and Sherlock may seem, it is the few similarities they share that allow their partnership to form and to develop into a friendship. Sherlock understands that Watson can be useful and is not as bothersome as everybody else. Over the course of the series, Watson evolves into Sherlock's spokesperson. Meanwhile, solving cases with Sherlock brings back normalcy to Watson's life. In this case, the genius and sidekick have formed a mutually beneficial symbiosis.

Hannibal suggests the existence of not one, but several sidekicks in various hierarchies and alternating relationships. The first genius-sidekick relationship develops between Jack Crawford, head of Behavioral Sciences at the FBI and Will Graham, his employee. This is unusual insofar as the genius is normally on par with his sidekick or at a higher level. Here, the genius starts out as the sidekick. Nevertheless, their relationship changes when Hannibal tries to manipulate Will. In "Amuse-Bouche," the mentally unstable Will tells Hannibal: "Jack thinks I need therapy," to which Hannibal replies, "what you need is a way out of dark places when Jack sends you there."[21] Will maintains his status as Jack's sidekick for a while longer, which is obvious when he proclaims in "Coquilles"[22] that "Jack hasn't abandoned [him]," yet Hannibal rears him as his own supposed sidekick.[23] Interestingly, Hannibal himself can be seen as antagonist, sidekick, and mentor to Will. Although he initially seems to be the genius-in-charge, whose crimes are unsolvable for the common FBI agents, he promptly realizes that he is not the only genius around and thus is keen to develop a friendship with Will, who he knows is his greatest threat. Hannibal the Cannibal literally feeds Will clues that help him solve some of the crimes. As a sidekick, he is unusual as he is both a genius himself and has a completely corrupt mind. Will and Hannibal complement each other more than Will and Jack do, yet Will secretly remains loyal to the man who arrests him for seeing the truth, namely that Hannibal is the killer they are chasing. The role of the sidekick is hence not a fixed position.

The presence of the sidekick on *Dexter* is also one of constant renegotiation. The position is partly filled by Dexter's sister, Deb, who also works for the Miami Metro, but Deb can never be the Watson to his Sherlock as she operates on different moral principles. Dexter is bound by what he calls "Harry's Code," which consists of two rules: never get caught, and don't kill innocents. These are the basic moral principles his adoptive father has equipped him with in order to channel Dexter's violent desires. Deb is of a much more black and white morality: she is a cop through and through, and even though she learns about Dexter's murders in the final seasons, and tries to support her brother, she ultimately cannot do so. Dexter tells Deb on her deathbed that "Ever since you found out who I am, I've screwed up your life,"[24] thus indicating that theirs was not a true partnership. Dexter's Code and Deb's more conventional morals could not be united, culminating in a growing estrangement between the siblings. The sidekick in the Sherlockian sense is someone who is utterly unshakable in his dedication and support of the genius, and Deb is unable to follow in these footsteps. As Dexter meets, season after season, new killers and occasionally befriends them, the sidekick position is filled again and again, but these platonic unions never last; they end, more often than not, in the demise of the prospective companion. This is partly because the other killers do not inhabit a complementary role and thus strive to fill the genius' role themselves. Because Dexter is shown as being the best at what he does, all sidekicks who become rivals must be eliminated sooner rather than later, thus drawing a parallel to the cat-and-mouse game Hannibal and Will engage in. The only exception to this pattern of ever-changing sidekicks is Harry, Dexter's adoptive father, who dies before the events of the series. Dexter turns his deceased father into an imaginary friend, who appears to reinforce the Code when Dexter is close to breaking it. In this way, Harry is the ultimate sidekick: his whole existence is based in the need to govern Dexter's behavior and keep him from abusing the power of his "Dark Passenger." Grodal calls the Harry/Dexter scenes "super-ego situations,"[25] while Santalauria identifies Harry's continued presence as "a form of patriarchal conscience."[26] Either way, it is not Dexter's genuine affection for his sister, but his belief in his father's moral dictum that keeps him on track. In the episode "Let's Give the Boy a Hand," Dexter deliberates a potential kill, but ultimately decides against it on the basis that "Harry wouldn't want it."[27] According to Donnelly, "the moral code by which [Dexter] dictates his own actions helps to establish a clear line between 'acceptable' and 'unacceptable' deviance."[28] It is thus the sidekick's influence, even beyond death, that reins the (criminal) genius in and maintains his position between good and evil, rather than veering off into the latter.

True Detective, in a surprisingly conventional act of storytelling for a show that is praised for its innovative delivery, assigns the sidekick role to the less brilliant, but socially far more capable Marty Hart, prompting Orr to conclude that "the pairing of Cohle and Hart, the misanthropic genius and the 'ordinary' observer who set his eccentricities in context, is not a novel one, of course. Holmes and Watson are the classic prototypes."[29] This division into genius and sidekick, however, is not comfortable for Marty. During their work, Rust and Marty come to blows frequently. In a memorable fight, Rust stresses his own superior intellect while putting Marty's down:

> RUST: You moron. God damn. You, these people, this place, it's like you eat your fucking yarn and that's all just fine as long as you got something to salute on. I have things to do. So type the report, man. It's how we do, I get people to talk, you write the stats, it's worked out well for you so far.
> MARTY: I'm the only one ever took up for you. Ever. You know what it's like being your partner? Heh? Fuck you.
> RUST: Oh buddy. Without me, there's no you. So type the fucking report, man.[30]

While the arrogant Rust is thus sold as a genius and remains as such for the entire narrative, his partner is by no means the bumbling fool. In fact, Marty is in a lot of ways shrewder than the genius. He has the people skills (even though these are not always put to best use) that haughty Rust lacks, especially in the 2012 part of the story. Marty, however, is assigned a more physical role, and is often shown as giving into the temptations and trappings of the normal life that Rust is no longer capable of living. True to his function, Marty eventually supports Rust in his endeavor to solve their 1995 case in 2012, when Rust himself has become the object of the investigation. Marty loyally tells the two new detectives on the case that "you weren't getting a read on him, he was getting a read on you," stressing his own belief in Rust's genius over that of everyone else.[31] Marty thus inhabits a perverted coming-of-age narrative as *True Detective* charts his happy acquiescence into a mere sidekick role. While Will, Deb and Harry, and Watson all provide a moral base in an attempt to regulate the genius' dangerous potential, Marty does not need to fill this role because Rust follows the trail of the unsolved murders into a corrupt society without any prompting. Rust may be proactive here but still, he needs the aid of his socially competent sidekick both to solve the case and to become more functional in everyday life. Marty ultimately serves to boost Rust's ego, but also to reveal his flaws, thus offering the genius, much like the other sidekicks discussed here, a mirror image. Importantly, the genius requires his sidekick to prevent him from straying too far over the legal and social boundaries he is wont to cross.

The Adversary

The genius may possess mental capabilities superior to those of the average human being, but he nevertheless needs challenges to demonstrate them. The adversary provides such an opportunity for the genius to distinguish himself and is hence a more than welcome gift. In order to qualify as a worthy adversary one has to arouse the genius' interest, which is not an easy endeavor as he is generally uninterested in his contemporaries. This becomes obvious for example when Sherlock hosts proper castings to find the next case worth being solved. Unlike the sidekick, the adversary challenges the genius and manages what most female characters in these shows cannot: intellectual seduction.

Depending on how childlike the genius' disposition is, the adversary is treated like a depraved playmate. This applies especially to Sherlock and his game of cat-and-mouse with the flamboyant Moriarty. Like Sherlock, Moriarty is well aware of his ingenuity as he ruminates, "Aren't ordinary people adorable? Well, you know. You've got John. I should get myself a live-in one. Must be so funny."[32] An essentially more serious adversary is Charles Augustus Magnussen, who appears throughout season three. Magnussen is a remarkable antagonist because, unlike Moriarty, he is not a professional criminal but a business man. While Moriarty matches Sherlock's childishness and his cynical humor, Magnussen also uses the mind palace technique, which allows him to store information and thus analyze Sherlock like he analyzes his opponents. Both main adversaries hence share significant characteristics and methods with Sherlock, but they fail to succeed, presumably because they lack the moral support of a reliable and resilient sidekick like Watson. At the same time they manage to bring out the worst in Sherlock.

What is special about *Hannibal* is that the adversary here is eponymous with the show's title. Although the series offers a variety of smaller adversaries, Hannibal remains Will's main opponent, as if to impart that no one can compete with Hannibal's ruthlessness and murderous creativity except a fellow genius. Will's tagline, "this is my design," is an explanation of what Hannibal does, namely designing his murders into culinary and sculptural pieces of art. Hannibal is highly dangerous because he serves as a mirror for Will and recognizes his weaknesses. By trying to mold Will into his carbon-copy, Hannibal reveals the crux of the evil genius: loneliness. Although they are surrounded by people, both the evil and the good genius suffer from an intellectual void that no lover and no amount of money can fill, only the adversary can.

On *Dexter*, Green finds that "The central narrative of the show does not offer a mystery—the perpetrator and the crime are already known," referring of course to Dexter as the murderer in question.[33] Much like *Hannibal*, *Dexter* thus also features an adversary in the title role. However, the show also functions as a classic detective narrative, as Dexter and the (slower) team of Miami Metro are solving a slew of other cases. Season one sees Dexter identifying the Ice Truck Killer, season four the Trinity Killer, season five the Doomsday killer, and season eight the Brain Surgeon. All of these are conventional antagonists and the process of finding and stopping them reiterates Dexter's dual position as both detective and killer; it is only because of his own dark side that he can catch killers that elude conventional policemen. Dexter connects to all of these adversaries on an emotional level: the Ice Truck Killer is revealed to be Dexter's brother, and when Dexter eventually has him on his kill table, he admits that he is "the only one I ever wanted to set free."[34] This situation is mirrored in the show's seventh season, when Dexter decides not to kill the poisoner Hannah and not only frees her from his kill table, but also chooses her as his new girlfriend. Similarly, he forges a connection with the Trinity killer, musing that "Trinity's a husband. A father. He's ... like me."[35] Finally, he also sees a part of himself in the Doomsday Killer's split personality. The Ice Truck Killer admonishes Dexter that "you can't be a killer and a hero. It doesn't work that way,"[36] but Dexter manages to do just that up until almost the end of series. Thus Dexter is often his own adversary.

The detectives on *True Detective* do not encounter such suave adversaries as Moriarty or Hannibal. Instead, they come face to face with an almost Gothic monster, complete with a remote and dilapidated lair in the woods. It is because of this lack of sophistication in the antagonist that Rust's genius fails to convince in the same way Sherlock's or Will Graham's does. Since the final battle on *True Detective* is a violent and archaic confrontation with more blood than brains, Rust's genius falls short of his potential. A true genius, it seems, is able to thwart the adversary with his wits alone, leaving the lesser, physical actions to his sidekick, as impressively showcased in Sherlock's "A Study in Pink," when Watson shoots the cabbie.

Conclusion

Geniuses in detective fiction are manifold. They can be self-proclaimed sociopaths like Sherlock, outright psychopaths like Hannibal and Dexter, and aimless souls like Rust Cohle and Will Graham. Some of them are well aware of their ingenuity and flaunt it; others obviously wear it as a burden. Either way, their worst enemy is not the adversary that challenges them, but their own inability to fit into society. The examples of geniuses discussed here are simultaneously functional and dysfunctional. Without the steady accompaniment of a trustworthy and morally just sidekick, they veer into dysfunction, aided by characters who should be their adversaries, but who are revealed to be soul mates. Romantic love is thus an insignificant component in the genius' social make-up; it fails to elucidate a great emotional or moral response from the genius. Instead, all of these shows advocate, in the spirit of Conan Doyle's archetypal Sherlock and Watson, a buddy romance that sits at the core of the genre.

But even in the context of the great platonic relationships the shows seem to advocate, the geniuses allow no relationships that are truly equal; they always have to be smarter, faster, and shrewder than everybody else, friends, foes, and family included. Nobody can measure up to the genius because nobody is to the same degree both as brilliant and as broken. In keeping with this, the genius detectives often reject criticism because they are unable to see the goodwill behind it and refute it as coming from 'lesser' minds than their own. The genius in detective fiction is thus a character that deliberately orchestrates and maintains his status as a lone wolf in society and prefers distinguishing himself to entering social commitments of any kind. By positioning himself beyond emotions, beyond good and evil, the genius creates a moral category of its own. This moral category is delineated by both the sidekick's good influence on one side, and the contrasted evil of the adversary on the other. In keeping with his susceptibility to the temptations of criminality, the genius also reveals the true root of his genius and his ultimate challenge: a constant struggle with himself and his conscience.

Notes

1. Torben Grodal, "Crime Fiction and Moral Emotions: How Context Lures the Moral Attitudes of Viewers and Readers," *Northern Lights* 9 (2011): 145.
2. This essay focuses exclusively on the representation of male ingenuity on the screen,

but it should be noted that within the detective genre, the female genius is by no means nonexistent. Both *Bones* (2005) and *The Closer* (2005), as well as its sequel *Major Crimes* (2012), portray female geniuses who are successfully employed in the police business.

3. Julia Kristeva, "Is there a Feminine Genius?" *Critical Inquiry* 30, no. 3 (2004): 503.

4. Marjorie Garber, "Our Genius Problem," *The Atlantic Monthly*, December 1, 2002, http://www.theatlantic.com/magazine/archive/2002/12/our-genius-problem/376720/.

5. Ashley D. Polasek, "Surveying the Post-Millennial Sherlock Holmes: A Case for the Great Detective as a Man of Our Times," *Adaptation* 6.3 (2013): 386.

6. Garber, "Our Genius Problem."

7. Kathleen Belin Owen, "'The Game's Afoot': Predecessors and Pursuits of a Postmodern Detective Novel," in *Theory and Practice of Classic Detective Fiction*, ed. Jerome Delamater (Westport, CT: Greenwood Press, 1997), 73.

8. Stephen Cooper, "Sex/Knowledge/Power in the Detective Genre," *Film Quarterly* 42, no. 3 (1989): 23.

9. Mark Gatiss and Steven Moffat, "A Study in Pink," *Sherlock*, season 1, episode 1, directed by Paul McGuigan, aired July 11, 2011, on BBC. *Sherlock: Season 1 and 2* (London: BBC Home Entertainment 2013), DVD.

10. Ibid.

11. Garber, "Our Genius Problem."

12. Stephanie Green, "Dexter Morgan's Monstrous Origins," *Critical Studies in Television* 6, no. 1 (2011): 27.

13. Isabel Santalauria, "Dexter: Villain, Hero or Simply a Man? The Perpetuation of Traditional Masculinity in *Dexter*," *Atlantis* 32, no. 2 (2010): 69.

14. Santaularia, "Masculinity in *Dexter*," 60f; Green, "Monstrous Origins," 25.

15. James Manos, Jr., "Dexter," *Dexter*, season 1, episode 1, directed by Michael Cuesta, aired October 1, 2006, on Showtime. In season 7, Captain Maria La Guerta too picks up on Dexter's dual nature, but is promptly shot by Dexter's sister before he himself can kill her. La Guerta, a former partner and lover of Doakes', inherits his distrust, but it should be noted that it takes over five seasons and countless murders to manifest.

16. Clyde Phillips, "Crocodile," *Dexter*, season 1, episode 2, directed by Michael Cuesta, aired October 8, 2006, on Showtime.

17. Cf. Emily Nussbaum, "Cool Story, Bro: The shallow deep talk of 'True Detective,'" *The New Yorker*, March 3, 2014, as well as Drew Grant, "Time is a Flat Circle: 'True Detective' Too Clever By a Shade," *New York Observer*, February 24, 2014, http://observer.com/2014/02/time-is-a-flat-circle-true-detective-too-clever-by-a-shade, and Mike Hale, "A Coupling as Bizarre as the Murder: McConaughey and Harrelson Star in 'True Detective,' on HBO," *New York Times*, January 10, 2014, http://www.nytimes.com/2014/01/11/arts/television/mcconaughey-and-harrelson-star-in-true-detective-on-hbo.html?_r=0.

18. Christopher Orr, "*True Detective*: The Best Show on TV," *The Atlantic*, February 11, 2014, http://www.theatlantic.com/entertainment/archive/2014/02/-em-true-detective-em-the-best-show-on-tv/283727/.

19. Nic Pizzolatto, "The Long Bright Dark," *True Detective*, season 1, episode 1, directed by Cary Joji Fukunaga, aired January 12, 2014, on HBO.

20. Gatiss and Moffat, "A Study in Pink."

21. Bryan Fuller, "Amuse-Bouche," *Hannibal*, season 1, episode 2, directed by Michael Rymer, aired October 10, 2013, on NBC.

22. Bryan Fuller and Scott Nimerfro, "Coquilles," *Hannibal*, season 1, episode 5, directed by Guillermo Navarro, aired October 31, 2013, on NBC.

23. It should be noted here that Will plays a dual role. In the course of the first two seasons Will gradually discovers that Hannibal is behind some of the crimes he investigates. In order to convict him Will enters a teacher-pupil-relationship with him and allegedly commits to a life beyond good and evil.

24. Scott Buck and Manny Coto, "Remember the Monsters?," *Dexter*, season 8, episode 12, directed by Steve Shill, aired September 22, 2013, on Showtime. *Dexter: Complete Series* (Munich: Paramount Home Entertainment, 2014), DVD.
25. Grodal "Crime Fiction and Moral Emotions," 154.
26. Santaularia, "Masculinity in *Dexter*," 65.
27. Drew Z. Greenberg, "Let's Give the Boy a Hand," *Dexter*, season 1, episode 4, directed by Robert Lieberman, aired October 22, 2006, on Showtime.
28. Ashley M Donnelly, "The New American Hero: Dexter, Serial Killer for the Masses," *The Journal of Popular Culture* 45, no. 1 (2012): 23.
29. Orr, "Best Show on TV."
30. Nic Pizzolatto, "Haunted Houses," *True Detective*, season 1, episode 6, directed by Cary Joji Fukunaga, aired February 23, 2014, on HBO.
31. Nic Pizzolatto, "The Secret Fate of All Life," *True Detective*, season 1, episode 5, directed by Cary Joji Fukunaga aired February 16, 2014, on HBO.
32. Steve Thompson, "The Reichenbach Fall," *Sherlock*, season 2, episode 3, directed by Toby Haynes, aired May 28, 2012, on BBC.
33. Green, "Monstrous Origins," 26.
34. Daniel Cerone and Melissa Rosenberg, "Born Free," *Dexter*, season 1, episode 12, directed by Michael Cuesta, aired December 17, 2006, on Showtime.
35. Tim Schlattmann, "Dirty Harry," *Dexter*, season 4, episode 5, directed by Keith Gordon, aired October 25, 2009, on Showtime.
36. Daniel Cerone and Melissa Rosenberg, "Born Free."

References

Buck, Scott, and Manny Coto. "Remember the Monsters?" *Dexter*, season 8, episode 12. Directed by Steve Shill. Aired September 22, 2013, on Showtime. *Dexter: Complete Series*, DVD. Munich: Paramount Home Entertainment, 2014.
Cerone, Daniel, and Melissa Rosenberg. "Born Free." *Dexter*, season 1, episode 12. Directed by Michael Cuesta. Aired December 17, 2006, on Showtime. *Dexter: Complete Series*, DVD. Munich: Paramount Home Entertainment, 2014.
Cooper, Stephen. "Sex/Knowledge/Power in the Detective Genre." *Film Quarterly* 42.3 (1989): 23–31.
Donnelly, Ashley M. "The New American Hero: Dexter, Serial Killer for the Masses." *The Journal of Popular Culture* 45, no. 1 (2012): 15–26.
Fuller, Bryan. "Amuse-Bouche." *Hannibal*, season 1, episode 2. Directed by Michael Rymer. Aired October 10, 2013, on NBC. *Hannibal Season 1*, DVD. Berlin: Studiocanal, 2013.
Fuller, Bryan, and Scott Nimerfro. "Coquilles." *Hannibal*, season 1, episode 5. Directed by Guillermo Navarro. Aired October 31, 2013, on NBC. *Hannibal Season 1*, DVD. Berlin: Studiocanal, 2013.
Garber, Marjorie. "Our Genius Problem." *The Atlantic Monthly*, December 1, 2002. http://www.theatlantic.com/magazine/archive/2002/12/our-genius-problem/376720/.
Gatiss, Mark, and Steven Moffat. "A Study in Pink." *Sherlock*, season 1, episode 1. Directed by Paul McGuigan. Aired July 11, 2011. *Sherlock Season 1 and 2*, DVD. London: BBC Home Entertainment, 2013.
Grant, Drew. "Time is a Flat Circle: 'True Detective' Too Clever By a Shade." *New York Observer*, February 24, 2014. http://observer.com/2014/02/time-is-a-flat-circle-true-detective-too-clever-by-a-shade/.
Green, Stephanie. "Dexter Morgan's Monstrous Origins." *Critical Studies in Television* 6, no. 1 (2011): 22–35.
Greenberg, Drew Z. "Let's Give the Boy a Hand." *Dexter*, season 1, episode 4. Directed by

Robert Lieberman. Aired October 22, 2006 on Showtime. *Dexter: Complete Series*, DVD. Munich: Paramount Home Entertainment, 2014.

Grodal, Torben. "Crime Fiction and Moral Emotions: How Context Lures the Moral Attitudes of Viewers and Readers." *Northern Lights* 9 (2011): 143–157.

Hale, Mike. "A Coupling as Bizarre as the Murder. McConaughey and Harrelson Star in 'True Detective,' on HBO." *New York Times*, January 10, 2014. http://www.nytimes.com/2014/01/11/arts/television/mcconaughey-and-harrelson-star-in-true-detective-on-hbo.html?_r=0.

Kristeva, Julia. "Is there a feminine genius?" *Critical Inquiry* 30, no. 3 (2004): 493–504.

Manos, Jr., James. "Dexter." *Dexter*, season 1, episode 1. Directed by Michael Cuesta. Aired October 1, 2006, on Showtime. *Dexter: Complete Series*, DVD. Munich: Paramount Home Entertainment, 2014.

Nussbaum, Emily. "Cool Story, Bro The shallow deep talk of 'True Detective.'" *The New Yorker*, March 3, 2014.

Orr, Christopher. "*True Detective*: The Best Show on TV." *The Atlantic*, February 11, 2014. http://www.theatlantic.com/entertainment/archive/2014/02/-em-true-detective-em-the-best-show-on-tv/283727/.

Owen, Kathleen Belin. "'The Game's Afoot': Predecessors and Pursuits of a Postmodern Detective Novel." In *Theory and Practice of Classic Detective Fiction*, edited by Jerome Delamater, 73–86. Westport, CT: Greenwood Press, 1997.

Phillips, Clyde. "Crocodile." *Dexter*, season 1, episode 2. Directed by Michael Cuesta. Aired October 8, 2006, on Showtime. *Dexter: Complete Series*, DVD. Munich: Paramount Home Entertainment, 2014.

Pizzolatto, Nic. "The Long Bright Dark." *True Detective*, season 1, episode 1. Directed by Cary Joji Fukunaga. Aired January 12, 2014, on HBO. *True Detective*, DVD. Hamburg: Warner Home Video, 2014.

Pizzolatto, Nic. "The Secret Fate of All Life." *True Detective*, season 1, episode 5. Directed by Cary Joji Fukunaga. Aired February 16, 2014, on HBO. *True Detective*, DVD. Hamburg: Warner Home Video, 2014.

Pizzolatto, Nic. "Haunted Houses." *True Detective*, season 1, episode 6. Directed by Cary Joji Fukunaga. Aired February 23, 2014, on HBO. *True Detective*, DVD. Hamburg: Warner Home Video, 2014.

Polasek, Ashley D. "Surveying the Post-Millennial Sherlock Holmes: A Case for the Great Detective as a Man of Our Times." *Adaptation* 6, no. 3 (2013): 384–393.

Santaularia, Isabel. "Dexter: Villain, Hero or Simply a Man? The Perpetuation of Traditional Masculinity in *Dexter*." *Atlantis* 32, no. 2 (2010): 57–71.

Schlattmann, Tim. "Dirty Harry." *Dexter*, season 4, episode 5. Directed by Keith Gordon. Aired October 25, 2009, on Showtime. *Dexter: Complete Series*, DVD. Munich: Paramount Home Entertainment, 2014.

Thompson, Steve. "The Reichenbach Fall." *Sherlock*, season 2, episode 3. Directed by Toby Haynes. Aired May 28, 2012, on BBC. *Sherlock Season 1 and 2*, DVD. London: BBC Home Entertainment, 2013.

"It's the age of the geek, baby"

The Intelligent Con Artist, Corporate America and the Construction of the Family in Leverage

Hannah Swamidoss

The pilot episode of Dean Devlin's *Leverage* (2008), "The Nigerian Job," appropriately begins at the bar of a high-end hotel at which the exceptionally intelligent and talented former insurance investigator Nate Ford (Timothy Hutton) sits alone and has a drink. The transitory nature of the hotel bar reflects Nate's instability; he has quit his job and his marriage has fallen apart following the death of his son. Consequently, when the devious Victor Dubenich (Saul Rubinek), a corporate executive at an aviation firm, approaches Nate to hire him to supervise a theft, Dubenich plays a pivotal role in reshaping Nate's identity. Bereft of family and purpose and driven to and by alcohol, Nate stands at a threshold, admittedly a luxurious one. As Dubenich pitches his idea to Nate, the camera moves back and forth between the two seated at a table, and the narrative plays on their similarities. Both are dressed casually, each wearing a brown jacket and black shirt. Over the course of the episode, it becomes clear that both men are strategists; while Nate gains the upper hand at the end of the episode, Dubenich will reappear in the series and wreak havoc and take one more member of Nate's already diminished family. Clearly unscrupulous and willing to engage in criminal acts, Dubenich moves Nate into the gray area of breaking the law and working with a team of impressively intelligent and successful thieves, all of whom Nate has chased as an insurance investigator. Ironically, through this act, Dubenich provides Nate with a new "geeky" family and purpose, and the "firm" Leverage Consulting & Associates is born.

Critical reviews of *Leverage* frequently focus on the team's mission to tackle corporate corruption by bringing down dishonest executives and aiding their victims. Two days before the series premier, Dale McGarrigle described *Leverage* as "capers pulled off by a Robin Hood–type crew, but with a modern twist."[1] Writing two days after "The Nigerian Job" first aired, Robert Bianco praised the second episode ("The Home Coming Job") but also cautioned, "Keep in mind, though, that despite the current economic relevance of its Robin Hood theme, Leverage is a corporately funded piece of entertainment, not an incitement to class warfare."[2] Joshua Alston provides a different perspective when he discusses television shows that focus on the antihero and includes *Leverage* with shows like *24* (2001), *Damages* (2007), and *Mad Men* (2007). Alston notes that a "narrative problem with antiheroes is not that they are flawed but that they are flawless. At least, they are infallible" and suggests that despite the political climate, "what TV needs now, in these uncertain times, is dramatic characters [...] characters who aren't trying to save the world or plunder it, but are just trying to subsist in it. After all, aren't the times we're living in dramatic enough?"[3] While *Leverage* does follow a basic Robin Hood schematic of taking down corrupt executives to help their victims, the series also constructs certain claims about *who* can play Robin Hood. Nate and his team members, Sophie Devereaux (Gina Bellman), Parker (Beth Riesgraf), Alec Hardison (Aldis Hodge), and Eliot Spencer (Christian Kane), all possess high-levels of intelligence.[4] Their collective intelligence covers a range of areas from book knowledge, street knowledge, corporate knowledge, military knowledge, and technological knowledge, to understanding and manipulating human behavior. With Sophie's presence on the team, the series also introduces her love for the theater (along with the ideas of illusion and the creation of narratives) as a form of intelligence.

In addition to this construction of intelligence being integral to a Robin Hood form of social action, money also plays a significant role. Bianco makes an important point when he discusses the irony the show's corporate funding presents; even more interestingly, the narrative itself portrays wealth as part of the reason why the team functions so well. Lisa Holderman's argument in *Common Sense: Intelligence as Presented on Popular Television* proves useful here; Holderman states that "constructions of intelligence intersect with constructions of other social statuses, such as social class, race, gender, age, and sexual orientation, among others, so that mediated stories about intelligence and the characters within these stories are not simply one-dimensional."[5] The intersection of intelligence and social class forms the basis of the *Leverage's* call to social action. Members of the team, for instance, come from different socio-economic backgrounds, but when they meet, they are, for the most part, financially well-off. After the first con, when the team decides to form the firm "Leverage Consulting & Associates," Nate, Sophie, Parker, Hardison, and Eliot have made so much money off of Dubenich's downfall that not one of them has any individual financial worries—each member now belongs to the select group of the very wealthy. While in some ways this engagement with wealth portrays money as a neutral force that can be used for good, it also constructs intelligence as belonging to or needing a certain social class in order to flourish.

Finally, the series also depicts a re-formation of the individual and the family. Although the characters on *Leverage* do fall into the category of anti-heroes, I would argue that the show tries to form a place for the essentially unstable intelligent subject. By creating a fluid familial space for the intelligent individual, the overarching narrative posits that this placement will enrich society. Since, *Leverage* constructs intelligence by connecting it with social action and the concept of the family, *Leverage*, therefore, interrogates ideas of integrity, identity, family, and community and juxtaposes these with corruption, wealth, and big business. Intelligence, consequently, becomes a powerful, subversive social force.

Intelligence, the Limits of the Law, Moral Integrity and Corporate America

In his discussion of Home Box Office's *The Sopranos* (1999), Horace Newcomb argues: "Drawing on film and radio presentations of similar material, television has long been the site of negotiated cultural significance of 'law and order,' 'justice,' 'authority,' and certainly 'violence' or 'crime.'"[6] Intelligence, of course, can occur with both the law official and the criminal, but *Leverage* manipulates the traditional sites or, to draw from Homi Bhabha, the cultural locations of law and order and criminal activity. *Leverage* demonstrates that the traditional locations of law and order—the police, the FBI, the judiciary— seem to struggle and need additional help. This moves the team of "good guys" into the traditional location of criminal activity: thieving, hacking, conning, and using force. As mentioned earlier, the transitory nature of the hotel bar of the opening scene of "The Nigerian Job" suggests the instability within Nate; additionally, it reveals a choice that he, as an intelligent, law-abiding individual, has to make. Nate can remain broken and drink himself to death, or he can transform into a new moral subject. In *The Location of Culture*, Bhabha convincingly argues that many of the sites in which culture is negotiated occur in processes between cultures and that "these 'in-between' spaces provide the terrain for elaborating strategies of selfhood—singular or communal—that initiate new signs of identity, and innovative sites of collaboration, and contestation in the act of defining the idea of society itself."[7] The in-between, interstitial, space that Leverage Consulting occupies, therefore, demonstrates a new strategy of identity for the individual and the team. The members of the team reside and move between the sites of the civil, the criminal, and law enforcement. This mobility in identity and action provides the team with its tremendous agency. Unlike rogue agents who may also traverse this interstitial space, Leverage Consulting offers a structure—as chameleon-like and fluid as the structure may be. This protean structure indicates that the type of high intelligence that the team displays also falls outside of traditional cultural locations and needs a new location in which it can thrive.

Examining typical television crime series proves useful in analyzing why *Leverage* makes this move into the interstitial space between law and crime. Newcomb notes that crime dramas are situated in "social contexts that can best be described as beleaguered, social contexts in which 'crime' is but one of a number of indicators of social decay or, at best, decline."[8] The types of social decay that *Leverage* addresses are the hegemonic paradigms that corporations have established through legal means over the middle and working classes, which need a new moral paradigm. "The Nigerian Job" introduces key ideas to this interrogation of integrity and morality that the rest of the series will develop. Dubenich, for instance, uses two significant arguments when he convinces Nate to take the job. First, Dubenich argues that since the airplane designs he is interested in were first stolen from him, stealing his intellectual property back does not cross any moral lines. Dubenich tells Nate that he needs "one honest man to watch [thieves]."[9] Although Nate suggests that legal means exist to recover this work, Dubenich argues that none of these methods would provide the timely assistance that he needs. Second, Dubenich suggests that as an added incentive Nate has a chance to take revenge on his former insurance agency, which would cover the costs of the theft. Dubenich manipulates Nate at a very personal level here: the agency refused to pay for a potential life-saving treatment for Nate's young son. Although Dubenich's claim that he owns the designs gives Nate a moral reason to use in overseeing the theft, the real reason that moves Nate into the interstitial area of Leverage Consulting is his son. At first, this reason may seem purely personal but the series' narrative establishes Nate's son as representing one of many victims of a systemic and rapacious element of corporate America that the law alone cannot eliminate or even curtail.

Interestingly, Nate himself has represented corporate America at its most successful when he worked for his insurance company, IYS. As an investigator, he recovered artwork for IYS and on one job alone saved them (as Dubenich points out) 20 to 25 million dollars.[10] Although Nate is betrayed by the insurance company at the deepest level, he also represents significant qualities that make a successful corporation: intelligence, drive, a work ethic, and innovative, adaptable methods. On later jobs with Sophie, Parker, Hardison, and Eliot, Nate frequently draws from his experience as an insurance investigator to understand the criminal mind of mob bosses, international gangs, and even other crews like Nate's own. The problem with corporate America does not lie with the success of individuals like Nate, but occurs at the deeper systemic level.

In the last episode of the first season, "The Second David Job," the series makes this problem explicitly clear. Nate's former boss at IYS, Ian Blackpool, explains to Nate why Nate's claim was turned down by stating, "I don't let my personal feelings affect policy." To Nate's response, "Your policy. This company never automatically turned down claims until you came along," Blackpool states, "I have a responsibility to my shareholders."[11] It is this responsibility of generating increasing amounts of profit and weighting this type of profit over human concern and human needs that makes the corporate moral paradigm so problematic. Nate tells Blackpool that this profit comes at a cost: "People lost their homes; children died."[12] While Blackpool's corporate morality technically does not break the law, it fails at a deeper ethical level. The responsibility toward shareholders does not take into consideration a different type of responsibility—the responsibility of taking care of the powerless and meeting basic human needs. Over the course of the first season, the episodes depict a wide range of scenarios that are similar in the fact that the characters have no legal recourse against corporate corruption. A veteran from Iraq who was shot by members of a private contracting firm has no restitution from the company and no access to the extended healthcare he needs ("The Home Coming Job"). Similarly, a church struggles to survive against the scheming of an unethical developer ("The Miracle Job"). Likewise, parents of a dead girl are stonewalled by a corporation responsible for her death ("The Mile High Job"). These examples establish the series' continued use of the interstitial nature of Leverage Consulting—the move away from traditional law enforcement—in ensuing seasons.

Fortuitously for *Leverage*, the line that is heard during the opening credits, "The rich and powerful, they take what they want" fits in well with national concerns in 2008.[13] Although initial press releases from Turner Network Television (TNT) and Dean Devlin suggest that the theme of corporate corruption always lay at the heart of *Leverage*, as Bianco and Alston point out the series' debut neatly coincided with financial upheaval and anxiety, and *Leverage* could capitalize on the premise that the law, government, and upstanding ordinary citizens had serious limitations.[14] The timing of "The Nigerian Job" in December, for instance, could not have been better as it came during the height of the financial crisis of 2008. David Wessel identifies three key moments in the financial crisis of 2008: In March, the Federal Reserve lent $30 billion to JPMorgan Chase to buy Bear Stearns; in August the Fed seized Fannie Mae and Freddie Mac, and in September, it let Lehman Brothers fail.[15] Wessel observes that after the failure of Lehman and the subsequent bailout of the American International Group, "Within weeks, the Fed would successfully press the rest of the U.S. government to guarantee the debts of all the nation's banks, to buy shares in banks to bolster their financial conditions, and to declare the government would not let another 'systematically important' financial institution go under."[16] Thereafter, numerous banks received government aid.[17] The "Nigerian Job's" narrative of corporate greed echoed American outrage and anxiety over corporate corruption and the mismanagement of financial institutions during the long months of the financial crisis. Four days after "The Nigerian Job" first aired, Bernie Madoff would be arrested for his Ponzi scheme. Law enforcement and the government itself seemed handicapped while, in the midst of the collapse and bailouts, top executives received raises.[18]

Unarguably, *Leverage's* narrative seeks redress for the excesses of corporate executives, but it also reflects a swinging pendulum of popular opinion in American culture toward financial institutions and corporations. David Wessel notes that the financial crisis of 2008 was not the first major crisis that Americans have faced but that the financial crisis of 1907 and the Great Depression created similar outrage and anxiety. Wessel observes that in such crises and in other lesser market fluctuations, "tension between borrower and lender, farmer and financier, worker and Wall Street didn't disappear. Hostility to big money ebbed and flowed, but American workers, farmers, and debtors had a recurrent suspicion that 'Wall Street' or the 'money trust' or 'the robber barons' were responsible for economic misery."[19] Wessel argues that the animosity changed more recently; he states: "this recurrent American suspicion went into remission during much of the 1990s and 2000s when Americans enjoyed rising stock prices and climbing home values but it returned with virulence during the Great Panic with multibillion-dollar bailouts of banks and bonuses paid to executives of failing companies."[20] In many ways, while *Leverage* does reflect "virulent suspicion" of the wealthy, the series also depicts a yearning to return to an earlier time period of seeming prosperity. The series certainly presents a high standard of living for Nate, Sophie, Parker, Hardison, and Eliot. Before they leave their criminal ways, Hardison owns a luxurious apartment in Chicago, and Sophie has several stashes of expensive artwork tucked away in different global locations. After they reform, Hardison can still purchase expensive property in Boston and Oregon. Sophie still maintains her collections even after she sacrifices one to help bring down a smuggler using child refugees ("The King George Job"). Likewise, after donating the bulk of his share from the first con, Nate drives an expensive but eco-friendly Tesla. Parker has a spacious residence in Boston, and Eliot faces no financial worries. Nate makes a telling comment when he reveals his purchase of a Tesla to the team; Nate states: "Just cause you're the good guys now doesn't mean you can't have a little fun along the way."[21] The series suggests consistently that when wealth is gained appropriately, it can be spent for pleasure.

One reason for this level of wealth may lie in how the series structures the characters of Sophie, Parker, Hardison, and Eliot. For the interstitial position that Leverage Consulting occupies, Nate has to move from the clearly demarcated space of working within the law to the interstitial area of being outside the purview of the law (and frequently breaking it) to do good, and likewise, he needs to lose his corporate character and take on the amorphous identity of being a morally good thief. This movement has to occur for Sophie, Parker, Hardison, and Eliot as well, but in the opposite direction. Sophie, the "grifter" (confidence trickster), Parker the thief, Hardison, the hacker, and Eliot, the retrieval specialist, all occupy a clearly demarcated space of criminal activity. At the end of "The Nigerian Job," the text offers three reasons for their willingness to leave criminal activity behind: they have made enough money to retire; each one of them has a drive to continue to work even if he or she does not need to do so, and all enjoy the rush of working together as a team. By being freed of financial concerns and having an inner drive to continue to work (with the added desire of wishing to work together), Sophie, Parker Hardison, and Eliot can give up criminal activity to meet Nate in the interstitial area of what the series will establish in later episodes as "picking up where the law leaves off."[22]

The second episode of the first season, "The Homecoming Job" offers a different reason for Sophie, Parker, Hardison, and Eliot to give up criminal activity and join Nate in his efforts to redress wrongs. When the team realizes that they face a private army in the form of government contractors in Iraq, each one expresses to Nate that the job is too dangerous but reluctantly agrees to see it through to the end. After they successfully accomplish their mission of bringing down the corrupt contractors and obtaining money for injured veterans at a hospital, the team watches an emotionally charged scene as the happy hospital staff and veterans take the money. To the incentives of financial security and the thrills of the job, Sophie, Parker, Hardison, and Eliot now also desire to do good for the less privileged. In the first episode of season two, "The

Beantown Bailout Job," Hardison refers to their increasing desire to be the "good guys" when he humorously tells Nate that "You took the world's best criminals, hitter, hacker, grifter, thief, you took us and broke us."[23] This desire to help others continues to grow in Sophie, Parker, Hardison, and Eliot, but the overarching narrative of the series cannot and does not try to move away from their motivations tied to wealth. *Leverage* firmly places the intelligent "bad/good guy" with the financial elite.[24]

Whether intentional or not, this aspect of wealth, as interconnected with the needs of the intelligent individual, reinforces existing class structures. The various characters that the team helps receive genuine aid, and almost always have different opportunities to move forward. In "The Homecoming Job" Corporal Perry and the other veterans receive enough money to meet their healthcare needs.[25] In "The Fairy Godparents," the team recovers the mismanaged funds of a healthcare clinic and adds an extra amount to it so that it can remain open.[26] Likewise, in "The Three Day Hunter Job" the team helps a slandered bus driver regain his reputation and in "The Runway Job" they make sure that the factory ownership of a former sweat shop run by the Chinese triad changes hands to good leadership.[27] The narrative of the series is careful to demonstrate that the victims of each episode are hardworking people of limited means, who are responsible in their financial commitments, and who try to do right in the face of oppression or injustice. In the episodes mentioned above, the bus driver did not want any money, while the veterans, the clinic, and the Asian workers in the clothing factory all receive some form of financial help from the team. Admittedly, while none of these characters express any desire to move upward in social class, their contentment is part of what maintains the status quo.

The series suggests that the average American needs certain things—a house, healthcare, protection from drug, food, and agricultural companies (as well as mob shakedowns), and the means to keep a business running—but this can be achieved without a major redistribution of wealth. Leverage Consulting & Associates is the ideal new corporation. It demonstrates a commitment toward meeting human need and battles corruption and injustice. The team makes no profit off of ordinary citizens, yet remains wealthy. If the opening credits were applied to Leverage Consulting itself, it might run as: The rich and powerful, as long as they don't take what they want dishonestly, can remain rich and powerful. The series does not suggest that this new category of the rich and powerful will have an expanding membership or promote upward class mobility. It does suggest, however, that the familial aspect of this new corporation, while still set apart in the interstitial space, can offer an inclusive model for American society and the global community.

Intelligence and the Construction of Family

In her 2008 discussion of the changing nature of depictions of families on television, Mary Ann Watson notes that between 1945 and 1995 American family demographics changed rapidly from children growing up in a two parent household with biological parents being the norm to single parent households and blended families becoming prevalent.[28] Watson argues that, "for the sake of pathos and plot, television has always presented non-traditional families," but these families have increasingly been depicted as the norm.[29] Watson concludes that "in the 1990s, the potential of popular entertainment to define the meaning of gender and family in the nation's collective consciousness entered the political arena ... because men and women across the political spectrum understood that strong families were essential to a strong country."[30] This framework is useful in understanding *Leverage's* portrayal of the family and the connections the series forges between the family and social action. Both Dubenich's use of Nate's son to manipulate Nate and IYS' lack of action on behalf of the child's medical needs create a strong connection between the family and corporate America. Nate moves from a traditional nuclear family to a strong non-traditional family made of the team members. Likewise, Leverage Consulting focuses on helping a range of families, both traditional and non-traditional. By helping the family (in whatever form) get back on its feet, Nate, Sophie, Parker, Hardison, and Eliot are nation building and, at times, strengthening the global community as well.

The narrative over the course of the series makes the case for understanding the team as a family. As early as the third episode of the first season, for instance, Eliot's former sweetheart, a girl he almost married, tells him, "You're never going to be the kind to settle down, but I am glad you found a family."[31] Meanwhile, Parker's initial displacement from family is even more severe than Eliot's. Parker is mentored and nurtured to a certain extent by a master thief, Archie Leach (Richard Chamberlain), and both Parker and Archie think of themselves as father and daughter. Archie, however, never takes Parker home to be a part of his own "normal" nuclear family because she would not fit in with them. When Archie sees her in action with the team and notes the change in her attitude, he apologizes to Parker for never making her a part of his family. He comments, "You went out and made your own [family]."[32] At the outset of the series, Nate and Sophie have a romantic interest in each other, but even before this turns into a mutually fulfilling relationship (and an engagement in the series' final episode), they act as parents towards the other three on the team. This parental aspect is especially clear in "The Ho, Ho, Ho Job" which is set during Christmas. At the end of the episode, Nate and Sophie give Eliot,

Hardison, and Parker Christmas gifts.[33] Through the staging of the scene, the choice of gifts, Nate's teasing of Parker by making her wait for her gift, and the clear pleasure and childlike enjoyment that Eliot, Hardison, and Parker display while they play with their gifts, the episode evokes a parent-child relationship. Finally, another deep familial bond is made when Hardison's romantic interest in Parker (indicated in the pilot episode) culminates in the final season when Parker casually informs the rest of the team that she and Hardison are dating.

Significantly, one of the primary bonds that transform the team members into a family lies in their high levels of intelligence and their love for the extraordinary aspects of their work. By centering the family around shared intelligence and work, *Leverage* manipulates traditional television portrayals of the public and private. Ella Taylor argues that the domestic space and the workplace can merge, stating, "taken together, the television family and workplace served to map out a social field, recasting the boundaries between private and public spheres and redefining the normative meanings within and between these spheres."[34] Taylor goes on to offer that "the interplay of short- and long-term cultural analyses suggests that television's juggling of the meanings of private and public, family and work, rehearses older questions in a new social environment."[35] In contrast, in his study of families portrayed on television, William Douglas suggests that families are often portrayed in isolation and that "television narratives normally [do not] integrate the family-at-home and the family-at work. As such, family life is privatized."[36] Douglas rejects Taylor's merging of the private and the public by arguing that workplace "relationships are inconsistent with a normative family model" and that "work groups are also governed by an often rigid organizational structure that obviates the negotiation of roles, increasingly common in modern families."[37] I have cited these positions at length to demonstrate what *Leverage* does with the private/domestic and the public/workplace. *Leverage* counters both Taylor's idea of a work family struggling against the corporation which employs them and Douglas's objections to Taylor. Taylor suggests that familial comfort in the workplace counters the harshness of work requirements, but *Leverage* shows that the team's work environment does not face stress from a larger entity because they all have an equal investment and standing in Leverage Consulting. Likewise, when one of the team members creates stress for the others, this stress occurs not because an organizational rule was broken but because a familial bond was strained. This merging of the public with the domestic stems from the team's intelligence and their need to move away from both the civil/legal and the criminal. When Dubenich puts together a team of four exceptionally intelligent individuals (Sophie being a later addition), each individual's appreciation of the intelligence of the others leads to the formation of a working relationship which deepens into familial bonds. The call to social action, consequently, becomes inseparable from the domestic and the public. The family in *Leverage* takes the interstitial position between clearly demarcated lines of work and family, public and domestic. The nature of this family structure and its positioning between traditional spaces of public and private endow the team with a subversive power against oppressive societal structures that separate the family from the corporation. Instead, Leverage Consulting invests in the team's family (with a high level of satisfaction for each member in the public sphere and the domestic sphere), which enables the team to invest in other families.

Leverage capitalizes on this new form of the "family business" by juxtaposing it with a different father and son relationship: Nate's relationship with his estranged father Jimmy Ford (Tom Skerritt). This aspect of the narrative not only creates a rich Irish-American heritage for Nate but also gives him mob connections, the ultimate "family business." Although Nate has strong ties to some people from his childhood community, he distances himself from his father's business and affections (and the mob) to pursue careers on the right side of the law. Nate's new role in Leverage Consulting, however, moves him closer to the space that his father occupies and reestablishes a connection between them. The narrative once again plays with the father and son relationship, thus reflecting a larger societal paradigm. Just as Nate's son ties Nate to the corruption of corporate America, Jimmy Ford brings in an element of corruption, but one that in the midst of its severe flaws provides a sense of heritage and belonging. Throughout the series, while members of the mob are brought to justice, the idea of the mob as an arm of law enforcement also emerges. This idea is most clearly articulated in season five's "The Real Fake Car Job." A mob boss tells Nate, "You know my organization in its original and purest form was law enforcement, neighborhoods where the police didn't have the ability to enforce the law."[38] More importantly, however, this scene depicts a shift in power; the mob boss makes it clear that he does not wish to tangle with Nate. The old form of the family business gives way to the new, morally reformed family business of Leverage Consulting.

Ultimately this move away from moral corruption is seen in all aspects of the family, even in the individual vices and struggles that *Leverage* frames through the concept of addiction. At the beginning of the series, Nate struggles with alcoholism; he sobers up for a short period, and then he takes to drinking again. Towards the end of the series, although he still drinks, the narrative suggests that he has it under control. The narrative emphasizes repeatedly that this drinking is symptomatic of a deeper problem which also manifests itself in Nate's need for risk taking and his drive to take on formidable foes. What Nate lacks—what the drinking is symptomatic of—is emotional closure regarding the death of his son. Each time he takes a greater risk, he reenacts the battle for his son. This rage and grief over his son's death lessens as Nate forges new relationships with the team members, particularly Sophie. Sophie, while criticizing Nate's drinking, suggests that the problem of addiction goes much deeper and that all of humanity suffers from an addiction to each person's desire for the past, the familiar.[39] In its presentation of the closure that Nate eventually receives as he works through his grief, *Leverage* suggests a connection between past and present, but also a need to leave the past behind.

Finally, this construction of the intelligent family and its location between public and private creates space for some of the social awkwardness stemming from each team member's intelligence. Even though the show capitalizes on prevalent stereotypes of "nerds" and "geeks," particularly when applied to Hardison, *Leverage* portrays a reformulation of the position of the geek. Christine Quail argues that "the nerd moniker has historically been used as a way of distinguishing, and discrediting, a particular expression of nonhegemonic masculinity and favoring the more hegemonic, consumer-viable contrast."[40] At several points in the narrative, *Leverage* positions Hardison against Eliot, with Hardison being awkward around girls and not as physically strong as Eliot, who is a natural ladies' man. In several different episodes (including the pilot and the series finale) Hardison and Eliot bandy back and forth the idea of the "geek" with Hardison holding his own and asserting consistently in several episodes that, "it's the age of the geek."[41] Whereas *Leverage* does not treat issues of race and gender as deeply as it does class, Hardison as a black male creates space in white male geek culture.[42] In later episodes, Eliot affirms Hardison's intelligence and the value of geeks. Not only does Hardison have a central role in his new family, but he also has a position of dominance over civilians, criminals, and law enforcement officials. This model applies to each of the other characters as well: the team makes allowances for Parker's emotional detachment, Sophie's multiple identities, Nate's need for control and risks, and Eliot's reserve. The family business can reflect the best of each member and negotiate what needs to be changed. In the midst of its call to social action, the narrative also demonstrates the importance of the intelligent individual. While Nate, Sophie, Parker, Hardison, and Eliot possess tremendous agency over other members of society, this power is framed in a non-hegemonic manner. Admittedly, the family of Leverage Consulting has a wealthy lifestyle, but the members of the team do not construct a formal structure to maintain their wealth or suppress others.

Tellingly, the series finale of *Leverage*, "The Long Goodbye Job" reflects the pilot episode at key places. Nate and the team once again take on corporate America at the deepest possible level as they go after a list of bankers and wealthy individuals who profit from the 2008 financial crisis. This time, however, Nate does not face the same instability that he experienced at the beginning of the series; instead, he has purpose and closure. Fittingly, one of the last scenes of the series takes place in a bar; this time however the team owns the bar—it no longer represents a place of transience but home. When Nate and Sophie say goodbye to Parker, Hardison, and Eliot (who will continue to run Leverage Consulting & Associates), this parting leaves each member grounded in family.

Notes

1. Dale McGarrigle, "Robin Hood-esque 'Leverage' a winning series," *Bangor Daily News*, December 5, 2008, C5.
2. Robert Bianco, "Critic's corner," *USA Today*, December 9, 2008, 08d.
3. Joshua Alston, "Too Much of a Bad Thing," *Newsweek*, 153, no. 2 (January 12, 2009): 58–59.
4. Parker, Hardison, and Eliot formed the original team selected by Dubenich while Nate requests Sophie to join them.
5. Lisa Holderman, *Common Sense: Intelligence as Presented on Popular Television* (Lanham, MD: Lexington, 2008), xi.
6. Horace Newcomb, "'This Is Not Al Dente': The Sopranos and the New Meaning of 'Television,'" *Television: The Critical View*, 7th ed. (New York: University Press, 2007), 563.
7. Homi Bhabha, *The Location of Culture* (New York: Routledge, 1994, 2004), 2.
8. Newcomb, *Television: The Critical View*, 564.
9. John Rogers and Chris Downey, "The Nigerian Job," *Leverage*, season 1, episode 1, directed by Dean Devlin, aired December 7, 2008, on TNT.
10. Ibid.
11. John Rogers, "The Second David Job," *Leverage*, season 1, episode 12, directed by Dean Devlin, aired February 24, 2009, on TNT.
12. Ibid.
13. John Rogers, "The Homecoming Job," *Leverage*, season 1, episode 2, directed by Dean Devlin, aired December 9, 2008 on TNT. Subsequent episodes have the same opening lines: "The rich and powerful, they take what they want. We steal it back for you. Sometimes, bad guys make the best good guys. We provide.... Leverage."
14. John Dempsey reports on March 15, 2007, that "TNT and Dean Devlin are developing 'Leverage,' a 'Mission: Impossible'–type action series in which six professionals in various fields pool their expertise to fight underworld mobsters, and corruption among international corporations and government officials" (John Dempsey, "TNT, Devlin gain 'Leverage,'" *Daily Variety Gotham* [Reed Business Information], March 15, 2007, 29). Again in August 2007, Dempsey describes *Leverage* as a team of five high-tech thieves who circle the globe to rob from wealthy criminals, corrupt businessmen and venal politicians" (John Dempsey, "TNT gets 'Leverage' with pilot greenlight," *Daily Variety Gotham* [Reed Business Information], August 31, 2007, 3).
15. David Wessel, *In Fed We Trust* (New York: Crown Business, Random House, 2009), 2.
16. Ibid., 26.
17. "Bailout Recipients," *ProPublica*, updated January 23, 2015, http://projects.propublica.org/bailout/list.
18. Edmund L. Andrews and Peter Baker of *The New York Times* report that "the American International Group, which has receive more than $170 billion in taxpayer bailout

money from the Treasury and Federal Reserve, plans to pay about $165 million in bonuses by Sunday to executives in the same business unit that brought the company to the brink of collapse last year." Edmund L. Andrews and Peter Baker, "A. I. G. Planning Huge Bonuses After $170 Billion Bailout," *New York Times,* March 14, 2009.

19. Wessel, *In Fed We Trust,* 30.
20. Ibid., 30–31.
21. Rogers, "The Homecoming Job."
22. Melissa Glenn and Jessica Rieder, "The Two-Horse Job," *Leverage,* season 1, episode 3, directed by Craig R. Baxley, aired December 16, 2008, on TNT.
23. John Rogers, "The Beantown Bailout Job," *Leverage,* season 2, episode 1, directed by Dean Devlin, aired July 15, 2009, on TNT.
24. Jason Mittell in his discussion of class portrayals on television suggests "that television reinforces a belief system that treats consumer capitalism as an unquestioned part of out common sense" and goes on to argue that "[t]he vast majority of shows focus on middle-class and upper-class characters.... Even characters who lack obvious economic success typically consume at a level beyond their means, as seen in the idealized apartments on *Friends* or the consumerist paradise of *Sex and the City*" (Jason Mittell, *Television and American Culture* [New York: Oxford University Press, 2010], 274). This tendency of television programs at large to focus on a wealthier lifestyle and *Leverage's* own particular link to corporate America, may explain some of the show's focus on wealth. Interestingly, in separate works, both Mittell and Michael Arntfield place police in the working class, perhaps one more reason why the *Leverage* team shies away from identifying itself with typical law enforcement (Mittell, *Television and American Culture,* 274; Michael Arntfield, "TVPD: The Generational Diegetics of the Police Procedural on American Television," *Canadian Review of American Studies* 41, no. 1 [2011]: 86–91).
25. Rogers, "The Homecoming Job."
26. Amy Berg, "The Fairy Godparents Job," *Leverage,* season 2, episode 4, directed by Jonathan Frakes, aired August 5, 2009, on TNT.
27. Melissa Glenn and Jessica Rieder, "The Three Day Hunter Job," *Leverage,* season 2, episode 5, directed by Marc Roskin, aired August 12, 2009, on TNT; Albert Kim, "The Runway Job," Leverage, season 2, episode 10, directed by Marc Roskin, aired January 13, 2010, on TNT.
28. Mary Ann Watson, *Defining Visions: Television and the American Experience in the 20th Century* (Malden: Blackwell, 2008), 77–78.
29. Ibid., 77.
30. Ibid., 82.
31. Glenn and Rieder, "The Two-Horse Job."
32. Geoffrey Thorne, "The Inside Job," *Leverage,* season 3, episode 3, directed by John Rogers, aired June 27, 2010, on TNT.
33. Michael Colton and John Aboud, "The Ho, Ho, Ho Job," *Leverage,* season 3, episode 14, directed by Marc Roskin, aired December 12, 2010, on TNT.
34. Ella Taylor, *Prime-Time Families: Television Culture in Postwar America* (Berkeley: University of California Press, 1989), 2.
35. Taylor, *Prime-Time Families,* 4.
36. William Douglas, *Television Families: Is Something Wrong in Suburbia?* (Mahwah, NJ: Lawrence Erlbaum Associates, 2003), 106.
37. Douglas, *Television Families,* 20. Douglas has a point that critics' perception of the familial at the workplace (such as Taylor's) is flawed. Taylor, for instance, provides several examples of the domestic and a private life outside of the office workplace for several characters in *The Mary Tyler Moore Show.* Taylor, *Prime Time-Families,* 114–126. While the workplace may provide support in such circumstances, it does not necessarily equate to the confluence of the domestic and the public.

38. Josh Shear, "The Real Fake Car Job," *Leverage*, season 5, episode 7, directed by John Harrison, aired September 2, 2012, on TNT.
39. See Rogers, "The First David Job."
40. Christine Quail, "Nerds, Geeks, and the Hip/Square Dialectic in Contemporary Television," *Television New Media* 12 no. 5 (2011): 461, doi: 10.1177/152747641038.
41. Rogers and Downey, "The Nigerian Job."
42. Ron Eglash argues that several key African Americans including Malcolm X and Samuel Ray Jackson have appropriated intellectual space in what was predominantly seen as a white male dominance of technological knowledge. Ron Eglash, "Race, Sex, and Nerds: From Black Geeks to Asian American Hipsters," *Social Text*, 71, no. 2 (Summer 2002): 49–57.

References

Alston, Joshua. "Too Much of a Bad Thing." *Newsweek* 153, no. 2 (January 12, 2009), 58–59.
Andrews, Edmund L., and Peter Baker. "A. I. G. Planning Huge Bonuses After $170 Billion Bailout." *New York Times*, March 14, 2009. http://www.nytimes.com/2009/03/15/business/15AIG.html?_r=0.
Arntfield, Michael. "TVPD: The Generational Diegetics of the Police Procedural on American Television." *Canadian Review of American Studies* 41 no 1 (2011): 75–95. doi: 10.3138/cras.41.1.75
Berg, Amy. "The Fairy Godparents Job." *Leverage*, season 2, episode 4. Directed by Jonathan Frakes. Aired August 5, 2009, on TNT. Netflix.com.
Bhabha, Homi. *The Location of Culture*. New York: Routledge, 1994, 2004.
Bianco, Robert. "Critic's corner." *USA Today*, December 9, 2008: 08d.
"Bailout Recipients." *ProPublica*. Updated January 23, 2015. http://projects.propublica.org/bailout/list.
Colton, Michael, and John About. "The Ho, Ho, Ho Job." *Leverage*, season 3, episode 14. Directed by Marc Roskin. Aired December 12, 2010, on TNT.
Dempsey, John. "TNT, Devlin gain 'Leverage.'" *Daily Variety Gotham* (Reed Business Information), March 15, 2007, 29.
———. "TNT gets 'Leverage' with pilot greenlight." *Daily Variety Gotham* (Reed Business Information), August 31, 2007, 3.
Douglas, William. *Television Families: Is Something Wrong in Suburbia?*. Mahwah, NJ: Lawrence Erlbaum Associates, 2003.
Eglash, Ron. "Race, Sex, and Nerds: From Black Geeks to Asian American Hipsters." *Social Text* 71, no. 2, (Summer 2002): 49–64.
Glenn, Melissa, and Jessica Rieder. "The Three Day Hunter Job." *Leverage*, season 2, episode 5. Directed by Marc Roskin. Aired August 12, 2009, on TNT. Netflix.com.
———, and ———. " The Two-Horse Job." *Leverage*, season 1, episode 3. Directed by Craig R. Baxley. Aired December 16, 2008, on TNT. Netflix.com.
Holderman, Lisa. *Common Sense: Intelligence as Presented on Popular Television*. Lanham, MD: Lexington, 2008.
Kim, Albert. "The Runway Job." *Leverage*, season 2, episode 10. Directed by Marc Roskin. Aired January 13, 2010, on TNT. Netflix.com.
McGarrigle, Dale. "Robin Hood-esque 'Leverage' a winning series." *Bangor Daily News*, December 5, 2008: C5.
Mittell, Jason. *Television and American Culture*. NewYork: University Press, 2010.
Newcomb, Horace. "'This Is Not Al Dente': The Sopranos and the New Meaning of 'Television.'" *Television: The Critical View*, 7th ed. NewYork: University Press, 2007.

Quail, Christine. "Nerds, Geeks, and the Hip/Square Dialectic in Contemporary Television." *Television New Media* 12 no 5 (2011): 460–482. doi: 10.1177/152747641038.

Rogers, John. "The Beantown Bailout Job." *Leverage*, season 2, episode 1. Directed by Dean Devlin. Aired July 15, 2009, on TNT. Netflix.com.

_____. "The Homecoming Job." *Leverage*, season 1, episode 2. Directed by Dean Devlin. Aired December 9, 2008, on TNT. Netflix.com.

_____. "The Second David Job." *Leverage*, season 1, episode 12. Directed by Dean Devlin. Aired February 24, 2009, on TNT. Netflix.com.

Rogers, John, and Chris Downey. "The Nigerian Job." *Leverage*, season 1, episode 1. Directed by Dean Devlin. Aired December 7, 2008, on TNT. Netflix.com.

Shear, Josh. "The Real Fake Car Job." *Leverage*, season 5, episode 7. Directed by John Harrison. Aired September 2, 2012, on TNT. Netflix.com.

Taylor, Ella. *Prime-Time Families: Television Culture in Post-War America*. Berkeley: University of California Press, 1989.

Thorne, Geoffrey. "The Inside Job." *Leverage*, season 3, episode 3. Directed by John Rogers. Aired June 27, 2010, on TNT.

Watson, Mary Ann. *Defining Visions: Television and the American Experience in the 20th Century*. Malden, MA: Blackwell, 2008.

Wessel, David. *In Fed We Trust*. New York: Crown Business, Random House, 2009.

About the Contributors

Jillian L. **Canode** received a Ph.D. in philosophy and literature from Purdue University and teaches courses in English, literature and philosophy at the Center for Global Education at Universidad San Ignacio de Loyola, in Lima, Perú. Her work and publications focus on popular culture, feminism, and Marxism.

Ashley Lynn **Carlson** earned a Ph.D. in English from the University of New Mexico and is an assistant professor at the University of Montana Western. Her research focuses on nineteenth and twentieth-century cultural studies, feminism, and intersections between gender, science, and popular culture.

Laura-Marie von **Czarnowsky** holds an M.A. in English studies, German studies and cultural anthropology from the University of Cologne, where she is an instructor in the English Department. Her research interests include contemporary British drama, fantasy literature and magical realism, representations of monstrosity in literature, and detective fiction.

Carol-Ann **Farkas** is an associate professor of English and director of writing programs in the School of Arts and Sciences at MCPHS University in Boston. She teaches first-year composition and literature as well as elective courses in the nineteenth-century British novel and literature and medicine.

Marian R. **Hjelmgren** is pursuing a B.A. in English at Monmouth College. She intends to pursue a career in editorial work after her graduation. Her interests include modern fantasy literature and how it pertains to society as a whole, contemporary re-imaginings of well-known stories, and classical music.

Jennifer **Kirby** is a doctoral candidate at the University of Auckland, New Zealand, where she is examining science fiction cinema's remediation of the aesthetics of other digital media. She holds a M.A. in film, television, and media studies. Her research interests include post-media aesthetics, genre evolution, and the representation of gender and sexuality in film and television.

Kristin **Larson** is an associate professor in the Department of Psychology at Monmouth College. Her areas of specialization are counselor education and applied ethics in research and treatment. She is also a licensed clinical psychologist with a private practice.

About the Contributors

JZ **Long** is an assistant professor of communications at Wilson College in Chambersburg, Pennsylvania. He holds interdisciplinary degrees in political and cultural economy, popular culture, and cultural studies. He studies the impact of popular representations across such genres as comic books, culinary arts, and reality programming.

Cecilia J. **Pang** is an associate professor and head of performance in the Department of Theatre and Dance at the University of Colorado at Boulder. She is also a documentary filmmaker whose work has dealt with such issues as immigrant Peking opera artists, women scientists, motherhood, domestic violence, and consumer rights.

Lisa K. **Perdigao** has a Ph. D. from Northeastern University and is an associate professor of English at the Florida Institute of Technology. Her research and teaching interests are in the areas of American literature, young adult literature, television, film, and Florida culture.

Jeffrey A. **Sartain** is an assistant professor of English at the University of Houston–Victoria, where he also serves as managing editor of *American Book Review*. He writes on issues of gender in technology, posthumanism, the image of the geek, and living authors.

David **Sidore** is an associate professor of English and media studies at Middle Georgia State College. He teaches courses on film, media studies and popular culture as a member of the Department of Media, Culture and the Arts and serves as the faculty advisor of the student-run campus television station.

Annette **Schimmelpfennig** received an M.A. from the University of Cologne in English, Spanish and German philology. Her research interests include contemporary film and television, postmodern fiction, poststructuralist theories, and violence in the media.

Hannah **Swamidoss**, an independent researcher, completed a Ph.D. in literary studies at the University of Texas at Dallas with an emphasis on British fiction, children's literature, and postcolonial studies. Her most recent publication is an essay that surveys the moral value of housework in British children's fantasy literature.

Index

Ackerman, Phillip 63, 66
addiction 1, 33, 39, 148, 158, 162, 165, 209–210
advanced degrees 4–5, 16, 51, 141
Ally McBeal 145
American Psycho 159
angel in the house 113
anti-intellectualism 32–43
Arrow 1
Asperger's syndrome 16–22, 40, 159, 161, 163–167, 176–177, 181 *see also* autism
autism 16, 18, 156–160, 163–164, 169; high functioning autism (HFA) 175–181; *see also* Asperger's Syndrome

banking model 56
Barthes, Roland 34–35, 42
Battlestar Galactica 106
The Big Bang Theory 1, 4, 5, 6, 17–19, 22–23, 36, 51, 53, 96–109, 126, 157, 158, 161–164
Binet, Alfred 3
bipolar disorder 6, 150, 156, 158–160, 163–165, 168–169
Bones 1, 4, 6, 19–22, 26, 36, 40–41, 50, 52–53, 150, 175–181
Breaking Bad 36
Bundy, Ted 7

Cagney & Lacey 140
Cartesian dualism 98–105
Cattell, Raymond 3
Charlie's Angels 113, 126
Chuck 36, 54
The Closer 5–6, 138–150
Community 6, 157–171
Conan Doyle, Arthur 12–14, 32, 80, 82, 84, 90, 187–188, 195
convergent thinking 141–142
creativity 49–50, 54, 141–143, 150, 156–157, 159, 167, 169, 175, 186, 187, 194

Criminal Minds 1, 6, 7, 36, 51, 53, 113–121
criminality 7, 166–167, 195
crystallized intelligence 3, 59, 63, 66, 69–70
Curie, Marie 138

Damages 200
Descartes, René 83
Dexter 1, 7, 185–186, 188–195
divergent thinking 141–142
Dr. Kildare 140
Dollhouse 1
Doogie Howser, M.D. 36

Easy Rider 39
eidetic memory 14, 18, 51–53, 59, 163
Einstein, Albert 1, 2, 50
Elementary 1, 7, 22, 32, 156–158, 162–163, 168
emotion 4, 25, 38, 49, 53, 56, 61, 66–67, 69, 72, 80–93, 124–134, 142–143, 149, 162–163, 167, 175, 177, 178–181
ER 140

fans and fandom 18, 36, 38, 40, 72, 85, 97, 132, 140
femininity 89–90, 99–101, 114–115, 117–121, 124–134, 139, 148–150
feminism 83–83, 106–109, 129, 130, 139–140
Fight Club 159
financial crisis (2008) 204, 210
Firefly 106
fluid intelligence 3, 59, 62–66, 69–70, 72
Foucault, Michel 32, 41–42
Frankenstein 59–61, 67
Fringe 1, 4, 36, 52, 59–72

Gardner, Howard 3, 62
Gates, Bill 126
Grey's Anatomy 5–6, 124, 133, 138–150
Guilford, J.P. 3

217

Index

Hannibal 1, 7, 187–195
Hawking, Stephen 1, 23, 105–6
Homeland 6, 150, 157–171
House 1, 7, 15, 22, 24, 36, 39–41, 52, 53, 56, 157–159, 162, 165, 168–170, 186

Intelligence 54
intelligence quotient (IQ) 3–7, 22, 24, 40, 51, 59, 61–64, 66, 67, 70, 72, 87, 103, 141, 149–150
IQ *see* intelligence quotient
The IT Crowd 36

Jobs, Steve 126

Kazynsky, Ted 7
Kristeva, Julia 186

Law and Order: Criminal Intent 7
Leverage 1, 7, 199–211
Lie to Me 22, 36
logic 19, 20–21, 22, 38, 80, 83
Lombroso, Cesare 6–7, 49–50

Mad Men 200
madness 32–33, 39–43, 60–61, 66, 68, 113–114, 116, 120, 159, 163, 166, 169
Marvel Agents of S.H.E.I.L.D. 1
masculinity 83–84, 96, 98–106, 114, 125–126, 128–129, 132–133, 139, 148–150
medical drama 36, 38–39, 124, 139–140
memorization 14, 51, 56
Mental 36
The Mentalist 1, 22, 36
mind palace 14, 55, 187, 193
misogyny 96–109
Monk 1, 65
murder (and murderers) 7, 20, 21, 39, 70, 92, 116, 119, 120, 142, 143, 148, 175, 176, 179, 188, 189, 191, 193, 194
murderers *see* murder
Murphy Brown 145

NCIS 6, 113–121
Numb3rs 36

One Flew Over the Cuckoo's Nest 159
Otherness 7, 13, 19, 25–26, 119

photographic memory *see* eidetic memory
police procedural 36, 38–39, 139
politics 34, 56, 84, 125, 159
post-traumatic stress disorder (PTSD) 40, 156, 158–159, 167, 190

Private Practice 140
Psych 1, 51–52
psychology 40, 179–180

race 125–128, 134
Rain Man 20, 21
reason (versus emotion) 1, 19, 33, 41, 49, 61–70, 80–93, 98, 117–118, 124, 128–129

savantism 16, 40, 119, 157, 158, 164, 166, 168–169, 178
Scandal 6, 7, 124–134, 140, 150, 157–170
Scooby-Doo, Where Are You! 126
SET (science, engineering, technology) 107, 113–114; *see also* STEM
sexuality 39–40, 42, 85, 90, 98–106, 114–120, 127, 133, 138, 139, 149–150, 159, 167, 179–180, 189
Sherlock 1, 4, 5, 7, 12–16, 22–26, 32, 49, 52–53, 55–56, 65, 80–93, 157, 158–159, 161, 162, 165, 169–170, 185–195
Silicon Valley 126
situation comedy 36, 103
Sleepy Hollow 65
soap opera 130–131, 133
Spearman, Charles 62
Stanford-Binet *see* intelligence quotient
Star Trek 37–38
Star Wars 106
STEM (science, technology, engineering, and math) 4–5; *see also* SET
Stern, William 3
Sternberg, Robert 2, 32
subculture 97, 116–118, 126

technology 1, 4–5, 35, 52, 54–56, 60, 63, 70–71, 84, 98, 105–109, 113–114, 117–118, 120–121, 200
Terman, Lewis M. 141
Thurstone, Louis 62
trauma 20, 22, 167, 176, 180–181, 187
True Detective 7, 185–195

Unforgettable 65

Weisberg, Robert W. 141, 145
Wilde, Oscar 12, 138
The Wire 133
work-life balance 139, 145–147

The X-Files 65

www.ingramcontent.com/pod-product-compliance
Lightning Source LLC
Chambersburg PA
CBHW032053300426
44116CB00007B/722